The Never-Quite-Ending War

*for dear friends,
Carl & Janet —
Love, Peace,
Nancy*

Praise for **The Never-Quite-Ending War**...

" *The Never-Quite-Ending War* deserves broad readership. While Nancy Corson Carter directly addresses the children of WWII veterans, she also speaks to the hearts of those swept into Vietnam-era service. Even more importantly, those born into the 21st-century's unending retaliation against the atrocity of 9-11 will find here crucially important ways to contemplate our best futures. If we can imagine writing a memoir from the perspective of 2051, can we foresee a reconciliation of Muslims with all other faiths? Can we hope to use love to confront war with the same contemplative honesty that this book takes up?"

– **George P. E. Meese**, Ph.D., Professor of Rhetoric Emeritus, and former Operations Officer on the USS Claud Jones DE 1033, Pearl Harbor

" In this graceful memoir, Nancy Corson Carter weaves through time the intersections of herself and her World War II veteran father. The war took him away during the first two and a half years of her life. Delayed bonding combined with her father's post-war anger and control issues became formative aspects of her life. Rich historical and cultural themes reveal universal issues stirred up by war. Prose, letters, and poems vividly bring a wholeness to this creative telling of a family finding ways to bond, love, and share."

– **Lynore Banchoff**, leader of the Autobiography Workshop of the Society for Values in Higher Education

" *The Never-Quite-Ending War* is a psychologically astute memoir describing the impact of a father's WWII service on his daughter. When her father returned from Europe to his home in Pennsylvania, he set about raising a family, building a business, and embracing civilian life. Nancy Corson Carter deftly reveals insights in dreams, letters, travels, objects, and symbols. She circumambulates the shadow of war during her childhood and her later travels to Normandy, the London Imperial

War Museum, Hiroshima, the Florida Holocaust Museum, and Pearl Harbor. She reflects on poignant details and universal complexity as she herself develops as a writer, professor, feminist, environmentalist and peacemaker. She shares dreams that unearth psyche's wisdom and bounty, even in puns. When she uses *haibun*, narrative interspersed with short poems, the haiku crystallize the chapter with a clarity twinkling through many facets.

"There comes a time when adults examine parents not only as father and mother but also as individuals who carried their own history, met challenges of their generation, chose their guiding truths, and built their own meaningful lives. The father who raised Nancy carried his experiences of WWII. They fueled his discipline, erupted in anger occasionally, and were sublimated into big-game hunting. Nancy Corson Carter brings honest self-reflection to memories, history, and symbolic keepsakes. Finally, she arrives at a balanced understanding of her father and herself that rests, after all, in gratitude."

– **Theresa A. Yuschok**, psychiatrist, Durham (N.C.) VA Medical Center

❝ With insight and clarity, Nancy Corson Carter shares her experience of growing up in the 1940s and '50s and how World War II impacted her and her family. With many folksy anecdotes, she explores how her father's and other soldiers' trauma was not addressed or processed after the war, but was deeply felt. Her reflections, told from a humble and loving perspective and a desire for healing and reconciliation, are inspiring and elucidating."

– **Patience Robbins**, on the adjunct staff of the Shalem Institute for Spiritual Formation and author of *Parenting: A Sacred Path.*

The Never-Quite-Ending War

a WWII GI Daughter's Stories

NANCY CORSON CARTER

LYSTRA BOOKS
& Literary Services

LYSTRA BOOKS
&c Literary Services

Published by Lystra Books & Literary Services, LLC
391 Lystra Estates Drive, Chapel Hill, NC, 27517
lystrabooks@gmail.com

The excerpt from W. C. Heinz's *When We Were One: Stories of World War II* (copyright © 2002) reprinted by permission of Da Capo Press, an imprint of Hachette Book Group, Inc.

The excerpt from Black Elk Speaks is reprinted by permission of the University of Nebraska Press, reproduced from *Black Elk Speaks: The Complete Edition* by John G. Neihardt. Copyright 2014 by the Board of Regents of the University of Nebraska.

"Dich wundert nicht.../You are not surprised..." by Rainer Maria Rilke; from *Rilke's Book of Hours* by Rainer Maria Rilke, translated by Anita Barrows and Joanna Macy, translation copyright © 1996 by Anita Barrows and Joanna Macy. Used by permission of Riverhead, an imprint of Penguin Publishing Group, a division of Penguin Random House LLC. All rights reserved.

Lines from "How to Be a Poet," copyright © 2012 by Wendell Berry, reprinted by permission of Counterpoint Press.

Quote from Peter Sawtell, August 18, 2017 *Eco-Notes*, used with his kind permission.

Quote from *The Flaming Bomb* used by permission from Stars and Stripes.

Material from Lydia Mayo used by permission of the U.S. Army Center of Military History.

Three lines from *The Narrow Road to the Deep North and Other Travel Sketches* by Matsuo Basho translated with an introduction by Nobuyuki Yuasa (Penguin Classics, 1966). Copyright © Nobuyuki Yuasa, 1966. Used by permission from Penguin Random House UK.

In memory of my parents
Harvey Fullmer Corson &
Dorothy Virginia Corson

Also for
my sisters, Marilyn, Bette, & Janet;
my husband Howard;
our daughter Rebecca &
our son-in-law Gustavo;
& all peacemakers

Contents

Preface

Daddy left for US Army service in northern Europe when I was six weeks old, returning two and a half years later, in 1945. During that time, like many other children with their caretakers, I waited at home with Mother, our future uncertain. After her death much later, when I was married, a mother and a professional, memories of him and our life after his return began to fill my thoughts and dreams. The war, I discovered, played a much larger role in my life than I'd allowed myself to recognize.

I began to write and to collect images, hoping to find some kind of wholeness. I covered a large bulletin board with photos and maps; I wrote poems and sketched stories; I experimented with form and wrestled with the intimacy issues of memoir. The war's remnants were tightly stitched into the fabric of my childhood, but I needed to alter them—to cut them apart and then to re-make a more suitable garment. After more than a decade of this process, I've found a kind of quilted pattern that fits me: the Japanese pattern of *haibun* juxtaposes short poems and sometimes illustrations with prose units of a narrative, usually about a journey. I write further about my adaptation of this form in the chapter "Japan: Anger and Art." I write letters to my father to open each prose section, with the intention to keep the honesty of personal exchange in our relationship, even beyond his death. The poems and photos extend the stories and evoke other dimensions of them.

Millions of people shared World War II, yet no two people experienced it in the exact same way. Our cultural expressions, in films, in the news media, in books and interviews, as well as in personal stories, will go on adding to the diverse whole. I write stories of the war touching me and my family in specific ways, yet I know my readers, especially my contemporaries, will find many points of commonality.

The war will always be a part of me, and it has mysteries that will never be solved. Veterans are disappearing and so are their children along with their stories, so I feel the pressure of time passing. I keep track of news that reveals new aspects of the war, raises new questions, and reports honors bestowed (many belatedly) upon those who soldiered and served. Such accounts interweave with my own; they are all part of a larger "never-ending war."

The war was considered to be a "just" one because it was fought to rid the world of a clear evil. Men (and a few women) who returned were generally honored, and they considered it a privilege to have served. But there were costs to families. In ours, homecoming meant an uphill climb for an ambitious man who was driven to make up for lost time. Daddy had gone as an older soldier at age twenty-nine, and he returned with the sense that he must start over. The urgency he felt sometimes boiled over in tense moments that now seem like flashes of post-traumatic stress disorder (PTSD), although we didn't know that label then.

It has taken me years both to forgive and also to fully appreciate Daddy's war. My intention as storyteller is to marry confidence and clarity with compassion. In my childhood home, we called someone who didn't speak up when she should a "Minnie Mouse"—I'm determined not to be one.

Daddy cannot answer my questions now, but I try to listen to him with my heart, my mind, and my imagination as I sort through angers, joys, confusions, and dreams. My search has yielded fuller understanding of him *and* of myself in the wider world. Ultimately, I agree with those who assert that the only force that is powerful enough to subvert the force of war is love. And that is a truly never-ending challenge.

I

Can We Talk?

One Name Not Crossed Off

(A Letter)

Dear Daddy,

"I was supposed to kill you," the German man told you when you met by chance at a bar during a big game hunt in Sudan in 1972. When you introduced yourself, he looked hard at you and pulled out a little black book from one of his pockets. He held out a page for you to see; it had ten names on it. All were crossed off except one—yours: Harvey Corson.

At the moment of this revelation, the war had been over for some twenty-seven years. You were happily married, with four daughters, and you had recently retired from a successful business career. This hunt in Sudan was one of many trips you took around the world for big game hunting over some twenty years. I remember how you told us of meeting this man, and then you recalled a time when you were a soldier in Europe and a woman invited you to join a hunting party at a chateau. Some instinct warned you not to go. The man at the bar confirmed it; that was quite likely an attempt to lure you to your death.

My unspoken first reaction was, "How bizarre!" Later it became a good story to tell my friends. Now you are gone, and I have so many questions.

Did you have an uncanny sense during the war that you had a special antagonist? Did your sharpshooter's skill lead to your being diverted from your ordnance assignment into serving as a sniper? And if so, did you kill someone(s) of importance to the enemy? Were your prodigious skills as a mechanic and problem-solver in keeping transport moving seen as a threat? Why had this particular man carried this book in his pocket even on an African safari? What was your immediate response to his message?

You kept notes about the trip, but in your usual bare bones way. You recorded mostly facts—dates and places, the game hunted and killed, and expenses, but rarely the settings and stories behind them. I note that it was April, in northeast Sudan. In that time, usually between the slight rainy season and intense summer in the Red Sea Hills area where you hunted, it still must have been quite hot and dry.

I conjure up a bar scene with slightly creaking ceiling fans turning, background talk, and street noises, maybe an open door and a chicken or two pecking through as you took in that stunning news. The biggest question is, Why were you considered by the Germans to be a particular menace?

I was at least in my late twenties when I heard this story. I assumed that the war was past and done in our family. I was proud of your being in it without much curiosity about what it meant to you, especially in any continuing way. Now I wonder. Did you truly feel you'd "gotten over it"? Enough to be able to shrug off that German's notebook message?

Because my questions come too late, I feel like an untrained taxidermist, handed a skin and skull with no instructions attached. I have to construct my own creature and pray that I approximate its nature. I've pieced together layer after layer of stories that begin to make plausible patterns. Some of them are easy to gather while others have involved dead ends and erasures of the war's secrets. Among your colorful ribboned medals is a simple WWII sharpshooter medal with its RIFLE bar. I wonder if it is a clue to why the German had your name on his list.

As I write to you, Daddy, I find it is helpful and challenging to envision your presence. I have delved deeply enough to uncover issues that were unsettled between us; I hold myself as rigorously as I can to an authentic exploration of these. I chose to begin with this story because it seemed somehow romantically shocking, a thread

I could unwind with a narrative coherence, but the further I go, the more I see that I'm on the list as well, my name not yet crossed off. In my seventies I'm asking the eternal question, Why am I here?, and I would guess that you had to ask that question again after the German's revelation. Although we cannot have a dialogue in the usual sense, I'm testing the limits of empathetic imagination as I tell stories about our life together, searching for meaning that isn't mine or yours alone.

We shared life in a time, mostly, of sanctuary between wars; I celebrate that time in its joys as well, in retrospect, as its opportunities to learn hard lessons (ones I keep learning). And I want you to know without question that the matrix of this writing is my abiding love and gratitude.

Love,
Nancy

Memorial Day No. 66, 2011

L uckily, I've always been a pack rat. Otherwise, I might have been totally gumption-trapped by my belated sense of urgency to fathom the mysteries of Daddy's war. At least I had a place to start.

My pack-rat habits are deeply engrained. I confess that I still have jewelry boxes of bric-a-brac stowed away, bins and bags of cloth and craft materials, slides, seashells, and scrapbooks. Once in a while I discover a cache I didn't remember I had—like grade-school autograph books and flamingo drawings from a third grade trip to Florida. There is, however, one special file that's basic to my hunt. I started it in about 1994 and stored it in the bottom drawer of a four-drawer metal filing cabinet in my office at the college where I taught. I labeled it "D-Day etc." I collected special editions of newspapers and magazines that commemorated the fiftieth anniversary of D-Day, June 6, 1944.

That summer Howard and I drove up to Pennsylvania to visit Mother and Daddy. The celebrations were televised, and we watched some of the ceremonies together. Old soldiers laid wreathes on graves, they wore uniforms either altered or miraculously still fitting. Some were accompanied by several generations of family. There were pictures of well-tended green fields crisscrossed with row after row of white crosses and Stars of David. The sounds of drums and bugles occasionally interrupted the voices of the commentators. I wanted to ask questions and to hear stories, but Daddy was so embattled by Parkinson's by then that he could not really engage. As he sat there in the living room, stolidly locked into the disease's "mask" with its erasure of his natural vitality, I realized it was too late for discussion. I felt sad.

When Daddy died in 1996, we'd never had the conversations I finally yearned for and now covet. By contrast, Janet, my youngest sister and our family archivist, knew to ask Mother questions. She made an eightieth-birthday book in 1999 with Mother's reminiscences; it's a valuable resource.

I saved more articles, but I didn't think much about them or even read them carefully, until 2004, the sixtieth D-Day commemoration year. By then, I had realized that the war had been a large part of our family's life, and I felt the urge to better understand it.

In a well-timed bit of good fortune, I was invited to present in the "Forms of Autobiography" group at the 2005 annual summer meeting of the Society for Values in Higher Education. I put together a sixteen-page draft of an illustrated memoir about Daddy and my family's wartime experience. Many people in the group had similar stories in their own families and were anxious to hear mine. They urged me to go more deeply into the "sense of absence" many felt. One woman simply said, "My dad didn't come home."

In the sixty-sixth year after Daddy came home from World War II, 2011, I committed myself in earnest to completing this project. That year, Memorial Day had extra meaning for me because I returned to Muncy, Pennsylvania, to celebrate the fiftieth reunion of my high school class. I remember when Daddy had *his* fiftieth high school class reunion, at nearby Hughesville High School, and I must admit, it seemed then that only *truly aged people* could reach that stage. I remember a late spring evening when Daddy dressed up handsomely in suit and tie before joining that small but important group of surviving classmates in that rite of passage. I can smell Old Spice shave lotion and hear his hearty laugh.

Before my class reunion began, I drove up to Twin Hills Memorial Gardens to visit Daddy and Mother's gravesite. From the little hill where it is located, I could look around and feel that their beloved valley (bordered by Bald Eagle Mountain beyond the Susquehanna River) embraced them.

I wondered if Daddy would feel properly honored as a veteran for this national holiday. I was glad to see that there *was* a permanent metal disk with a spread-winged American eagle and "WWII (1941–45)" stamped on it by their site marker, but it was overgrown. I found a groundskeeper working nearby and asked for his help. He did a great job of weed whacking away the tough grass and weeds I hadn't been able to pull. He said there were more than three thousand veterans buried in the Gardens. Daddy's small American flag, specially put out for the occasion, was one of many waving brightly in the sunshine that day.

Before the reunion, I had emailed my classmates, telling them that I was working on a memoir and I hoped they would be willing to share their experiences of the war and its after-effects. One who responded is a Vietnam vet. Although he said that his own father was too old to be in World War II, he remembered, "Many of my male adult interfaces were WWII vets. A priest, teachers, Boy Scout leaders, and employers. Today I realize that they were only ten to fifteen years off the battlefield and many were still suffering from the emotional aftershocks. It never showed. And they were great models."

Other classmates told me of fathers who returned with wounds that either took a long time to heal or never really did. Others recounted stories of "our war"—Vietnam; their home-comings had not been publicly celebrated—the troops bore the brunt of that unpopular conflict.

I haven't stopped being a pack rat (as I collect and sort, I hope to separate the "real stuff" from the chaff). I have a whole new box of newspaper clippings about such things as soldiers being belatedly recognized and decorated, new films related to World War II, and secrets at last being told; I keep adding to it. I just clipped an article about France bestowing the Legion of Honor, its highest award, on American soldiers for their roles in liberating that country seventy years ago. The eight North Carolina recipients of the award were told by the Consul General of France, who came to honor them, "You will forever be our heroes."[1]

I thought of Daddy. To be eligible for the Legion of Honor, a veteran must have fought on French territory in one or more of the four main campaigns of the liberation of France: Normandy, southern France, northern France, and the Ardennes. He amply qualified, having served in three out of four of those campaigns, all but southern France. Although the award is given only to living veterans, I consider him now as one of those deservedly decorated heroes, a true *chevalier*!

I have to say, though, that the statement that affected me most from that article was uttered by a ninety-nine-year-old former paratrooper as he received his medal. "It's nice to know people haven't forgotten. And it's important, because the reason we have wars is we forget the last one."

When Ken Burns's fourteen-hour documentary series about

World War II appeared on TV in 2007, I didn't miss a single episode. I kept scanning for Daddy's face, almost afraid that I would see it in the grainy black and white 1940s film footage. Still, I had an eerie sense of his presence, as though I were looking through his eyes at things he didn't—or *couldn't*—talk about during his lifetime.

When asked why he'd made the series, Burns said, "It was really a couple of statistics that got me: one was that we're losing a thousand World War II veterans a day, and the other is that our children just don't know what's going on."[2] He said he'd found "terrifying, just stupefying" the fact that so many high school graduates believe that the US and Germany were allies in the war.

I've learned much about what soldiering in World War II cost. This expense in life and treasure extends, with few real differences, to all wars. There's a truism that "no soldier who has been in battle escapes without wounds." I know now that whatever Daddy endured had to be slowly sloughed and healed—as much as it could be—after he came home. And that is surely true for all who served, as well as for their families and larger communities.

Truth-Telling

At Home

In a scrapbook I made as a teenager, I glued a cut-out paper rose between photos of Daddy and Mother taken in 1936. They both graduated that year, Daddy from Penn State University and Mother from Altoona High School. To me, these photos project such health and beauty, even innocence. I saw my parents as the ideal couple, in a marriage fulfilling a mid-twentieth century American girl's dreams. It is an image I loved and depended upon. Our family was grounded in their relationship and it undergirds my stories, even though I focus on Daddy.

As I look back upon this composite image now, it seems like a perfect place to begin my storytelling, with the two of them. This symbolizes the ideals Mother and Daddy had then—they were young lovers about to be married. And when I assembled my scrapbook as a teenager, I saw them through rose-colored lenses of my own ideals.

Now as an elder, I gather facts and wonder about their meanings for myself growing up and for my family, and even for my country, as we weathered the war and its continuing after-shocks.

Early in my writing, I had an important dream as I struggled with questions of truth-telling:

Apparently I am in a Habitat for Humanity house, having some difficulty finding a place where I can fit into the ongoing project. I notice one set of cupboards in the kitchen is slightly askew, and I suggest changes, but they are rejected by the overseer. Someone comes in to work on them in a way I'm sure is wrong, but I have no authority to interfere. I walk outside where some men are using a truck in the midst of deep mud of different colors; that mud is everywhere, and I think it's sure to wreck my shoes. Then I return to the kitchen and notice that the cupboards seem fixed, but there's no visible way to open the doors. Suddenly Mother appears before me, in her young forties, I'd say; she looks serene and lovely. I'm ecstatic to see her, and I give her a big hug and ask her why she's there. She says she's attending a class reunion nearby. My mental map indicates that we are in New Jersey, having crossed over water to reach this place. She mentions Tel Aviv. I want to show her around, but I barely know the place myself.

In my journal I wrote: "All of this leads me to wonder about deeper probing of the past in this memoir—it's going to take courage as well as confidence in my own authority. I am going to get muddy shoes. If the mud 'wrecks' them? At worst I'll be greatly hindered, at best, I'll clean them as well as I can. I'm getting into the dirt, confusingly of different colors (diverse grounds or bases of truth? ground colors of a rich palette?). If I think in alchemical terms, I seem to be getting into the basic stuff of transformation—the gritty *prima materia.* Will I have the patience and fortitude to persist in getting those cupboards open so that I can let light into their dark corners?"

That it's likely a Habitat for Humanity project heartens me. I've helped to build a Habitat house and found it rewarding. I want to be part of a similar team in my dream even if it hasn't been decided exactly how I'm to contribute. Later I add, "Isn't that what I want—for Earth to be a fit habitat for humanity *and all life*, instead of a world war battlefield?"

Mother appears in the kitchen, the heart of the house, as I am wondering how to open and activate its qualities of nurturance and generously offered hospitality—things she epitomized in life. She visits me as she celebrates the past in the present, letting me know that I can "attend to" a re-union of past-present-future in my writing, even with some obstacles.

I often find puns in my dreams, so "New Jersey" might be about sewing or weaving something new—from jersey, a soft, plain-knitted fabric? But Mother's mention of Tel Aviv is better, I think—"*Tell a* life—[make it] *vivid/lively!*" Even though I didn't know the place well enough to show her around—I didn't yet have my stories mapped out at that point—I was determined that in the end, I would!

Mother's appearance radiates a blessing. She is ever-present in this work, even though Daddy is mostly on center stage. This dream reminds me of the power of the feminine in building and restoring health to our lives; it is often under construction and sometimes muddied by being overpowered or rejected by the masculine.

I recall that truth-telling was a basic theme of my childhood. My sisters and I always remembered that Mother and Daddy's wedding anniversary was the same as George Washington's birthday, February 22. In an elementary school spring curriculum typical of American public schools in that era, our teachers read to us in February about our first president and his courageous exploits, especially in the Revolutionary War. Valley Forge, Pennsylvania, was often mentioned as a site in our state of a terrible, morale-testing winter for him and his troops. When Congress in 1968 permanently changed the legal holiday of Washington's birthday from the February 22 to a movable date, the third Monday in February, and generically called it "Presidents' Day," it felt to us like a personal family loss.

I still have a book that Mother and Daddy gave me for Christmas, *Heroes and Holidays* (1948), which showed how important President-General George Washington was in the American heroes' pantheon then; he was featured along with Christopher Columbus, the Pilgrims, and Abraham Lincoln. The last sentences of Washington's section exemplify the patriotic prose of that era: "A man you could count on. There will never be a day more worth celebrating than the birthday of George Washington—February 22, 1732."[3]

In school, the familiar cherry tree story was reduced to simple images for his birthday art projects: we brought home mimeographed cherries and hatchets and sometimes a Washington silhouette that we'd proudly colored and cut out for display. Daddy liked to tell the cautionary tale of young George cutting down the cherry tree and then bravely confessing his misdeed to his incensed father—"I cannot tell a lie."

Daddy considered lying a cardinal sin, and I, unfortunately, told fibs. My sister Marilyn, three years my junior, was often the target. I lied to blame her for things I'd done wrong. I wasn't exactly an angel in school either since I loved to talk. So when the "Good Citizenship" cards were passed out in first grade, I didn't always get one. Once or twice I found one dropped on the playground by another student, and I presented that at home as mine.

My worst school-related fibbing happened when I was in second grade. For some reason, I got temporary care of a small plaster bust of Abraham Lincoln, and I brought it home. I didn't want to give it up, so I told the teacher that I'd lost it, and I hid it in the linen cabinet in a corner of our playroom. Another girl, my main scholastic rival, won a writing contest, and it was to be her prize.

A week or so later, Mother found it and asked, "Nancy, where did this little statue come from?" I reluctantly confessed that our teacher had given it to me to bring home, but now I was supposed to return it to the girl who won it.

What an irony—Honest Abe entrapped by my lie! Mother's discovery led to my finally returning it to school. This was hard to do, but I was relieved afterward.

One of Daddy's business acquaintances, Mr. M, often got caught in lies; he was an Allis-Chalmers representative and came around regularly to check inventory at our place of business just outside Muncy. He was a jocular man, round and red-headed. I remember him bellied up to the counter, telling jokes and chuckling. Naturally, based on his "stretchers," Daddy used him as a prime negative example for us. His all-time biggest lie came out after he died, that he had been a bigamist.

Daddy demanded of us girls that we tell the truth no matter what, but sometimes his own truth-telling seemed too unvarnished. Once when I complained that a school class photo was unflattering, fishing for a compliment, he said, "Well, it looks like you!" I was embarrassed to hear him joshing the shop's head mechanic, who hated it, that his ears stuck out.

Like most children, we enjoyed telling stories like those truth-telling ones as we grew older; they are part of our family bonds. We have a certain cache of stories about Mother and Daddy's parenting that are part of this. But I noticed that as my sisters and I moved away to go to college, to marry, and to begin our own families, it was hard to keep our new stories interwoven with the old. I know this isn't unusual between generations, and this happens particularly if there are long distances and maybe only one time a year when everyone gathers. I credit Mother for keeping us connected as well as possible with her dedication to sharing news from each of us on a regular basis in her newsletters. But I wish we'd all been able to share stories more freely as we matured. This is particularly critical to me as I consider Daddy's part in our family story-telling.

Truth-telling always relies upon the filters of language, and I've thought about the ways in which Daddy's and my training and experience represent different "languages." He'd grown up on a small farm. With a degree in Agricultural Engineering, he knew of agricultural matters that ranged from seed choices to bringing a crop to harvest with the right equipment and the savvy to sell it. He could design equipment and use a multiplicity of tools for automotive and farm equipment services. He mastered the economics of running a complex business and provided for a family of six. Then too, the language of his Army war experience— mostly "men's talk"— is one I can know only vicariously; of his expert knowledge of guns and hunting I know next to nothing.

I learned the languages of growing up as a dutiful daughter in an entrepreneur-farmer's household and as a good public school student, but the added languages of my adulthood came from my graduate training and teaching in art, literature, and cultural history, and later from involvement with Earth care and contemplative practice.

Much later I came to an understanding that although I sometimes felt frustrated and somewhat lonely as I wished for more open exchanges of ideas and stories that would allow us to relate adult to adult, that was just how it was. I knew, however, that there was a language of the heart that would always keep us connected.

After Daddy and Mother died (in 1996 and 2001), it gave me comfort to remember that Ira Progoff, one of my journaling mentors, firmly asserts, "Death ends a life, but it does not end a relationship." This idea is my basis for writing letters now to Daddy in combination with my essays. In another vein, I trust the wisdom of the American Transcendentalists who claim this: in any fully authentic creative expression where we are deeply truthful to our experience, we speak a universal language. Both beliefs undergird my writing as a whole, as ideals and as practical guides.

In a number of passages, I've had to struggle to write with "tough love" since there is a "nice Nancy" who would prefer to write an unblemished encomium. But she would not be truth-telling if she followed that urge. Daddy was human. He was a strong and extremely able person, the indisputable head of our family; he was basically generous and kind, an extroverted, charismatic person with a good sense of humor. But he could also be opinionated, controlling, and angry, even violent, especially in the years just after the war.

Even as I write that last phrase, I'm hedging, almost ready to stop and say with a little give-myself-away smile, "It wasn't so bad." But for a while, to tell the truth, *it was hard*, and that "while" occurred during a formative time for me and for Marilyn, his two eldest. What little girl feels she can contradict a large adult man who is angry and speaking in a loud, menacing tone? When Janet was born, fifteen years after me, there had been sufficient time for mellowing, for enjoyment of success. By then, in many ways, he was a different father.

Writer and memoir editor Charles Baxter's words help me set some boundaries: "If your memory of your experiences is precious, then your father has, at least in a patriarchal culture, a special and almost sacred power to confirm a history. He can also distort or corrupt history and the past and your place in it."[4] I don't believe that Daddy aimed to "distort or corrupt," but in our patriarchal culture I felt myself long in his shadow—men in his world seemed to be in charge, the ones to listen to and to obey. I accepted that world without question for quite a long while.

But Daddy believed in education, and he and Mother provided that for each of their four daughters. Education was my path to freedom; I followed it all the way to a Ph.D. When I began to teach, a vocation I love, I had the good fortune to be companioned by the feminist movement of the 1960s forward, to be able to teach courses like "Women in the Arts," and to have space and time to read and to write about inspiring women. The developing process of asserting my own voice, with strength and confidence, is a central part of this account as it is of my entire life. In terms of the public as well as the private world, even in the second decade of the twenty-first century, speaking as an adult female can be fraught with biased, discouraging responses. I have learned not to let that stop me, though I still have some stumbles.

About War

Conflicting points of view make telling the truth about any war difficult, if not impossible. The privileges of class and power allow some people to escape, while those on the wrong end of the economic and political spectrum are caught in war's harshness.

We see that happening now as millions of people risk their lives fleeing their beleaguered countries for supposedly safer havens. The word *war* has an Indo-European root, *wers*, which means "to confuse, to mix up." How can we achieve a peaceful cessation of the confusion that even a "just war" stirs up for years and even generations afterward? There is a French proverb, *Tout comprendre, c'est tout pardonner*, "To understand all is to forgive all"—but when the moral order is upended, who can even begin to understand?

There is great contemporary interest in ferreting out the truths of World War II. Many "baby boomers" (including my three sisters)—some 79.6 million US residents born in the years *after* the war, 1946–1964—want to know more. We see this hunger for understanding in Hollywood blockbusters like *Saving Private Ryan* (1998) and in bestsellers like Tom Brokaw's *The Greatest Generation* (1998), a phrase that's come to be commonly used for American World War II soldiers and their compatriots.

We now have hundreds of films about World War II. Those that I've seen and admired, besides *Saving Private Ryan*, include *Sophie's Choice*; *The English Patient*; *Hiroshima, Mon Amour*; *The King's Speech*; *Empire of the Sun*; *Schindler's List*; *Patton*; and *The Imitation Game*. I almost forgot *Casablanca* and *The Bridge Over the River Kwai*! New films will undoubtedly keep appearing as time passes, along with new interviews and stories, commemorations, and releases of classified information.

When I taught general humanities courses, beginning in the 1970s, I encountered new perspectives on World War II. I saw films like *Night and Fog*, a gritty thirty-three-minute documentary Alain Resnais made in 1955, ten years after the liberation of the Nazi concentration camps. The effect of juxtaposing color images (I seem to remember green lawns) of the camps as they were in 1955 with the authentic black and white footage of earlier scenes—such as those showing lines of emaciated prisoners and piles of naked bodies being shoveled into mass graves—was unforgettable. I was impressed to meet and learn from the Nobel

Peace Prize winner and Holocaust survivor Elie Wiesel while he was a visiting scholar at our college.

When I saw Pierre Sauvage's *Weapons of the Spirit* (1989), I felt gratitude and even relief. This documentary focuses on a village in southern France, Le Chambon-sur-Lignon, where, during the Nazi occupation, five thousand Jews were sheltered by its five thousand Christians, bearers of the staunch peace-making values of their French Huguenot ancestors. People used to ask "Why didn't anyone *do* something to stop the horrors?" The people of Le Chambon-sur-Lignon and many others who risked their lives to provide sanctuary and safe passage for the Jews *did just that!*

Many Americans probably first learned about the concentration camps after the war when they saw *LIFE* magazine photos of the skeletally thin inmates being freed. This topic was omitted from public schooling for decades; this was true in my white, Anglo-Saxon, mostly protestant Pennsylvania hometown.

I have wondered many times if Daddy and other soldiers knew about the camps. Seventy years later, in a 2015 Veterans Day column in our local newspaper, a son relayed this story of his father being one of a group of GIs taken to Buchenwald a few days after its liberation:

> They were taken by truck to Buchenwald and given a tour. Then each man was handed a set of photographs, 10 copies of each picture, and instructed to take them home after the war, to bear witness to what they had seen and to give sets of pictures to 10 people.... Someone in the Army had realized immediately that witness and documentation were called for.[5]

Important stories about the Holocaust keep emerging. Göran Rosenberg, in his memoir *A Brief Stop on the Road from Auschwitz*, first published in Sweden in 2012, tells us of "the other death—the death after the camps, the death from damage that proves insuperable"; his father's post-camp life ended in suicide.[6] Sarah Helm's 2015 *Ravensbrück: Life and Death in Hitler's Concentration Camp for Women* is a history of brutality researched barely in time to gather testimony from camp survivors.

In 2016, a ceremony in Israel posthumously designated the first American serviceman, US Army Master Sgt. Roddie Edmonds, as a "Righteous Among the Nations," the highest honor for non-Jews who risked their lives to save Jews during World War II. It's a story that remained untold for decades, but now we know that as the highest-ranking noncommissioned officer held in a German POW camp, Edmonds ordered more than one thousand of his fellow Americans held captive to step forward with him and boldly declared: "We are all Jews here." The German commander threatened him at gunpoint but then withdrew. Thus more than two hundred Jewish-American soldiers' lives were saved. More than twenty-six thousand are now counted among the "Righteous Among the Nations," the most famous being Oskar Schindler and Raoul Wallenberg, a Swedish diplomat. They and many whose names will never be known remind us of human goodness arising in the midst of evil.[7]

Still, names of the evil as well as the good continue to emerge. June 17, 2016, brought news of a former Nazi guard, ninety-four-year-old Reinhold Hanning, who was sentenced to five years in prison as an accessory to the murders of at least 170 thousand people. Alison Smale's article in *The New York Times* online (June 18, 2016), "A Front-Row Seat to Germany's Long Reckoning With Its Past," mentions other Auschwitz and Birkenau guards and soldiers tried in the last few years ("seven decades too late") while others are in ill health or dead. On the other hand, in the previous month (May 29, 2016, *The New York Times* online), William Grimes wrote "Hedy Epstein, Rights Activist and Holocaust Survivor, Dies at 91." Ms. Epstein, saved because her parents put her on a Kindertransport out of Germany in 1939, lived a life persistently devoted to justice, especially for refugees. Arrested as a protestor over the fatal police shooting of Michael

Brown in Ferguson, Missouri, in 2014, she said, "I'm Jewish and I was born in Germany, so I think I can understand what it feels like to be African-American in this country." Her concluding words in the many addresses she gave about the Holocaust were: "Remember the past, don't hate, don't be a bystander."

Many of us are now searching for understanding about that war, claimed as the deadliest war in human history, with estimates of lives lost reaching fifty-seven million, more than four hundred thousand of them American. Paul Fussell, a noted historian-author who fought in the Army in Europe when Daddy did, became a dedicated "warrior against war." His statement about psychological wounds is often quoted: "Wars damage the civilian society as much as they damage the enemy. Soldiers never get over it." Alarming suicide rates among soldiers from America's wars in Iraq and Afghanistan, and increasingly among Vietnam vets, underline this statement.[8]

As to damage to civilian society, in late December 2015 South Korea finally received an apology and a pledge for $8 million from Japan's prime minister to settle the issue of WWII "comfort women." Historians say that tens of thousands of women from around Asia, many of them Korean, were sent to frontline military-run brothels to provide sex to Japanese soldiers. There are said to be only forty-six surviving former Korean sex slaves, now in their eighties and nineties.

Many other survivors of that era, also in their eighties and nineties, are breaking the silences so long kept. They are getting their stories down before it's too late. On February 6, 2012, *NBC Nightly News* featured a "Living History" piece about fifty-six residents in a New Hampshire retirement community who published a memoir collection, *World War II Remembered.* One of the writers, Kesaya Noda, spoke of helping her father, Lafayette Noda, to document his experience of being held in an internment camp for Japanese-Americans.

That those internment camps were set up in the US during the war was another truth never mentioned in my schooling; I discovered it only when I was teaching, decades later. My students and I read *Citizen 13660* by artist Miné Okubo. As a result of President Franklin D. Roosevelt's Executive Order 9066, she had to spend the years 1942–44 at Topaz War Relocation Center, Utah. Her words and sketches paint a surprisingly sweet portrait of a tough experience.

Such stories and images are rare and important; they are part of our national and world history. They reveal to us the heights and the depths of our humanity. Telling Daddy's and my family's story with all the truthfulness I can muster, I feel I have both opportunity and obligation to share in this history.

II
War Years

The Testing Begins

(A Letter)

Dear Daddy,

As I write about the war years, I see how your life and Mother's radically changed after Pearl Harbor. I am proud of the brave way that you both, joining so many others, accepted the call to service. As I look back, I know you had to go, Daddy—I remember you saying that there had been no Corson men in the previous war (World War I), as though that was a patriotic debt that you felt obliged to pay. For that reason you decided to go, but that conclusion was not easy, for you or for Mother, that's certain. You stepped out into a great unknown as a soldier. Mother had me, a baby, to care for pretty much by herself while she waited at home for two and a half years, hoping and praying for your safe return.

The things I've learned suggest how scary a time it was. Hitler offered bounties to German U-boat crews for sinking Allied ships like the one that carried you across the Atlantic. In contrast, the books, postcards, and letters you sent from Europe to Mother and me are precious shadow-chasers. When I read them now, I feel as though I am receiving them all over again, and I am so grateful for the love and delight they bring!

The war was brutal and you must have been scared, sad, and lonely, not to mention hungry, thirsty, dirty, and exhausted much of the time, yet you found a way to keep in touch. I begin to understand more deeply than ever before the disturbed energy you had to slough off when you returned, Daddy. I want to think of you now and forever surrounded in blessed Light!

Love,
Nancy

Drafted

The image of the two young lovers in my teenager's scrapbook page returns to me; in their 1936 portraits they seem
sweetly content. Yet nine and a half months after Mother and
Daddy married, the catastrophe of Pearl Harbor, on December
7, 1941, catapulted the US into World War II. Their lives, along
with millions of others, would be unalterably changed by this
turn of the wheel of fate.

It's hard for me to imagine how suddenly their lives were no
longer their own. Daddy was drafted into the US Army in May
1943. After less than a year of intensive training, he crossed the
Atlantic on a troop ship, on his way to the European theater for
the duration of the war. Perhaps I, even as a baby, served as a bet
against high odds in a risky time, a brave hope that our family
would be reunited soon in a reasonably normal world.

How Mother must have wished my arrival would spare him
from going to war. But Daddy was proud and wanted to bring
our family honor. It seems that his American man's idealism and
a staunch patriotism kept him from taking an agricultural deferment like his brother, my Uncle Harold. At twenty-nine, Daddy
was older than most of the recruits, and he was indeed working
in an agricultural field, as a salesman for Allis-Chalmers farm machinery. Thus a deferment made sense, if he had argued for it, but
instead he accepted being drafted six short weeks after my birth.

I see no other choices for Daddy. Draft dodgers were considered traitors and even conscientious objectors were viewed as

suspect. Poet William Stafford describes a harrowing experience as a conscientious objector in a small Arkansas town in 1942 in his essay "The Mob Scene at McNeil."[9] Any man "who was a man" signed up; any "real woman" stood behind her man and her country. And Daddy, always a person of strong opinion, had made up his mind; anything else would have been, I'm quite sure, a betrayal of his convictions.

Mother was unable to breast-feed me, even though she tried—that's what she told me years later. I'm sure it was because she was so nervous about the war and what it might mean for her and her child. It would have been good for both of us if I *had* been able to nurse; instead, I was fed a formula sweetened with Karo corn syrup, a sad substitute for Mother's milk. Studies have shown, as we'd expect, that both children and adults who have loved ones in service are vulnerable to stress and depression from the prolonged sense of danger and uncertainty. I'm sure that *everyone* felt the general atmosphere of tension as the war encroached further and further upon their lives.

When I learned to read, I grew to love the elegantly illustrated Greek myths in *The Book of Knowledge* that Mother and Daddy bought for me and my sisters. Much later, I chose to teach a course, "Goddesses in Art and Literature," in which we studied the ancient myths. Reflecting upon the disordered world I was born into, I found one of those stories quite relevant to my life: since my birthday is close to the spring equinox, in late March in the northern hemisphere, I see myself as the young goddess Persephone, expecting to be joyously welcomed from the dark otherworld of winter by her Earth Mother Demeter. Instead, Daddy's departure in May of my first year seems to replay Pluto's refusal to release Persephone from the underworld for spring and summer. I can feel in this story the deep yearning of a parent for her child, and the desire that healthy life be restored to Earth when it is held in thrall by violence.

Mother must have felt great ambivalence about her circumstances. I can think of nothing in Mother's character and her sense of faithfulness to her husband and to her country that would allow her to fight the inevitable. Further, she and Daddy had been toughened by the Depression years. Mother, a city girl, enrolled in business programs, for a year at a state teachers college and then at Altoona School of Commerce; she took a variety of jobs in Pennsylvania cities and in Washington, D.C., using her court reporting and secretarial skills to earn her way before she married. Daddy, on the other hand, came from a farm family, and—this is so amazing—he graduated from Penn State in the midst of the Depression, in 1936, with *several* job offers.

But who could imagine raising a first child alone in wartime? Mother had only recently moved to a new community. Daddy's family lived in the general area, but she hadn't gotten to know them very well, nor did they live nearby. I remember her telling of one discouraging time that she made the effort to bundle me up and drive for some distance into the country in the wintertime to visit them, but they weren't home.

Daunting questions lurked around the edges. What if she or I needed medical help, especially in winter storms, with dangerous roads into town and maybe no electricity or phone service? How would she make do without Daddy's earnings, his skills and energy to maintain the big new shop building with apartments over it that they had just moved into? Knowing she had to put on a brave face and be a competent and loving anchor at home, Mother had to have secretly wondered, *What if Harvey doesn't return?*

There she was, tending an infant, alone, with only occasional visits with her mother, in an upstairs apartment inside a big empty building out in the country along a highway! Since Mother had only one sibling, her brother Jimmy, nine years older, I'd guess that she'd had little if any practice with babies.

There'd been an arrangement for Daddy's younger brother

and his wife to stay in an adjoining apartment, but after several months, they decamped to the family farm to assure his exemption from military service. That upset Daddy's careful plan for them to help run and maintain the building and to give Mother security while he was gone. I never heard him complain about this, but Janet recorded Mother's words about their departure:

> This left me ALL ALONE in the large building when Harvey went to the Army on his birthday, May 17, 1943, leaving from the Pennsylvania Railroad Station near Muncy. (Nancy was six weeks old.) With new baby, new location, and [now] an apartment to rent, most especially so someone could fire the large steam boiler in the building, I had a lot on my hands. Somehow, we managed…. Can't say that it was exactly easy.[10]

In the worn copy I own of Daddy's *Brooks's Readers: Sixth, Seventh, and Eighth Years*, I found many pieces that helped form the patriotic disposition of his generation. They range from poems saluting the American flag, like Oliver Wendell Holmes's "The Flower of Liberty," to prose such as Alfred J. Church's "Horatius at the Bridge" (accompanied by an illustration of the brave defender) and Patrick Henry's "An Appeal to Arms." Because he signed the volume and kept it, I assume that Daddy had thoroughly digested and approved of its themes.

Furthermore, the US propaganda machine was in full action; American citizens were deluged with persuasions to join in the war effort. The folksy art of Norman Rockwell became a powerful part of this appeal. He was commissioned to participate in the campaign to sell US War Bonds by illustrating the four essential human freedoms named by President Franklin Delano Roosevelt in his 1941 State of the Union address. These posters were published in 1943, and must have been visible in post offices and public places everywhere. Of the four freedoms illustrated—freedom of speech and of worship, and freedom from want and from fear, the last two must have tugged especially hard at the hearts of parents of a newborn. "Freedom from Want; Ours to fight for," a now iconic American Thanksgiving portrait, shows happy grandparents offering a feast to their family gathered around a big ceremonial table—grandmother holds a huge turkey on a platter while grandfather looks on proudly. The fourth poster, "Freedom from Fear: Ours to fight for" shows a middle-class white couple tenderly tucking their ideal family of a boy and a girl into bed. The dad has a folded newspaper under his arm with partial headlines visible, "BOMBS KI…" and "HORROR HIT."

For a long time, I owned a small certificate of proof of Mother and Daddy's ready response to this call for patriotic faith, a Series E United States Savings Bond. Designated as a United States War Savings Bond valued at $25, the handsome certificate was dated December 1943 for "Miss Nancy V. Corson or Mrs. Dorothy V. Corson, R.D. #2, Muncy, Penna." After Howard and I married, we considered it as one of our treasures and kept it in a safety deposit box wherever we moved. Finally, in 2004, we decided to cash it in. At the bank we learned that it had stopped accruing interest after forty years—in 1983. While we waited, the young teller phoned around to various offices to learn how to deal with it; he had never seen such a document. Redemption value: $105.09. Intrinsic value: priceless.

Still, I think, in spite of Daddy's resolve to go off to war, Mother continued to blame a local dentist, Dr. P, head of the local draft board, for cold-heartedly calling him up to serve in the Army when he had a new baby and useful work to do to support the country at home. Once, years later, when Mother drove us by his little office on Water Street, I asked, "Wouldn't it be nice if we could have pretty pink trim on our windows like his?"

She answered with a firm "No."

Honestly, I can't imagine now what it would have been like if

Daddy had *not* gone to war. That was a war that people believed in, a righteous or just one. The general public did not intellectualize about this—it was led to believe it was a matter of good versus evil and required their participation. Women became "Rosie the Riveter," used coupons, conserved scarce items, and found other ways to serve. For men of that generation, it meant the chance of a lifetime to have a real initiation into manhood— that's clear from the number of young men who lied about their age to go and the older men who could not go and felt deprived and even ashamed. In the end, I am proud that Daddy went. I think he'd have been sorry all the rest of his life if he hadn't; he would have felt diminished in his own and others' eyes. Without the war's harrowing focus, his zeal for life and success might have been lesser. Luckily in Daddy's case, the cliché, originally from German philosopher Friedrich Nietzsche, seemed to be true: "That which does not kill us makes us stronger."

Waiting at Home

your hand
my anchor
in a cold white sea

Here's a photo I'm sure Mother sent to Daddy. From what I can tell, he also saw a lot of snow that winter of 1944, in the Ardennes in France, so far away from us. What he saw certainly must have contrasted with the serenity of this scene, but surely it made him happy to see Mother's beautiful smile and to know that she and I were safe. American soldiers had the comfort that *their* wives and small children, unlike those of the men on whose soil they were fighting, were far from the front and its dangers. It was a mixed blessing: we were half a world away from the war *and* from each other.

Someone took this photo of Mother and me out by the shop, so we weren't entirely alone, but our communal circle was small. Nanaw sometimes visited from Altoona; I vaguely remember visiting a woman named Evie, a friend Mother made in our neighborhood—I loved the little mice she made by attaching eyes, ears, and tails to walnut shell halves. Of course there were shopkeepers in Muncy, our doctor, and perhaps a minister, but beyond that, our network was small and we were rather isolated.

Another myth, this one from the Greek *Odyssey,* helps me to imagine myself as that little girl in the photo. For those two and a half years, my father was King Odysseus, the far-voyager of many adventures, and Mother and I held the fort, as we said colloquially, at home, just as Odysseus's wife, Penelope, and child, Telemachus, guarded their hearth in the long-ago Ithaca. After anxiously waiting for Daddy to return from the dangerous journey, thankfully not the *Odyssey*'s twenty years in length, we had the good fortune that he *did.* As I was growing up, I never considered how different my stories would be if he had not.

* * *

Much as Penelope and the women of her household practiced the art of weaving while waiting for their men to return from war, Mother and Nanaw practiced the art of sewing. By the time Daddy came home, I had outgrown the delicate cotton dresses with tucked bodices and pretty moiré sashes they made me for summertime or the woolen pleated plaid skirts for wintertime. You can see the warm woolly snowsuit, a "makeover" I wore with my special white rabbit muff, in the photo. Mother and Nanaw were great at altering older garments to make new ones—frugality was needed to survive on what Daddy earned, the Army's dependent allotment of about $85 a month.

Accessibility also determined the need to re-use: wool was needed for military uniforms, silk and nylon were needed to make parachutes, and leather and rubber were needed for a variety of uses. Americans were restricted to buying three new pairs of shoes per year. But they *could* use sequins; these popular pretties weren't needed for any wartime use. The black hat Mother is wearing in the wintry photo has sequins on its looped "fascinator."

Mother visited twice at Camp Breckenridge, Kentucky, before Daddy was shipped out, and both times her parents kept me at their home in Altoona. Once, when she went on the train, it was so crowded that she had to stand on the back platform all the way to Indianapolis, more than five hundred miles, before getting inside to stand and eventually get a seat. The other time, she drove the Pontiac sedan, "which was a lemon," and worried about having enough gas coupons for the return trip.

How brave Mother had to be to set out on these trips. What if the car had broken down on some lonely stretch of road? What if she'd been robbed? I can voice these worries now, in retrospect, but I imagine that Daddy, like all soldiers on duty, had to discipline himself not to worry about such "what-ifs." In general, that was Daddy's way, to think of the best and to confidently march toward it, an attitude necessarily held by many in those years.

After Camp Breckenridge, Daddy was sent to Fort Ord in California. Mother said, "After he arrived there, they were given leave to come home and he had to spend about half of his leave time traveling to and from the west coast. It was just before Christmas 1943, and we had our Christmas early that year."

Again, in Mother's words recorded by Janet:

Harvey was then sent to New York for embarkation to Europe. Prior to that, he thought that he was going to be sent to the South Pacific, and I am glad he wasn't! When Harvey got to New York, he called and said that I could come down to see him there before he left. But after I had almost completed arrangements to drive to New York, he found his way out and called to say not to come—they were going to leave before I would have a chance to see him. He said that some of the other soldiers' wives had come fruitlessly to New York. I was so glad that I didn't make the trip!

That was the beginning of his journey into the war. What a forbidding threshold he had to cross, with Mother and me held in thrall at home.

I've never doubted that Mother and Nanaw took excellent care of me, but we all lived in an atmosphere of anxiety. I have a memory of standing at Mother's side after we'd said good-bye to someone at the Williamsport station. As the train pulled out, I dropped my new doll on the sidewalk, and its porcelain head shattered. It may have been a present from Nanaw, who had just left to return home. Mother's reaction, as I remember it, was to tell me rather sternly not to cry; she probably realized it wasn't fixable and may have felt like crying herself.

Even small emotional moments like that one were harder in the context of running a wartime household. Appliances were hard to find, so the hope was that the ones you had would last. Many necessities were rationed: meat, canned goods, sugar, coffee, and margarine, along with cars, gasoline, bicycles, and oil. American women shared these daily stresses, along with the largest one, their worries about their absent men.

Mother helped me say my prayers at bedtime; at the end of them we said, "Goodnight, Daddy." I barely understood what that meant, though I could tell it made Mother sad. As I overheard radio reports of the war and conversations of worry and concern, how could I not have suspected things were not as they should be?

On the lighter side, Mother said she whiled away the long evening hours by listening to radio shows; one of her favorites was *Fibber McGee and Molly*. She also told of "reading to Nancy and feeding her all the best of food." It's true, I'm sure, that I was well fed. I found a most comprehensive list she'd typed out of good foods to feed me; I'm sure she followed it scrupulously. Later, when Mother proudly announced that she gave me no candy until I was two, I added this to my list of disadvantages of being the oldest, since my younger sisters, born after the war, enjoyed sweets with no such rule.

I can, however, blame the shortage of chocolate in my diet on the war. Hershey Kisses, one of Pennsylvania's trademark candies, weren't available because the aluminum foil used to wrap them was diverted to the war effort. Besides that, World War I introduced American soldiers to chocolate, and during World War II almost all the chocolate produced in the US was earmarked for the military as a part of standard rations. Four Hershey bars sweetened the emergency rations carried by paratroopers dropping behind enemy lines just before D-Day. Tootsie Roll candy, another chocolate, was added to every soldier's field rations because it could hold up in a variety of weather conditions.

Who would have guessed that chocolate, along with cigarettes, would become the coin of friendship? There the soldiers were, with kids in foreign countries running after them when there were lulls in fighting calling out "Chocolate! Chocolate!" In a very different time and circumstance, I remember chocolate's lure for me and my sisters. When business associates brought Whitman's Sampler chocolates at Christmastime, Daddy carefully doled them out. We took our choices very seriously, studying the diagram in the box lid for just the right ones.

* * *

I waited with Mother for the war to end. A whole generation of American children, a special cohort, shared this experience. In one sense, we were safe and secure, but we were also burdened by the involuntary abandonment of our soldier parents. Unwittingly, we were called to make our own patriotic sacrifices at young ages. Many of my contemporaries were born either just before their fathers left, as I was, or soon after they left. We lived two to five of our first years without our fathers (or mothers in a few rare cases).

So many exciting and challenging things happened soon after the war that my cohort was sometimes overlooked—parents were reunited, overjoyed (or not) to make new plans for their lives; new sibs were born; new houses, cars, and other things were acquired. All this re-settling went on around us while we kids who had waited out the war were often left to tend to our strangely mixed feelings of joy, sadness, and resentment, by ourselves. The psychological, spiritual, and physical toll of war upon families and upon children is always high even after supposedly happy returns home.

Our twenty-first-century American wars, like those in Iraq and Afghanistan, have also left children at risk for depression, bed-wetting, and other stress disorders due to fears for military parents in dangerous places. In 2011, a military mom with two small children was quoted as saying: "The kids deserve a lot of praise and a lot of credit. If I decide I don't like this life, I can divorce my husband. They can't. They were born into it. Nobody ever asked the kids, 'Is that something you want—to have your father in the military?'"[11]

As I review materials about children and war, I realize that the feelings surrounding World War II were different from those in later wars. Research shows that kids do best when they believe there's a good reason for the war that has disrupted their lives—that was something I and my contemporaries could take for granted. But I think it's harder for children with military parents since then.

Before I knew its connotations, I referred to myself as a "war child." I was shocked, then, to learn that in the 1940s the term designated children condemned by fate to a life very different from my privileged one. It was commonly used in Europe for children fathered by occupying forces. As the war ended, these children and their mothers were shunned and persecuted by isolation, bullying, and even arrest, forced labor, and deportation. In an interview for the Swedish newspaper *Dagens Nyheter,* war children from an orphanage in Bergen claimed they were forced to parade where the locals whipped them and spit at them. An article in the April 8, 1946, issue of the US Army newspaper *Stars and Stripes* summed up the official US policy on war children ("Pregnant Frauleins Are Warned!"). It reflects the mores and the economics of the time, all legalistically worked out:

> Girls who are expecting a child fathered by an American soldier will be provided with no assistance by the American Army. If the soldier denies paternity, no further action will be undertaken other than to merely inform the woman of this fact. She is to be advised to seek help from a German or Austrian welfare organization. If the soldier is already in the United States, his address is not to be communicated to the woman in question, the soldier may be honorably discharged from the army and his demobilization will in no way be delayed.[12]

What if, in different circumstances, I'd been stigmatized as a "war child"? How scary and unfair. The more we learn of this war or any other, it seems to me, the more we are obligated to respond with compassion.

Passage to Chaos

winter blackout
Orion the Hunter
stalks the sky

My Orion haiku suggests a sense of fate looming heavily over us all in that time. From what I've gleaned, Daddy's ID, photographed above, was a ticket into chaos—his loved ones could only pray that it would be a round trip.

I'm fascinated by Bill Mauldin's cartoons, drawn while he was in the Army infantry. I hope Daddy saw his work in *Stars and Stripes* in Europe, that it gave him some chuckles amidst the mayhem. In his book *Up Front*, Mauldin wrote:

> I'm a cartoonist, maybe I can be funny after the war, but nobody who has seen this war can be cute about it while it's going on. The only way I can try to be a little funny is to make something out of the humorous situations which come up even when you don't think life could be any more miserable.[13]

One of his cartoons depicts the misery of weather woes. As usual, it features his two war-battered buddies, Willie and Joe; they are leaning against a small tree in the midst of driving rain, surrounded by mud. Willie turns to Joe and says, "This damn tree leaks."[14]

Mauldin's sentiments echo so many other soldiers':

> You can't understand it by reading magazines or newspapers or by looking at pictures or by going to newsreels. You have to smell it and feel it all around you until you can't imagine what it used to be like when you walked on a sidewalk or tossed clubs up into horse chestnut trees or fished for perch or when you did anything at all without a pack, a rifle, and a bunch of grenades.[15]

Mother told Janet that just before Easter 1944, in the first week of April, Daddy landed in Gourock, Scotland, after crossing the Atlantic on the Queen Mary from New York City. He told us later that his ship took a zig-zag course to avoid German submarines, and that he could hear and feel the changes of giant engines while he lay in his bunk far below deck; this would be especially noticeable to a trained mechanic on high alert. I try to imagine all those young men—very few who had ever even thought of crossing the US, let alone the Atlantic—making that hazardous passage.

Ocean maps now show where hundreds of American ships were sunk by the German U-boats along the east coast of the US, especially off North Carolina's Outer Banks, and farther out in the Atlantic. In fact, an area off Cape Hatteras, North Carolina, where some ninety ships were lost is known as the "Graveyard of the Atlantic"; it is the only US battlefield of World War II. Churchill called the entire campaign, which lasted from 1939 until Germany's defeat in 1945, the Battle of the Atlantic. The US Navy's resources were severely strained; men, machines, and material needed to protect shipping were in short supply. In 1942, perhaps the bleakest point, Allied ships, including many in the US merchant marine, were sunk by German U-boats at the rate of one per day. This loss of lives, ships, and raw resources represents one of the greatest maritime disasters in history. That information was kept secret for morale reasons at the time and then for a good while after for national security.[16]

When Daddy's troop ship crossed in 1944, however, the Allies had gained the upper hand, with substantial victories by mid-1943. Still, the U-boats continued to threaten the high seas. Mother's details of Daddy's crossing led me to a website on troopships, which lists specific crossings by the merchant ship Queen Mary. Studying the 1944 crossings with Mother's remembrance that he arrived "just before Easter 1944, in the first week of April" in mind, I found that since Easter that year was April 9, Daddy must have been on the March 21– 27, 1944, crossing. If so, he spent his first whole day on English soil on my first birthday, March 28. I was excited to find details about that exact crossing posted by a man named Richard Faulkner, who researched the Thirty-Fourth Photo Recon Squadron. His work had led to finding notes from a memoir by the unit commander of that squadron shipped to England aboard the Queen Mary:

Under cover of darkness on 21 March 1944 "Shipment 5254-Y" bedecked in full battle dress, detrained once again and marched aboard our "North Atlantic Cruise

Ship." And would you believe it! We had drawn the "Pride of the Seas," the Queen Mary....

With "no delay" the "Queen" steamed from her berth out of the narrows of New York harbor during the night hours and was well to sea by the time we saw daylight once again. It was a rough but rapid crossing. With 17,000 plus troops aboard there was little time or room for parading the upper decks. It was a mass of mankind in a relatively confined area. Even the seasick, and there were many, had to elbow their way to the rail—few making it. But I assure you, the "Limey outfit" running this "show" really knew what was going on and what had to be done. It was organized to a "T."

Other than the gales and continuous high seas, the only incident occurred on the third night out. Rumor had it that a German "wolfpack" was hard on our tail. At any rate during the night the "Queen" did make a sudden 90 degree turn to the North and drawing full steam must have headed direct for the "Ice Pack" before turning eastward once again. If one dared stick his nose out for a bit of fresh air it was cold, cold, cold. (Incidentally, one of the least publicized but also more reliable post-war secrets attributed that Hitler had posted a $1,000,000 reward for the "U-boat" skipper and crew that nailed the "Queen" in one of her fully-loaded east-bound crossings—Pleasant Dreams.)

No matter how fast or uneventful our crossing was it wasn't fast enough. It was, indeed, a great relief when we heard the rattle of anchor chains running out on the morning of the sixth day in the Firth of Clyde just outside Glasgow, Scotland.[17]

A later posting on the same site states that if the Thirty-Fourth had not been "bumped in schedule," they would have sailed on another ship that was attacked by a U-boat en route: all soldiers and crew on that cargo-troopship perished.

As an aside, I was on the Queen Mary with my daughter Rebecca in Long Beach, California, where it was permanently docked, about a decade ago. I wish I'd known more then to tell her about her grandfather's time on board this grand ship. I do remember, though, that despite the fact that we were with a relatively small group of tourists, unlike the thousands of men Daddy was bunked with, it still felt claustrophobic below deck, and we couldn't stay down there for long. We heard stories of ghosts that are sometimes seen there.

Right after his crossing, Daddy's company was taken by train from Scotland to somewhere in England, where they waited for two months while the Allies' leaders planned the invasion of France. Mother said that Daddy was stationed near Malvern in the Midlands. In that interim, which must have been a weird limbo time, she said that he used his mechanical skills to repair bikes for the English and that he sent his small earnings home.

Soldiers were probably kept busy with routine exercises, guard duties, and the like, but in their off time, while playing cards, writing to loved ones, or having a smoke, all must have felt their adrenaline rising as they tried either to imagine or to block out thoughts of the future. What would it be like in battle? Would they be wounded? Would they survive? Would the Allies be victorious? How soon? I wonder if Daddy had dreams or nightmares.

Since so much depended on the weather, everyone must have scrutinized it day and night, wondering, "When?" General Dwight D. Eisenhower, Supreme Commander of the Allied Expeditionary Force, said, "The big question mark always before us was the weather," and he, with the advice of his chief meteorological adviser, James Stagg, had to make the fateful decision. One of my D-Day fiftieth commemoration clippings describes how difficult this weather choice was:

> The right conditions of tides, moon phase, and time for an invasion existed only three days each month. Also, the

wind had to be between 12 mph onshore and 18 mph offshore, visibility had to be at least 3 miles, cloud cover no more than 60 percent and above 3,000 feet. The odds of all these conditions occurring together were no better than 50-to-1.[18]

Wherever Daddy was located before the invasion, it was under highest secrecy. He might have been at Lepe, one of the major places on the south coast of England used for the embarkation of troops and equipment for the invasion. Troops spent previous weeks in camps all along the coastline; roads and woods were crammed with men and materiel. Many of the troops ate, slept, and lived in or under vehicles, only moving when sent out on practice exercises. After more than two years of planning, Operation Overlord, the D-Day invasion, was about to begin, and Daddy was in the midst of it. The operation was kept so secret that even local people didn't know what was going on; the essential providers were issued passes allowing them to continue their daily business. A "D-Day at Lepe" website says, "Even the local milkman had to sign the Official Secrets Act before he was allowed to deliver milk to the site canteen."

As a member of an ordnance depot, Daddy was likely involved in the task of loading tanks and other heavy vehicles, as well as munitions and fuel. Mother said that he crossed the English Channel on D-Day plus five, arriving at Utah Beach on June 11, 1944. Undoubtedly it was the strangest, most intense boat ride of his life. So much blood had already been shed; no matter how soldiers steeled themselves for what conditions would be like, it had to be shocking to see death and ruin spread around on the beach and sloshing in the tides. The German installations on the hills above the beach must have seemed like forts of doom. When I saw them, decades after, they were still forbidding.

I wish I could have heard Daddy's comments on these things. His enlistment card and fading photograph give witness to immersion in a wartime military world that was foreign to those who remained at home. The blurriness of the photo and its foxing with age hint of much that will never be clear.

I can only guess what that time was like from war films and newsreel images: noise and sleeplessness, low-grade or little food, cold, wet, and muddy conditions, and alternating feelings of hope, depression, boredom, and fear. Still, what we *do* know is that it was one hair-raising, high-risk time.

Books Across the Sea: Bridges to Home

Line one, above: in French: "I would like to be one of your guests." Line two: In Dutch: "I too would like to be invited sometimes." On the back of the card Daddy wrote:

November 29, 1944 Somewhere in Belgium

Dear Nancy,

This little card says "I would like to be one of your guests" That goes for me too. To be yours and Mamma's guest sure would be swell.

Lots of Love,
"Daddy"

Of all the postcards Daddy managed to send, this is the one that delights me most. He couldn't tell where he was, except in the most general way. Rules enforced by Army censors protected the whereabouts of troops. I don't think he knew the languages, but he sent us a translation of the French (a Dutch friend recently translated the second line for me), to tell us how much he missed us. Calling himself a "guest" might sound strange, but the word *hospitality* comes from the root word *hospes* which can mean either "guest" or "host. " So he was yearning to join in loving hospitality in our home, a place where he was usually host, but now would be so happy to be even a guest. Not that he'd dream of going AWOL to be with us, but the fantasy of his joining us at the table, accompanied by a family of toy playmates, especially comforts my child self.

I love the eager expression of the little boy-man on the right; I see him as Daddy's surrogate, approaching with sprightly step to join the party. While I sometimes lost sight of his playful humor in those early years after he returned, it was always part of him. I happily recall the times after supper when he would stand on his head and help Marilyn, Bette, and me wobble up into place for headstands; he'd play "wheelbarrow" with us and show us how to do front and back somersaults. He'd take us on "horsey-back" rides too. What fun!

I have a little stack of Daddy's childhood books that I keep, along with my own, in my cedar chest. His copies of *Mother Goose Rhymes in Words of One Syllable* and *The Story of the Little Red Hen and Other Favorites* are filled with quaint illustrations similar to this child's party postcard drawing.

The more I study this postcard and others like it that he sent back from Europe, the more I imagine that this was one way he kept *his* child soul alive in the midst of carnage and chaos— what could contrast more radically with such images than a battlefield strewn with stinking corpses? At the same time, I feel the damage to our relationship that the war imposed. These cards, storybooks, and letters were substitutes for my father for the first years of my life. They were the only way he could reach me with his love and concern when he could neither see nor hear nor touch me—nor I him. I did not know how much I missed him. If a picture is worth a thousand words, as the cliché goes, how many postcards or storybooks would it take to equal just a few ordinary days together or even sharing one big hug?

How do we restore and heal the child selves who are thus abandoned? It's a challenging task, and I know I'm not alone with it. It is one that many must undertake, no matter what the cause of their being orphaned. As I go back and read Daddy's messages now, I find them very moving. When he sent them, I barely comprehended who he was. When he returned, our lives went into high gear as a whole new family era opened up, and such messages were laid aside. Part of his impulse to write them must have been to ensure that I would know that he loved me in case he did not return.

———— ◦ ————

One of the books he sent for Mother to read to me is the British *Bo-Peep Book of Nursery Rhymes,* with charming color illustrations, signed from "Daddy Somewhere in England April 17, 1944," seven weeks before D-Day. Holding this little book, I wonder how he came to find and send it. It may have afforded a brief respite of ordinary life in the midst of the huge military machinations going on around him.

In my mind's eye, I see Daddy getting a pass to go off base into the surrounding town, finding a little shop, and going in. A bell tinkles over the door, announcing a customer, and a saleswoman stands up from her stool behind a narrow counter. They greet each other—Daddy with his gregarious and charming demeanor—six feet tall with a strong mesomorphic physique, in his US Army uniform—and the Englishwoman glad to do business with one of the Allied troops, a Yank. After he asks to see children's books, she and Daddy exchange a few companionable words about their kids; he finds a book he likes and pays for it. Since earlier he had come around offering his service as a bike repairer, the woman smiles as he leaves and says, "John's bike works fine now!"

It occurs to me that my life-long love affair with words, and secondarily with images, began *because* they were the sole vehicles of love from my dad to me during his absence. And of course Mother reinforced that message in her diligent reading. She read bedtime stories to me in her lovely expressive voice from the books Daddy had sent. Mother also bought Little Golden Books (first published in 1942) when she went shopping at the A&P grocery. I adored *Rose Red and Rose White, Cookie,* and *Mumpsy Goes to Kindergarten,* and the sweetly comic drawings of picture books like *Bouncing Bunnies,* with its droll couplets.

One special story involved a velvety cat that got into a terrible mess in a paint pot, like me one time when I got my hands and hair in the roofers' tar on a hot summer day and had to be cleaned up. Decades later Marilyn found a copy for me: *Miss Sniff* by Jane Curry with fuzzy illustrations by Florence Sarah Winship.[19] Two of my sisters in adulthood argued about ownership of one of those beloved books that Mother read to each one of us in turn. They both declared that it was their favorite and that it rightly belonged to them. It got snitched back and forth and was a point of contention for several years. Was it Mother's voice they wanted, instead? *That* I can understand.

> *icy panes rattle*
> *Mama's story voice*
> *holds me warm*

"To Nancy Dear from Daddy Somewhere In Belgium, Christmas 1944." Mother made this inscription for Daddy in her elegant cursive inside the cover of one of my favorite books. On its back cover is a joyous circle of children from different lands holding hands as they dance, a beguiling image that pleased me as a solitary child. In its multi-national gathering of children, it's like a mini-UN, that idealistic problem-solving organization birthed soon after, in 1945. On the front cover a wheel is attached at center by a brad so you can turn it: a wedge-shaped opening reveals information about fifteen European countries, one at a time, each with a colored drawing of some landmark, a postage stamp, and its flag.

From it I learned of unfamiliar worlds—Mother translated its French text for me, and I pored over the drawings inside the book of children dressed in folkloric costumes doing exciting things I'd never imagined; how strange to ride a gondola in Venice or a toboggan in Switzerland. I especially admired the drawing from Holland—life there looked so *foreign*.

C'est en Hollande que près de l'eau s'amusent les bambins;
Ils dansent avec leurs petits sabots et tournent comme des
moulins.
(In Holland the little children are having fun near the
water;
They dance in their little wooden shoes and whirl like the
windmills.)

When I read through this charming *beau voyage* now, I realize that it—and all the books, cards, and mementos Daddy sent—conveyed one message: at war's end, *all* parents, like mine, hoped to be reunited with their children in a world as safe and happy as the one depicted in the pictures. The caption for Denmark implies this in a quaint but penetrating way. Three children, two pigtailed girls and a boy, in high boots and traditional garb exclaim:

Voyez! La cigogne a fait son nid, tout près de la cheminée;
Et ne prendra son envolée qu'ensemble avec ses petits.
(Look! The stork has made its nest right on the chimney;
It will fly away only if accompanied by its little ones.)

Our parents were like the faithful storks, ready to give their all to reunite us.

No Atheists in Foxholes

O Lord, how many are my foes!...
But you, O Lord, are
a shield around me....
                            – Psalm 3:1,3

It was standard operating procedure in the US Armed Forces during World War II to give the troops a special copy of the Bible, which was actually the New Testament only. Edges of the metal front cover of Daddy's copy are turned back to clip a piece of thin cardboard to its back. Dated 1943 from the Know Your Bible Company of Cincinnati, Ohio, it announces, "THE HEART-SHIELD BIBLE *Fits Snugly in Uniform Pocket/* THE ENGRAVED GOLD-FINISHED STEEL FRONT COVER PRO-TECTS HIS HEART." In one photo of him in Aachen, Germany, circa 1945, I detect a bulge in his left shirt pocket, over his heart, which may be Daddy's Bible. I can imagine that even if he didn't read it often, it was a powerful talisman.

There are no markings in this Bible, besides the childish scrawls of Janet, who probably discovered it in Daddy's desk drawer and wrote her name in big capital letters in pencil on a front endsheet in the early 1960s, when she was just learning to write. Two ribbons, unattached, are tucked inside the Bible, possibly for a US

Army Good Conduct Medal and a sharpshooter's decoration—the same ribbon is used for both, judging from images I've seen: red grosgrain with three thin white stripes paralleling each edge.

There's a 3 x 5 card penned in Daddy's handwriting left inside. It reads: "1) The Lord's Prayer: 6 chapter of St. Matthew, and 2) Red at Night Sailor's Delight—fair weather. Red in morning bad weather: Taken from 2 & 3 paragraphs of 16 Chapter of St. Matthew," and then, under a wavy line, a faint pencil line, "19th Chapter, St. Matthew." Were these notes from a chaplain's sermons? In Matthew 16, Jesus rebukes those of "an evil and adulterous generation" who know how to interpret the appearance of the sky but can't interpret "the signs of the times"; he says they will get no sign except the sign of Jonah and departs. It's not a very encouraging text. Matthew 19 begins with the Pharisees' tricky questions about what constitutes good reasons for divorcing a wife and goes on to include Jesus's reminder of the commandments, including, "Thou shalt not murder." Probably any soldier with a faith background knew that commandment and hoped somehow for a pass in combat. Perhaps the second part of verse 26 clears all away: "but with God all things are possible." I don't think we ever asked Daddy right out, "Did you kill anyone?" but every soldier has to wrestle with this question and try to come to peace with an answer.

The Psalms were not included in this Bible—how much comfort they might have offered.

The gold plating is pretty well worn away from the steel front; the etched words, "May this keep you safe from harm," are scratched and just legible. Other covers of the Heart-Shield Bibles, now for sale on eBay, have such inscriptions as "God's Weapon," "May the Lord Be With You," and "To My Loved One." Many, although not Daddy's, have a message from President Franklin D. Roosevelt inserted in the binding just inside the cover. It begins: "As Commander-in-Chief I take pleasure in commending the reading of the Bible to all who serve in the armed forces of the United States...." It doesn't sound like non-Christians were provided with *their* sacred texts. Someone on a website focused on the Heart-Shield Bibles asked, "What about Buddhists?" and a soldier's child answered: "Dad used to say that in the foxhole, everyone is a believer and it didn't matter who you believed in, it was all the same god."

———— ⚬ ————

There are stories that these Bibles served as miraculous breast-plates, saving soldiers' lives by stopping bullets. That seems un-likely unless a bullet was fired from quite a distance and lost much of its momentum—the steel case is thin. Though I never heard Daddy talk about his faith, I know that Grammy Corson was devoted to hers and must certainly have given her children a sense of its import. President Roosevelt's statement in the Bibles, along with the general war rhetoric, showed how close-ly Christian faith and patriotism were linked in the American mind of that day. From the wear on the cover, I'd guess that Daddy carried his Heart-Shield Bible all during the war. I am honored to have it.

Mother's counterpart to the Heart-Shield Bible was a ster-ling silver locket, heart-shaped with the wingspread eagle of the Great Seal of the United States in relief on the front. Inside (see back cover photo) are two photos, one of me held by someone's strong adult hands, likely Nanaw's. I'm wearing a fuzzy coat and a knitted cap with pompoms. On the other side, the side with the chain attached, is a photo of Daddy in his summer beige uniform with US overseas cap, facing inward toward me from the right. Maybe Daddy gave this locket to Mother as a gift? That thought reminds me of the lovely poetry of *Song of Solomon:*

> Set me as a seal upon your heart,..
> for love is strong as death,
> passion fierce as the grave.
> —Song of Solomon 8:6a

I also think of the Psalms of Lament in the Hebrew Bible and wonder if they were a solace to Mother, raised in the Episcopal Church with The Psalter in *The Book of Common Prayer.*

> You have kept count of my tossings;
> put my tears in your bottle.
> –Psalm 56:8

Daddy, with his country Baptist background, and Mother, with her city Episcopal upbringing, chose to join the Lutheran church in our small town. I remember that we attended regularly, going from children's Sunday school through catechism to confirmation. I always felt proud to file into the pew together as a family. Mother, whose clear soprano voice sounded so pretty singing the hymns, would occasionally mention how she missed the elegance of the Episcopal liturgy of her youth.

I know that Sunday school provided early socializing for me; in contemporary parlance it was rather like a regular play date. Mother played the piano and often helped teach the lesson from our regular Lutheran study flyers with front pages in beautiful color. We didn't notice that all the people portrayed were Caucasian—a mirror of our town. There were one or two "act-out" kids whose loud or goofy disruptions fascinated the rest of us.

> *"Yes, Jesus Loves Me…*
> *Little ones to Him belong"*
> *bratty Jimmy too*

I remember one shy girl I secretly pinched and shoved— ah, the eruptions of original sin! We all loved belting out the "Good-bye Song" and racing out at the end to find our parents and go home.

III

Starting Anew

Confusions of Homecoming

(A Letter)

Dear Daddy,

When you came home from the war, it was as though our world gyroscope, too long out of whack, began to right itself again. We just had to get used to it. You and I really needed to get to know each other, but it was difficult because you concentrated on starting up the new business and "making up for lost time" in a hundred ways. You practiced being my Daddy, sometimes with fun, but sometimes there were shadows of harshness I found frightening.

My Nanaw, Mother's mother, who'd been such a companion for us while you were gone, suddenly disappeared, and then in a short time I had a new sister—a most confusing change of players on my stage!

In this writing I am clarifying my own history, and as I think back, I am impressed by the resilience and competence you and Mother demonstrated as you made a new start in business, planted trees and lawns, and generally put everything in high gear. Another newness was the sanctuary we enjoyed at Grammy and Grandpap Corson's farm—what a gift to spend our Sunday afternoons and holidays there.

About what I called "shadows of harshness," this is what I now know: because you were the one who was immersed in war's confusions, the one who could not turn aside from any of its danger and ugliness, you had the hardest role of all, to undo that experience as well as you could. Even when we had to suffer with you after it was presumably over, we all had, and continue to have, the opportunity—and grace—of forgiveness and reconciliation.

Love,
Nancy

Missing Nanaw

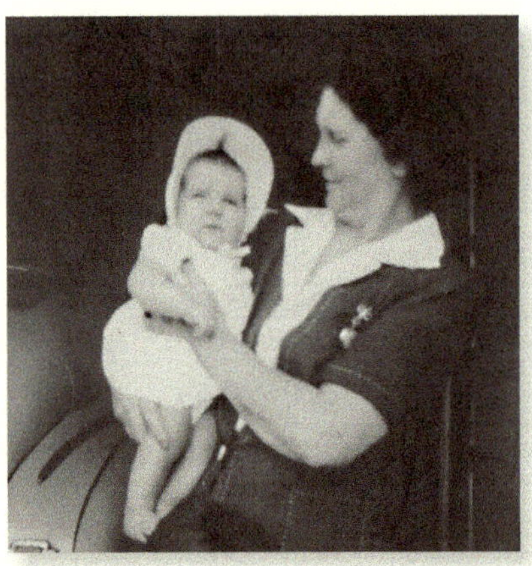

Overnight our worlds changed. The Allies were victorious, and Daddy was coming home at last. I must have been aware of the surrounding jubilation, but the time also had its confusions for me. "Finally," Mother said, "the war in Europe ended and Harvey returned to Fort Rucker, Alabama, on an Italian troop ship. While he was there, my mother died suddenly (the summer the war ended in Europe—1945), and Harvey was able to get leave to come home briefly."

Nanaw embodied love and support for Mama and me during

the war, but when it was over, she was gone. It must have been a great blow to Mama to lose her mother, her close companion and supporter, but knowing that her husband was back in the States surely was a huge compensation, even though for a short while it looked like he might have to go to the Pacific theater.

As for me, I'd lost my own dear ally, my Nanaw. She had been the one who'd taken care of me in Altoona when Mother needed to make trips to see Daddy. I had no idea what had happened, but someone very important in my world abruptly disappeared, never to return. At two and a half, I was only dimly aware of the epochal events swirling around us.

What caused Nanaw's death, I don't know, but one factor may have been depression exacerbated by the fact that Grandpap J wasn't the most supportive of mates. Of all our relatives, he was perhaps the most enigmatic. He was a laconic man with a distant mien; his main love was tennis, and he was an ardent player and supporter of the sport, a winner of many trophies. Nanaw didn't play, as far as I know. Mother did play, some. We had rackets and a few cans of tennis balls around the house, but it never quite caught on with any of us sisters. I don't recall him spending any energy to introduce us to the sport. Grandpap J didn't even seem to remember his grandchildren's names, or else he had a weird sense of humor. Oddly, he called us all "Rover" or "Snicklefritz." One nice thing I remember is his sending me birthday cards; they were usually funny, and I liked his handsome, mostly printed handwriting.

Another peculiarity about Grandpap J was that everything about him smelled of smoke. I don't remember that he smoked so much during the day, but he spent hours listening to the radio, especially after dinner, with his eyes shut, smoking and dozing. Daddy may have smoked some cigarettes during the war. He occasionally smoked a cigar with a friend, and for a while he had some pipes, but generally smoking was frowned upon in our household—especially for "good girls." It was stinky and *dangerous*. Mother remembered that her family had to watch out that Grandpap J didn't burn the house down by falling asleep in his chair at night, dropping live ashes from his cigarettes.

Some family photos from our visits in Altoona show a girl who appeared in age to be another of my cousins, but I'm now quite certain that she was Mother's illegitimate sister, from Grandpap J's liaison with a younger woman.

When I was about two, Nanaw took a trip to Florida, alone. In those days that was a rather unusual thing for a married woman to do. I liked the gaudy hand-colored postcards she sent to us. They presented a storybook world of exotic gardens with flamingos and parrots. Grandpap J re-married just a few years after Nanaw's death to a woman we never got to know very well. Once, when she and he were visiting us, I had the devilish, perhaps Freudian, notion at the breakfast table to blurt out to her, "Virgie, in your reflection in the toaster, you look like a witch!"

We'll never hear Nanaw's side of any stories of her life and marriage; her secrets are buried with her. There was an air of mystery and silence around her; we girls knew somehow that we were not to ask about her, and we didn't. I do know that she dearly loved Mother and me. I'm so sorry that I can't even remember the sound of her voice.

I remember that her rather somber portrait stayed for many years on one side of Daddy's desk in the study. My sense is that Daddy had a good relationship with her as a mother-in-law. I believe he appreciated her and her kind ways, as the person who had taken such good care of Mother and me when he was gone and who taught Mother to be such a great cook.

Veteran Entrepreneur

Mother said, "Finally he was sent home and arrived in the middle of the night on Columbus Day in 1945! That was a great day!" Even though Daddy returned from war in late autumn, it must have seemed like a most joyous springtime, long delayed.

As for me, a whole new relationship loomed. At first I was afraid. "Mommy, who is that man?" I asked, hiding behind her, when he climbed the wooden porch stairs to our second floor apartment and back into our lives. This man's largeness, the strange Army uniform with scratchy wool overcoat I could feel when he lifted me up and hugged me, his strong voice, and all his different smells—aftershave, damp wool, perspiration. What an overwash of conflicting emotions my father's presence created.

I hadn't quite finished my "terrible twos," but clearly whatever space my child self might have claimed with my autonomy-building "No!" was now in question. The king had clearly returned to his castle. With Nanaw mysteriously gone, I had to learn to share my first love, Mother, with him. A whole world had been swept away and a new one emerged, full of excitements and challenges.

And away we went! What an enormity of transitions this man was making—so much joy and relief, so many plans, so much to catch up on, including me.

I'd guess that the photo I've included was taken very soon after he returned. Mother and I are wearing summery dresses and shoes—perhaps it was a warm late-autumn day; we all look healthy and tan, though Mother looks a little thin. I link my uncertain feelings with remembrance of that corner of our living room as having scratchy surfaces—the fiberglass wallboards and that itchy green upholstered chair barely visible to the right. I note familiar objects there too: I'm sitting on a stool Daddy made for me to stand on to reach the sink in the bathroom, and there's just a corner showing of a glass coffee table that got broken later in sisters' horseplay. Even that tiny picture of a pretty country scene, hung too high, is still familiar. What was *not* familiar to me then was my father, gone since I was only six weeks old, and, moreover, his being in Army uniform. Perhaps he hadn't yet had time to shop for civilian clothes?

Comparing photos before and after the war, it's clear that Daddy was losing his beautiful wavy hair when he came home. He blamed this on wearing a heavy steel helmet so often and in tough conditions, though Grandpap Corson's baldness suggests that genetics played a role.

Here are Bill Mauldin's comments about helmets; he doesn't exactly support the baldness theory, but a reader can at least infer that they were uncomfortable to wear:

Those who look carefully at newspaper pictures have probably observed that many Germans are captured at the front without helmets, while our guys wear them almost all the time. One of the reasons for this is that we were taught very thoroughly that a helmet is a good thing to have around, but the main reason is because the American helmet is a handy instrument even when you're not wearing it. You can dig with it, cook with it, gather fruit with it, and bathe with it. The only disadvantage of the helmet is that it is drafty in winter and hot in summer.[20]

About ten or fifteen years later, when Daddy lost nearly all his hair and began to shave his head, he got kidded that he looked like Yul Brynner, famously bald in the movie *The King and I*. But that look wasn't quite "in" yet, and he tried all sorts of things to restore hair growth, including mange cure, a nasty-smelling concoction that I got to massage into his head. A futile effort.

He also told us that he felt that his loss of hearing in later years was in part caused by the sounds of explosions, gunfire, and other loud noises in the war. Even though he learned to wear ear protectors for such things as chain sawing and shooting, the hearing aids he wore in both ears were a bane of his last decade. They never seemed to work as well as he wished, and I noticed that he was embarrassed at not being able to hear conversations clearly, especially as a person who'd always loved banter and storytelling.

From the day he returned, like almost all those men who'd spent years in the military, Daddy was determined, as he often said, "to make up for lost time"—that really was a central theme of his hard-working life. He and many others apparently intuited that immersing themselves in the American protestant work ethic meant not only a chance at economic success, but also a way to direct mind and energy away from the shocks of war and into the balm of normal life. Many, like Daddy, quickly found employment. While he had already finished his formal education at Penn State, as an educator I'm proud to note that the GI Bill gave about 7.8 million others the chance to advance theirs by returning to the classroom.

Daddy told us later that he felt that his old job as an Allis-Chalmers territory manager required him to be on the road too much to be a good father, so he wasted no time in establishing his own business, in January 1946. The first lines of the ad placed in the local paper read:

HARVEY CORSON
Muncy Veteran of World War II
Announces the opening of his place of business
at the
GULF SIGN l Mile North of Muncy
On the Road to Williamsport.

"Muncy Veteran of World War II"—in that one line he proudly announced himself as a trustworthy local son ready to serve. In the photo above, Mother and I are pleased to pose beside the first business sign along the highway. Beginning with maintenance and repair services and the sale of large and small appliances, cars and farm machinery sales and services were soon added. Mother said that at first cars and machinery were scarce due to wartime restrictions, and that being in business was difficult.

At some point, Daddy dropped appliances from the inventory and the business focused on sales and service of cars and farm machinery. After that, the signs and stationery, the ones familiar to me as I was growing up, read:

> *Harvey F. Corson*
> *Sales and Service*
> *Chrysler and Plymouth Autos*
> *and Allis-Chalmers Farm Machinery*

In the final years of the business, when I was off to college, yet another transition led to selling and servicing only Allis-Chalmers and New Holland farm equipment, Remington chain saws, and, once again, some home appliances, but no more cars. Snowmobiles got on the list too, but I missed that era.

Daddy and Mother were a great team. In twenty-two years of business, Daddy was the intrepid chief salesman, mechanic, and planner. Mother did all the secretarial work. There were usually two or three mechanics on the payroll. Daddy farmed various crops on the side too, from seed corn and soybeans to hay, sorghum, and crown vetch.

I vividly recall Daddy's work uniform of heavy dark green cotton twill with the Allis-Chalmers insignia and "Harvey" written over the breast pocket in orange machine stitching. The business uniform was very democratic—the hired mechanics wore the exact same uniform, with their own names over the pockets. What a pleasure it must have been to have the freedom to choose his uniform instead of wearing whatever ones were assigned by the Army. Mother taught me how to iron them. I must have been about eleven or twelve when I proudly mastered the particular steps of pressing the shirts, and I was pleased to contribute to our family business in that way.

Daddy worked right along with the other mechanics, and often needed to use strong abrasive soaps like Lava or Twenty Mule Team Borax to clean the grease from his hands at night before supper. He was physically strong and skilled at manual labor; his welding, which may have been perfected in his Army Ordnance Depot, was expert. Years later when Howard and I owned a VW Rabbit (he told us he wished we'd buy American), Daddy saw that the dipstick was far too short to use easily, so he took a spare one and spot-welded it onto the original. When a gas station mechanic saw it as he checked our oil, he praised the ingenious solution to an obvious design weakness from VW and added, "Whoever welded these two thin pieces of metal together sure knew what he was doing!" We were glad to relay that comment to Daddy.

Daddy was seldom sick, though he had to be hospitalized for several hernia surgeries, probably as a result of over-lifting. I remember visiting in the hospital on those occasions. It was so strange to see him in a bed or in a chair wearing jammies and bathrobe during the daytime, something unheard of for his usually vital, busy self. I admire his staying active and in good shape all during his life; it was only that miserable Parkinson's that slowed him down at last.

Through determined entrepreneurial skill and lots of hard work, along with Mother's help, Daddy became an exemplar of the Horatio Alger myth of the American self-made man so admired in our twentieth-century culture—he was the American boy who began humbly, worked hard, dreamed big, and achieved success. As a result, our family lived out the post-war American dream—comfortable with the basics, able to keep up with new technologies like TV and even the latest cars, thanks to our Chrysler-Plymouth dealership.

In my child's eyes, we were rich, and we *were* in so many ways. Whatever Daddy did was on a large scale, whether it was building a business or buying land, raising a family of four girls and sending them all to college or, later, in retirement, becoming a world-class game hunter.

From the point of view of American culture, his success involved many of the signature transitions of the twentieth century in the US. He began as a rural farm boy whose family used horses to draw machinery and grew up to be a seller of tractors. He was the first in his family to go to college. As a salesman of American-made cars, he participated in the automobilization of the country. I think of Eisenhower, his commanding-general-become-president, who speeded this up by pushing for an interstate highway system.

Clearly Daddy's agricultural engineering degree coupled with a sound knowledge of economics helped him keep up with the enormous technological and market advances in his lifetime. Ironically, economics had been a subject Daddy deemed unimportant in college. A Penn State economics professor, who saw signs of his indifference to his subject, asked him, "As an agricultural engineering student, how do you think you're going to *sell* what you design and produce?" That question marked a critical turning point—Daddy changed from an about-to-fail economics student into a high-grade one. He put those lessons to good use.

With my American Studies background, I'm fascinated to learn that the central franchises of my parents' business, Allis-Chalmers, along with Chrysler and Plymouth, represented corporations that rose from humble roots in the nineteenth century to become twentieth-century American industrial giants. Besides that, Chrysler's manufacture of tanks, bombers, anti-aircraft guns, and military trucks was crucial to national defense during World War II. For better or for worse, Mother and Daddy's small business was enmeshed in the expanding military-industrial complex of our nation.

> *fireflies blink*
> *outside showroom window*
> *neon lights blink back*

In his 1961 Farewell Address, President Dwight D. Eisenhower said:

> We must never let the weight of this combination [of the military-industrial complex] endanger our liberties or democratic processes. We should take nothing for granted. Only an alert and knowledgeable citizenry can compel the proper meshing of the huge industrial and military machinery of defense with our peaceful methods and goals, so that security and liberty may prosper together.[21]

This was a wise warning of our president, who was formerly the Allied Supreme Commander. In retrospect, I feel that these words challenge us to deal much better with serious problems than we are currently doing as a nation and as a planet. They seem to me as a direct rebuttal of the current corporation-coddling of the US Supreme Court's "Citizens United" ruling. But in those boom years right after the war, it seemed, at least on the surface, that life had returned to normal, and Americans could devote themselves to families and to peacetime progress. We took for granted that "the sky was the limit."

Like the lucky others who were reunited after the war, Daddy and Mother were certainly energized by the chance to live out dreams deferred. In 1946, in the first spring after Daddy returned, he and Mother seeded lawns and planted the first of many gardens on the "home side" of the big building where our second-floor apartment could be reached by outside stairs. Trees, mostly maples, and bushes like forsythia, lilac, beauty bush (kolwitzia), and bridal veil spirea soon flourished. In the great burst of grateful-to-be-home energy, Daddy organized the shop and inventory while Mother organized the office and accounting system, and they were soon ready for customers.

I am so grateful for all those long hours, all that careful planning, all the risks our parents took to realize a dream my sisters and I had the privilege of sharing. Surely this is part of what inspired Tom Brokaw when he gave them and their contemporaries the name of "the Greatest Generation."

Sibling Rivalry

You can easily imagine this visual cliché. In a wartime photo taken where the picket-fenced yard with trees and bushes would later be, there I am, a baby on a blanket, basking in the sunshine. Soon, like lots of other soldiers' kids left at home during the war, I had a new sibling, born just about nine months after my father's return. Our own post-war boom!

Ever the entrepreneur, Daddy earned extra money by growing sweet corn and peddling it in town. Mother remembered him bringing in bushels of fresh corn to sell to the doctors and nurses at the Muncy Valley Hospital the day Marilyn was born.

Shortly after she was brought home from the hospital, I crawled amidst the dust bunnies under her crib when its side bar was down and announced to Mother that I was in jail; her angry order for me to get up from there "Right away!" marked this in my memory. Had she been reading warnings about sibling rivalry? When she was old enough to walk, Marilyn got a little wooden pull-toy bear that played a simple xylophone melody as its wheels went around. She would circle the dining room table with it, giggling at its jolly noise, her curly long auburn hair bouncing as she ran. Daddy would laugh with delight.

She had blue eyes like his and was such a happy little kid. I felt somber and dumpy in contrast to this bundle of cuteness that was my new sister. I had learned to talk fluently quite early as Mother's constant companion while Daddy was away, and language became my pride and refuge, but for awhile I felt silenced. My center stage role was now doubly usurped, first by my father and then by my sister, until I figured out how to either share it or find a new one.

I know it's quite normal for elder siblings to have some resentment toward a new sibling, but these weren't normal circumstances. I needed some reassurance that it wasn't a competition, and that I was special too. The intensity of my feeling made me think for a long while that I was just a jealous person: that was my personal flaw. I couldn't articulate the heaviness I felt, but I think it had a lot to do with the shadow of my father's absence when I was at this stage of "cute" babyhood. In psychoanalytical terms, our identity needs to be reflected back to us or we don't have it; if this is so, there are missing parts of my father-seen self that I needed to gather together and revive. This isn't something I blame him for. It was something that I didn't understand for many years. And it's pretty natural right after the war years that a just-returned soldier would be delighted with a new child full of happy spirit.

What's clear to me now is that I took on some of the shadow of the war without any understanding of the relationship of my own microcosm with the disturbed macrocosm. I can't blame all my jealousy and mean moments on the war, but it didn't help. It was a contamination of sorts that I, like so many others, have had to work to bring to consciousness and then to hoped-for healing.

Obviously the wartime absences and returns played out in many complex, differing ways in families. One of my friends told of her experience, which is an exaggerated form of my situation. Born in Germany before the war, she has photographs of that period showing a happy, smiling family. When her father, a scientist, was deported to the US after the war as a defeated enemy, she noticed that, in contrast, the faces in the photos of *that* time are downcast and unsmiling. She said that one of her father's prime joys was the post-war birth of her sister.

She felt she had become, in her father's eyes, the child who carried the burden of the war, even to the point of his being jealous of her time alone with her mother while he was forced to be absent in wartime service. The new daughter symbolized a new beginning; his obvious preference for her sister marred my friend's young life. Her later creative life as a teacher and her befriending of her sister *and* herself demonstrates the lifetime work of a "wounded healer." The term, from Carl Jung, refers to those brave enough to face their life wounds consciously and to follow them through the darkness of suffering until they yield a way to light and recovery. I find this idea very helpful. I want to join those who intentionally avoid the traps of bitterness and victimization in personal wounds by working to make them doorways to healing in the outer transpersonal realms as well.

On the other side of the coin, Marilyn had to suffer through manifestations of my resentment toward her as the child of the new beginning. When she was about five, Daddy warned her not to tell that she might have a party for her upcoming July birthday, that if she did, she wouldn't have one—I never knew why, because it's so hard for kids to keep secrets. Marilyn went ahead and bragged to the neighbor kids about her upcoming celebration. I tattled, and the party was canceled. (Did she not think Daddy would keep his word?) I quickly saw how wrong I'd been. How could I be so mean as to have had my own party earlier in the year, then go and ruin hers? She was such a loyal younger sister, despite the times I mistreated her.

> *her: post-war kid*
> *long curls, giggles*
> *me: dour wartime kid*
> *having to "set an example"*

I wasn't very good to her in lots of ways, trying to cheat her out of toys, piggy bank coins, and such when we played. Luckily, this jealous or resentful phase didn't last much beyond the time I began school. Marilyn was overjoyed when Bette was born three years after her, and she loved being a big sister. They played together—Marilyn even joined her in the playpen to share Fig Newtons and games with her toys—and I was free to be my independent bookworm self.

Since Marilyn is closest of my sisters in age with me, she is the only person now alive who remembers the earliest years I write about. I trust that as grown women we are both forgiving and forgiven for some of the hard places of our childhoods. The German poet Rainer Maria Rilke offers these words toward healing: "perhaps all the dragons of our lives are princesses who are only waiting to see us once beautiful and brave. Perhaps everything terrible is in its deepest being something helpless that wants our help."[22]

Shadows

I know that the war's trauma lingered in strange and often hidden ways. Mother told of Daddy's leaping out of bed and getting under it when he heard airplanes going over or scrambling down into a combat-ready crouch at the slightest nighttime noise for months after returning. Clearly, the passage from being a warfare-trained soldier to being a peacetime citizen again simply couldn't happen at once. Kevin Powers's 2012 novel about the Iraq war, *The Yellow Birds*, gave me some clues about this when I read it. The "Traditional US Army Marching Cadence" used as an epigraph for the book showed me how hard it would be to shake the cut-throat mindset continually hyped for combat. "A yellow bird/ with a yellow bill,/ was perched upon/ my windowsill./ I lured him in/ With a piece of bread/ And then I smashed/ His fucking head."

This theme is repeated in a Library of Congress anthology about World War II:

For besides being hell, without those letters [from home, especially at the holidays], war entirely replaces one reality with another. On the battlefield, paranoia is often a sign of mental health. Dirt is normal, and it is everywhere; coarseness is part of everyday demeanor; and a little callousness is a shell that helps keep one whole. Without it, a soldier couldn't go on in the midst of grief over buddies dying all around him. These are survival skills to fit an extreme situation, but in the long run they are not life skills.[23]

The recommendation for helping a GI back to normal life, to make him smile again, was to send ordinary good news. How are the kids, the dogs, the neighbors? What's coming up in the garden? Who won the latest local high school basketball game?

Facing the deadly weaponry of war, Daddy learned protective stratagems to be a survivor. I'm sure that he had to discipline himself when he returned to civilian life to slowly transform reactions from a world of violence and chaos to conventional behaviors of society. I've talked with some of my contemporaries about their fathers, and they acknowledge the lingering effects. Even though one girlfriend's father was willing, uncharacteristically, to talk a lot about the war and to watch war films with his family, she said he still had nightmares for the rest of his life. If Daddy had nightmares, he never mentioned them.

Daddy did tell us that he had detested the German V-2 missiles. Nazi propaganda presented the V-2s, along with V-1s and V-3s, as *Vergeltungswaffe* or "retaliation weapons," to get back at the Allies for bombing German cities from 1942 until war's end. Tragically, most of these weapons were assembled by concentration camp prisoners, many of whom were killed while producing them. Unlike the V-1 missiles, called "doodlebugs" in British slang, which gave some warning—about thirty seconds between the motors' stopping and their plummet to earth—the V-2 took only four seconds to reach its target at up to 2,205 mph (3,550 km/hr) and came down from the stratosphere, with its two thousand pounds of explosive, without warning.[24] No wonder Daddy hated them.

cool shade
shrapnel in tree bark
almost hidden

The war, however, seemed to have stirred up in him some angers and harshnesses that were hard to understand. One of my earliest memories is of a disturbing incident that occurred when I was about three. It was one evening after supper in our dining room; Daddy, Mother, and I were sitting on the floor in a space behind the big table with the long cotton lace tablecloth. Spread out like pieces in a game on the pink plume-patterned rug with its grey background was an assortment of American coins, and Daddy was giving me a lesson in counting with them.

I suppose I knew something about counting at that age, but certainly nothing about counting with the numerical values of different coins—why was one coin equal to five, another to ten, and so on? He explained and explained, but then got angrier and angrier as I kept failing the lesson. I was tired of this imponderable task and had to pee. I said so, but he apparently thought I was whining or lying, and sternly insisted that I was going nowhere until I "got it right." Mother tried to intercede, but it was too late, and I peed on the rug. He was disgusted, and I was ashamed of myself (I *was* potty-trained after all!) and very afraid of this angry person, my father.

I go back to that episode and think it over and over, puzzling at its dynamics. I remember that economics was a subject that first gave Daddy trouble, and then gave him an important key to success. Was he trying to give me that lesson from the start so that I would properly value money? Also, I wonder what kind of disciplining he received as a child from Grandpap Corson. Maybe there were resonances of some harshness in this situation. Parents reflexively pass on what they've experienced, particularly with first children, until they catch themselves repeating patterns they regret, and then they may try to change. I know something about that as a parent myself.

This was one small but memorable experience for me of Daddy's anger; there were others dotted through my childhood that created a tension between my knowledge of him as a father who was ordinarily steady and good-humored and as one who could be angry and frightening. I don't know if he had always had anger issues, which were, to some degree, exacerbated by the war experience, or whether they began then. All my life I've had this dilemma of sorting the wheat from the chaff of our relationship, like the princesses or peasant girls in the fairytales—it *is* almost always females doing the sorting, isn't it? In this incident I recognized how powerful this man, my father, was, and how much I needed to figure out how to please him to avoid, if I could, repetitions of such a painful scene.

Of course, working to please Daddy was not all bad—he said he wanted us "to see things to do" and to do them well; he expected us to meet high standards in our school work, and in family loyalty, responsibility, and truthfulness. All four of his daughters were raised to be "young ladies" who knew how "to be seen and not heard." We were complimented for our good manners by folks who observed us in public and at family visits.

And yet, I have felt a strong need to overcome what might have been a lifelong subservience to the power of the father in a patriarchal culture. Again, I owe much to Carl Jung's insights, this time about what he labels the process of "individuation." I am urged to honor my father *and* my own unique self as parts of an integrated whole. Once more, I find resonances with Jung's concept of the "wounded healer," one who has empathy for others gained through personal suffering, as well as with the Christian second great commandment, to love one's neighbor as oneself (Matthew 22:39). In short, I want to be able to say to Daddy that I understand my pilgrimage through life as aiming for living with a loving heart *and* a whole self with others.

The Grandparent Farm

dusty henhouse gold:
warm brown eggs in little bins
piggybank pennies

It was only after the war that I got to know Grammy and Grandpap Corson; then we began regular Sunday visits to their farm. I loved that drive up into the Muncy Hills; it was really a passage to another world, to an old-fashioned farm filled with surprises. What a blessing that Daddy was able to return with his growing family to the place where he was raised and find his parents still carrying on their lives much as they did before the war. It was, in many ways, a sanctuary for us all.

I like to think that Grammy's version of "swords to plow-shares" was to braid bright-colored rugs from the coarsely woven Army salvage flag fabric Daddy brought back from Europe. They were a great contrast to the somber-toned ones she made from old black, brown, and white stockings. Grammy's garden provided much of the food we ate together there, and in the summer we rarely left the farm without a bag of vegetables, fruit, or flowers. The garden was surely a place of solace as she waited and prayed for the war to end. Now it could be a celebration place with her Harvey safely home.

Before we went "up to Grammy and Grandpap's," we had a Sunday ritual of going to Sunday School, eating lunch, reading the Sunday papers we bought at the Grange News Agency on Main Street, and taking naps. Then we'd all load into the car. I remember the ride as a sequence of recognitions: places where friends lived in town, and then further out in the country, where our school bus went before it came to get us on the "second load," a hill peculiarly dotted with dark cypresses, a passage through a farmer's woods with a gently meandering stream where I saw my first great blue heron, and the old Frenchtown one-room schoolhouse Daddy attended as a boy.

Sometimes in the summer we'd stop on the way for him to shoot a groundhog, sworn enemy of farmers, because their holes posed threats to horses, which might step into them and break legs, or to machines, which could be damaged when tires lurched into them.

> *gun in the car trunk*
> *Groundhog*
> *I'd hide if I were you*

At the farm we loved chasing the wild kitties—Grandpap wanted them to be good mousers, not dependent on hand-outs, so he encouraged their being skittery. If we got there early enough, we could watch the piggies feeding in their pen and the cows being milked. Sometimes Grammy would take us along to gather eggs in the tar-papered chicken coop.

My sisters and I loved our snowy winter visits. There were times when our car had barely been able to make it up the last hill, on the sparsely-cindered dirt road, with our wheels, even with chains on them, slipping and sliding on ice and snow. We cheered Daddy's expert driving; I recall only one time when it was so bad that we couldn't make it and had to turn around and go home. When we reached the farmhouse, we'd greet Grammy and Grandpap. Mother would check to see that we had our boots, mittens, hats, and coats secured, then we'd race up one more hill past the house and pile on the biggest sled, its runners well waxed.

We loved it when Daddy would be on the bottom of the sled with one or two of us piled on top to get maximal weight for speed. He'd steer. That first hill, coming back down by the farmhouse, was pretty easy; we could even do this by our-selves, but we got the biggest thrill if we'd round the corner by Grandpap's garage and coast through the flat part of the road by the cemetery and then the church with enough momentum to go down that second, much steeper hill beyond (the one that gave us trouble to climb in the car). We'd have a long, jolly hike back, coaxing, "Daddy, let's do it again *just one more time!*"

Those occasions sometimes called forth his remembrance of a sled he'd paid to have sent from the Netherlands for me, with my name on it; he regretted that it had never arrived. We might suspect bad faith, but maybe some tragedy befell the seller. We will never know. That sled may have signified a childhood joy Daddy wished to pass on in a tangible way, or perhaps an even deeper desire to restore innocence after the shocks of the war. I like to think of our sledding together and playing snow games as somehow materializing the intent of that lost gift.

> *on the snowy wheel*
> *"Fox and Geese" tests runners' skills*
> *breathless race for home*

That farm house was a second home to me. Details flood in—from the smell of the Cashmere Bouquet soap in the cold, unheated bathroom upstairs (fairly new after years with just a wooden outhouse) to the springtime pleasure of soft, grey pussy willow catkins on bushes wedged between the kitchen and the milk house. We looked forward to playing games like Kick-the-Can with our cousins when visits coincided, an opportunity to scout out unusual nooks and crannies. At Christmas, we had gift-openings around the spindly tree Grandpap had chopped down in the woods and Grammy had decorated with fragile old-timey ornaments. One of our aunts always sent underwear or cheap perfume. Although we were in the company of adults mostly, we children had freedom to find our own special places inside and out.

Grammy's big black Easter Dockash wood stove in the kitchen was a presence in itself. It was uncomfortably hot in the summer but warm and welcoming in the winter. The dining room adjoined the kitchen, and centered on the big table that nearly filled it up. After we'd eaten, I helped to scrape leftovers into the slops bucket for the pigs and to dry dishes.

On the wall behind the table, portraits of President Eisenhower and Jesus as the Good Shepherd hung side by side. When Eisenhower ran for president during the fall of my fourth-grade year, we all wore "I LIKE IKE" buttons. I wondered if Daddy ever met him face to face or had seen and heard him exhorting the troops. In 1952, we were part of a grateful and admiring nation that elected him thirty-fourth president of the US. Pride in his leadership reflected upon all who had served with "Ike."

After Grandpap died and Grammy moved to town, she took those portraits along and hung them on her kitchen wall. I'm sure she felt that both delivered us from evil.

> *Grammy dines*
> *with Ike and Jesus*
> *allies in chaos and calm*

IV

Home:
The Castle

A Great Place to Grow Up

(A Letter)

Dear Daddy,

From "Somewhere in Belgium 1944" you sent a beautiful Christ-mas and New Year's card to Mother and me, "your two brown-eyed girlies." You labeled its cover, a colored drawing of pretty houses in a little village by a river, "Corson Castle on the Susquehanna," the image of your hopes and dreams. When you returned, it still repre-sented central goals of your life. I was lucky to share in your two "castles," the first one, which we dubbed "The Building," and then, in retirement, the more fully realized Corson Castle.

The Building was an interesting place to grow up. My sisters and I had many adventures there—inside, with all its stairs and rooms—our apartment upstairs, and outside in the garden and surroundings. We loved associating with the cars and farm machinery you sold in the business area downstairs, Daddy, especially bright orange Allis-Chalmers equipment. And we got to meet so many different kinds of people.

Years later, The Building burned down and Corson Castle was sold, but we have fond memories. Spring pleasures inspired this haiku:

> *first robins arrive*
> *mailbox forsythia sparks*
> *soon cotton dresses*

Thank you for all that gave us such a warm sense of security there.

Love,
Nancy

The Castle on
the Susquehanna

Daddy and Mother both spoke fondly of the Susquehanna River. Mother had spent happy summers with her family on a houseboat along its shores near Muncy. A small sepia-tone photo I've inherited shows five-year-old Harvey (in 1919) standing on a sledge in a snowy street in Muncy. He's apparently waiting with the horses while his dad makes one of their regular deliveries of milk and eggs. I made a silk screen enlargement of that scene, and Daddy was pleased to hang it beside the original on the living room wall. He must have enjoyed remembering a long day's adventure in his youth, traversing nearly ten wintry miles to town and back home again.

"Susquehanna" was a native Indian word; the English Romantics considered it one of the most beautiful words in the English language. It *is* a splendid river, with its wide, wide reaches and tree-hung banks and coves, with great rocks strewn about, creating riffles and little islands. Its vistas would inspire any painter of nature's wonders or make anyone want to live near it, just so they weren't located where spring floods reached. Although we never lived *on* the river, we lived in a valley of rich soil deposited long ago in the ice ages and now drained by the river; it was a presence in our community.

When I study the image of Daddy's card, however, it shows a cold, closed-up landscape. The boat looks frozen in. Although the houses are a warm yellow color, all their doors and windows are battened down. Not a single person has ventured out. Everything, from the mountain and forest in the background to the foreground village and river, is static; the dynamic of warmth and movement can only be anticipated for the future. And that must have been how Daddy felt then, on hold, hoping for the logjam of winter to give way to a safe and spring-freed world, with the end of the war and resumption of his life back in the US.

Upon his return, the castle became an abiding image in our family. I imagine he was drawn to it through stories about knights and kings and queens he'd heard as a child, as well as through the strong image from our mother culture in western Europe and the British Isles, where we traced our ancestors. The American adaptation of English common law on individual privacy commonly meant that "a man's home is his castle." So it's natural that Daddy thought of creating a kingdom upon return to his native land. It's an archetypal story in its echoes of classic tales like that of Odysseus returning to his own great castle-fortress in Ithaca after *his* ordeals in the Trojan War. Later on, I was a bit less sanguine when I recognized the castle as a patriarchal image, one I viewed with some skepticism as a daughter-become-feminist.

When I found this card, I realized how important the image of Corson Castle was to Daddy as he dreamed of life after the war. As Henry David Thoreau famously said in the conclusion of *Walden*, "Do not worry if you have built your castles in the air. They are where they should be. Now put the foundations under them."

Daddy and Mother did just that.

The Building

tire-tracked oil
spreads colors on a puddle
splashes rainbow sky

Home, until my late teen years, was the structure we called The Building. I knew from the Corson Castle on the Susquehanna card that it was a talisman of my dad's return, his keep, his stronghold in the world.

It was an intriguing place to grow up because of its layer of intimate home spaces— second floor apartments—over the public spaces on the first floor below. The Building had multiuse land around it—from play yard and garden to a large field behind, from loading ramps and miniature junkyard out back to car lot and gas pumps in front. And of course there were the many people who came as customers, as well as friends and family. All of this gave me a sense of a vivid and complex world, one that fostered creativity. The Building for me is also a place marked by childhood adventures, many fun, as well as some frightening ones.

How I'd love to have a good talk about it with Daddy. I'd want to know how he selected and bought the land, how he designed The Building's proportions with the functions of living and working spaces under one roof, who built it. I'd like to know how much it cost and what things, if any, he would change if he started over. How could he have imagined what it would be like when and if he returned to live and work there after the war?

I sometimes wonder if my being near-sighted made me especially attentive to its details. Even today I can walk through The Building in my imagination, through doors, into each room, and up and down the stairs. I could tell many stories as I go. My walking is like a circumambulation of sacred space, a ritual of recognition and renewal. This reminds me of one of my favorite films, *Walkabout*. In it a young Australian aborigine undertakes his initiation rite of a long walk through land that holds sacred history. In my imagined analogue, I walk through The Building and re-tell the history it and the surrounding land will always hold for me.

Gaston Bachelard's *The Poetics of Space* helps me speak of the mystery of special spaces and places; it serves as an invaluable resource for exploring the inner life through the physical world. He says:

We are very surprised when we return to the old house, after an odyssey of many years, to find that the most delicate gestures, the earliest gestures suddenly come alive, are still faultless. In short, the house we were born in has engraved within us the hierarchy of the various functions of inhabiting.... The word habit is too worn a word to express this passionate liaison of our bodies, which do not forget, with an unforgettable house.[25]

As I thought about special moments in our "unforgettable house" I wrote these haiku:

electric fan blows
back and forth
iced tea sweats in tall glasses

April night
sound of tractors plowing late
somewhere a skunk

Let me introduce The Building. Luckily, we have a few photos, invaluable documents Daddy or Mother thought to make. From them you can see that the outside resembled an airplane hangar with windows; inside it was clearly divided. Downstairs was the business part; the showroom area with its large plate glass windows took up most of the front half, the half toward the road; the garage or shop filled the back half. Upstairs were two apartments on the front half, over the showroom. Our apartment was on the west side, and private stairs led up to its porch with a "front door." The other front apartment, on the east side, was occupied briefly, as I've noted, by my uncle and aunt at the war's beginning. There may have been one other tenant just after the war that I don't remember, but after that it was empty, a storage space, until our family grew and we annexed it.

Customers entered the main door of the business, into the showroom with a parts counter and offices, on the front or road side. The shop doors opened on the east side, toward Muncy; that side included a loading platform for farm or other big equipment and cellar doors for coal deliveries for the furnace.

On the west side, toward Williamsport, where the Star*Light Drive-In would later be built across a grassy field, we had yards and a garden. You can see one of the newly planted maple trees in the photo. They grew up to create pools of shade. There was, for a while, garage activity on that garden side with a grease pit, but service work was shifted entirely over to the shop side when hydraulic lifts replaced the grease pit.

The Building was located on what was then Route 14 (now 147 and Interstate 80). Since it was the main connector of three towns in our vicinity, Muncy, Montoursville, and Williamsport, this was a good place to be located for a new business. We were warned as children not to cross this road without adult supervision because it was busy. But once Marilyn had a scary close call as she chased a ball that rolled across it.

Mother said that in the war years, when she and I lived alone upstairs in The Building, it interested some unsavory characters. They'd probably been initially lured by Mom's Lunch, a truck stop on the opposite side of the road, maybe a couple hundred feet from our property. She'd sometimes hear somebody trying our doors downstairs, snooping to see what was inside the showroom. While Daddy was away, it was rented out for storage and the big windows were covered with brown paper to keep the furniture inside from sun damage. Later, this became our car showroom.

There were intimations that the few buildings in a row behind Mom's Lunch constituted a whorehouse. A few years after Daddy returned, he spoke to the owners about that, concerned about the environment for his family and business. What he said must have had some effect; the place seemed calmer afterwards.

> *after thunderstorm*
> *loud Jezebel night cools down*
> *the birds sleep soundly*

If you looked closely around The Building, you could find

numerous resonances of the war. On Mother's dresser stood a pretty glass bottle of amber-colored perfume from France labeled *Latitude 45*. I remember finding it bedded in curly, aromatic wood shavings in one of the rare wooden boxes of treasures Daddy sent to us from Europe. The story Mother loved to tell was that it represented one time the censors failed to keep his location secret: *Latitude 45—Paris!*

> *dream-flowers*
> *on the Rue de la Paix*
> *the smell of your skin*

She kept that bottle for a long time on her dresser; we girls loved to open it and smell its special smell. I can almost catch the fragrance now—it lingered in bronzy stains in the bottle even after the liquid had entirely evaporated.

Daddy's big winter Army coat, the one he'd worn when he came home, hung for a while in the back of the closet in the study. We used Army blankets for years, those itchy olive-drab, all-wool ones that were warm, but so heavy that they weighed you down in bed like wet carpets. In summertime we took them out on the lawn for sun-bathing.

Daddy bought Army trucks to transport machinery and do the heavy work of the business in the early years. No one else I knew had anything like them. I recall the loud sound of their gears shifting; they were like Belgian work horses—large, powerful, efficient, and slightly exotic.

When a new shipment of machinery came in, Daddy got up very early, perhaps about 4 a.m. Mother had packed sandwiches wrapped in waxed paper bags along with a thermos of coffee, and he drove one of the Army trucks the eighty or so miles along the Susquehanna to meet the train at Harrisburg. He would get the truck loaded up and drive back in time for business that day. In good weather the trip must have been fairly easy, but the road could be treacherous in winter. Places where the road had been cut right through the high cliffs at river's edge drained downhill, creating icy run-off glazes. Also, there was always the threat of poor visibility with fog in the early morning hours on that narrow two-lane road.

> *windshield wipers sweep*
> *rhythmically across the glass*
> *ghostly hedgerows taunt*

That drive surely provided reminders of the hard winter of 1944, of the Battle of the Bulge in the Ardennes and of ordnance's many jobs to keep the troops mobile, such as making improvisations for the tanks to give them traction on ice. "Ghostly hedgerows," alludes to the now-famous hedgerows of the northern European farm countryside where the Allies could easily be ambushed by German troops. That kind of déjà vu was probably inescapable in the early years after the war for Daddy, although I never heard him mention it.

As much as I try to imagine what it must have been like to go to war and return, I cannot. But I do know that even the simple conversion of an Army truck to domestic use and the ability to drive it down a road with no fear of gunfire, bombs, or sentry posts with guards making threatening demands in foreign languages must have seemed amazing at first. It meant, at least subliminally for a former soldier, that he'd survived.

Daddy brought back few Army souvenirs. There was that rough and garishly colored "flag cloth" Grammy made into rugs. Marilyn thinks there might have been a flag with a swastika on it, but I don't remember that. Also a German helmet, a medal or two, some foreign money, a bayonet, and at least one gun—all kept upstairs in the gun cabinet, a big glass-door cabinet that smelled of gun oil and leather. Although it was forbidden territory, sometimes Marilyn and I sneaked into it just to have a look. Some seventeen years after later, when we moved to the new house across the fields, most of these things did not come along. I wonder what Daddy thought about them, did he have some small ritual of disposal or did he just throw them out for the junk man to haul away?

> *hunter's moon*
> > *deer carcass*
> > > *gone without a shadow*

The fact that he did the necessary work to transform his castle dreams into a new life in an outward way was evident all around us; I hope that the work proceeded inwardly as well.

Building Tales

If The Building could talk, it would recall that it was a stage of diverse activities: the usual car and machinery sales and repairs, all the events of the business, as well as skating, player piano playing, selling Girl Scout cookies, explorations for us girls, and even a dramatic rescue Daddy made to keep the roof from blowing away during a great windstorm.

Mother recalled that in the busy years of 1950–55, cars were sold not only during the daytime business hours, but also at night out in the front lot under a string of blue lights. Daddy joked that customers could choose whatever color car they wished—either blue or green; I guess that meant that the lights made them all appear blue-green, perhaps a variation on the saying that at night all cats are grey.

Sometimes we kids helped wash the cars to prepare them for display. In summertime we loved putting on our swimsuits to hose them down in the driveway. Polishing the cars was harder work, and Daddy gave close inspections.

In the showroom, one of our periodic tasks was to sweep the floor with some strange-smelling green powder that we scattered around to settle the dust, then cleared off with big wide shop brooms.

When we got roller skates for Christmas one year—the kind that clamped onto the bottom of your shoes—we found that the cement showroom floor made a dandy roller rink. We had a great time wheeling around and around, but were sternly warned: "Don't scratch the cars!"

The showroom floor was painted battleship grey. How do I know that? Did I once help paint it or at least have the job of cleaning up the paint cans? At any rate, my recollection of this led to another wartime connection: this was an important camouflage color for ships at sea since it blended with fog, spray, and sky. Whether Daddy crossed the Atlantic in the Queen Mary or the Queen Elizabeth, he crossed in a battleship grey troopship. Both Queens had to be transformed from cruise liners to military transports, and painting them to cover their previous bright Cunard-line colors was an important part of the modification. In fact, the Queen Mary was called the Grey Ghost due to her well-camouflaged exterior.

Back to skating: showroom skating was quite different from skating at Trout Pond Park Skating Rink. We went there with Brownies or an occasional birthday party group. I remember it as a special place set back in the woods on the way to Hughesville. For us children, it had a slightly tawdry but alluring carnival atmosphere. The main building was surrounded with little bridges over algae-scummed artificial ponds where real ducks paddled. Inside, lights flashed and loud recorded organ music blended with the rumble and whir of skates over waxed boards. We "little kids" got to wear shoe skates with long laces, and we hugged the guard rails in wide, wobbly circling until, by the end of the time, we'd improved enough to let go and join the general flow. We watched the "big kids" with awe.

skating rink hot-shots
red lipstick, tight jeans, black leather
ooo-la-la

For a time, Daddy bought old player pianos to sell and displayed them on one side of the showroom; we thought that was a super idea. There was a big cabinet filled with piano rolls that came along with one trade-in. The music incised on the paper rolls in funny little square and rectangular cuts included everything from Irish jigs to opera. We had a great time pumping away, especially at long-playing triple-sized ones, which Marilyn loved, but our noisy performances were soon restricted to non-business hours.

When Daddy returned in 1945, my March birthday was redeemed from being the time of impending departure for war; now it happily coincided with the beginnings of spring. We felt the intoxications of sun melting the giant icicles that hung like stalactites from the eaves. We didn't mind having cold hands from scooping up wet snow for the last snowballs or wet feet from wearing leaky boots or rubbers, those funny low-cut shoe-covers that nobody wears anymore. Soon tiny green shoots and the first delicate flowers poked up; first robins appeared; and we even welcomed the characteristic odors of various manures wafting in from nearby fields.

I remember the pleasure of having several grade-school birthday parties at home. Mother stitched crepe paper hats on the sewing machine and hung crepe paper streamers, which I helped to crimp, over the table where we had cake and ice cream on special paper birthday plates with napkins. There were favors too, noisemakers or "crackers," with little trinkets inside. Of course there were neat gifts and the chance to have girlfriends from town (it was two or three miles away via the highway; we weren't allowed to walk in and we didn't have bikes) come out to the country to play. Once a good friend stayed late after the others had left and Mother had gone back downstairs to work. We ran around so raucously upstairs that Mother called up on the intercom: "Stop thundering overhead!"

I'm embarrassed to think of our noise interrupting business that day.

spring fever
red-cheeked and sweaty
hijinks

Since we lived in the country and houses were far spaced, there were not many potential neighborhood consumers of Girl Scout cookies. Therefore, Marilyn and I, as Brownies, were allowed to peddle our wares to the customers. One afternoon after school I brought my box of cookies downstairs and awkwardly asked someone standing at the counter with Daddy, "You wouldn't want to buy some cookies, would you?" Daddy laughed and said that was no way to make a sale. I got a few pointers from a master salesman: "Tell them how many kinds you have and how good they are; assume they'll want to buy some!"

Though I knew I could improve, I also realized that this was *his* forte, not mine, *and* that he had just sold some cookies for me to a bemused and put-on-the-spot customer.

There was an intriguing outer office, with counters open to the showroom and a big Remington typewriter on a metal typing table across from a desk, cash register, and the receipt machine. That typewriter was a big draw for us girls. We pecked out notes on the blank sides of used paper Mother gave us, enjoying the sound of the bell's *ding!* at the end of lines and the *whang!* of the carriage as we whacked it back with the return lever. We pretended we were secretaries while eavesdropping on conversations Daddy had with customers.

> *gossip stopped*
> *just before it got good*
> *not for little girls' ears*

The inner office, separated from the outer area by a door with windows on the top half, was Mama's. There was a huge safe against the wall opposite her desk. Above it on the wall hung Grandpap J's insurance company calendar with a picture of Horseshoe Curve, a big railroad landmark near Altoona—famous in our family because it was the place where Daddy and Mother first met, on a double date. Her office was toasty warm in cold weather due to a grated vent on the floor that allowed heat to come up from the coal furnace in the cellar below. A few times we had stray kittens staying in that cellar where they'd be warm and contained. My sisters and I always wanted to keep them. Mother said that if you buttered their paws, they wouldn't run away. With the nearby road and so much traffic around the shop, however, none of them lasted very long. (Their living in the apartment upstairs with us was not an option.)

From the cellar, you had to climb three sets of stairs to reach the highest place in The Building. We sisters had to be careful in the rare, usually supervised times we went up to the third-floor partial attic because much of it was unfinished and was traversable only by walking on planks between beams; the big metal roof arched from the edges to high above. Daddy placed buckets here and there to catch a few leaks.

The whole unfinished back half of the second floor (behind the apartments) was a mysterious space. It was unheated, of course, but we sometimes played in the section right behind our apartment when it wasn't too cold. When it rained, you could hear the sonorous beat on the metal roof; there were only some fairly dim lights, so it was a rather somber place to be.

A short passageway between our apartment and this unfinished section led to a door to our porch; just before the door were two opposing windows. The inside one opened into Daddy's study and the other opened out to a section of the roof that slanted upward to meet other, more sharply angled roof planes rising toward the peak.

When we first got TV, probably in the early '50s, Daddy climbed up to put the antenna on the peak of the roof for best reception. Our job was to help orient it by calling from the outer window, relaying the news that came through the study window from the screen-watchers inside about the reception quality as he moved the antenna (I seem to remember that the show being watched was a very "snowy" puppet show, "Kukla, Fran, and Ollie"). At one point, I was told to climb out on the roof to better communicate the messages since Daddy couldn't hear our voices from the window. I obeyed. No wonder I remember this incident. I am an acrophobe. I feel queasy even writing about it.

Once, in a heavy windstorm, Daddy found that a section of the roof over the back part of The Building was loose and threatening to blow away—perhaps to take the whole thing off. He grabbed a hammer and spikes, had Mother hold a ladder so he could reach the gap, and nailed it down just in time. I remember standing by, awe-stricken. It looked for one terrible moment like the wind would lift the roof and Daddy and fly them both away. I still wonder how he knew to go to that exact place, not to mention how he summoned the strength and quick know-how to locate and use tools to save our roof.

At the far back of that same unfinished second-floor space was a seldom-opened door. It was a simple top-hung sliding door built to access the storage space for large parts that were lifted by a pulley from trucks parked below. When that door was open on a summer day to cool out that big space, we had a beautiful view of the fields and countryside stretching out from behind The Building. I was always careful not to get too close to the edge!

Gardening

To be complete, any description of The Building must include our garden, from its spring rituals of plowing and planting through to its winter fallow time and the ordering of seeds for the next year. We learned there about seeds and how to care for the plants that grew up in the neat rows we made in well-prepared earth. Daddy's farming and selling farm machinery connected us with the rich alluvial soil of the Susquehanna River valley and with the four seasons. It seemed that the earth itself gave healing balm to us, and I'd guess that was so for other soldiers and families who worked the soil at their homes. Daddy arranged for the plowing and soil preparation, he and Mother chose seeds, and then kids joined in planting with our major tasks coming later, the weeding and harvesting. Mother was in charge of freezing and canning.

Another springtime ritual indirectly involved the land: the spring cleaning of winter garments. Mother supervised as we carried piles of woolens to the porch to be brushed and aired. Then we hung them on the rainy day clotheslines on the porch.

soap mothballs sunshine
winter doesn't stand a chance

Mother set off "spray bombs" in the closets, and we had to keep them shut for several hours to fumigate any lurking moths.

It was my job to use the small hand-held pump sprayer on the clothes on the porch. I conscientiously applied the maximum dosage of DDT and other toxins in that chemical mist. I know I did a good job on the clothes *and* on myself, even though I thought I could reduce the damage by holding my breath. I've learned since that DDT as insecticide saved many lives in World War II, particularly in the tropics, but Rachel Carson's 1962 book *Silent Spring* alerted us its to harmful effects on the land and its creatures. DDT was banned in the US in 1972. It was banned for agricultural uses worldwide by the 2001 Stockholm Convention on Persistent Organic Pollutants, but it is still permitted in small quantities in countries that need it for mosquito and other pest control. We're still struggling to find the right balance of harms and benefits of many chemicals like this one, even for our gardens.

The folk saying "knee-high by Fourth of July" was often quoted as a benchmark for sweet corn in a good summer. Daddy loved to have "firsts" in the garden and in the fields and often succeeded. We never out-did Uncle Clete's sweet peas, however, because his seeds were always in the ground by St. Patrick's Day. In other categories of garden produce we competed good-naturedly with Grammy Corson, with Aunt Viola, and with Uncle Roscoe, who didn't always take it so well when he was bested.

Marilyn and I spent hours in our garden. In the spring, after the ground was plowed and harrowed with a tractor and then rototilled, we planted the bigger seeds like peas and limas, while Mother planted tiny seeds like lettuce and carrots; there were usually a few "let's try" ones like burpless cucumbers or peanuts. I was to be the record-keeper, diagramming what we planted, when and where. Marilyn and I had the job of weeding when the plants began growing. Sometimes we cultivated with hoes, but mostly we had to hunch over the rows handpicking, a task we heartily disliked. We got scolded when we let the weeds get so high in late summer that we could tunnel out secret rooms— that happened only once.

Marilyn and I got sent to the fields to hoe corn after it was too big to cultivate with the tractor; other times we were to weed out mustard, crabgrass, prickly wild radish, or sticky milkweed from crops so they weren't crowded out and to keep seeds un-contaminated. We'd take a water bottle, some Triscuits or Ritz crackers with peanut butter, and spend the morning. The twelve o'clock whistle at the Sprout Waldron plant in town, audible when the wind was right, brought the good news of lunchtime. Once Marilyn accidentally chopped down a big corn plant; she carried it to the end of the field and buried it as I urged her to, but somehow Daddy found it. She got a good scolding. Those sharpshooter eyes! Then we saw the nest of a bird we wished we'd been able to imitate:

> *killdeer's speckled eggs*
> *nestled among some pebbles*
> *hidden in plain sight*

Still, summer was the best season. Even if we'd spent all morning weeding in the fields, the afternoon was free for us to explore, to read, to maybe, on a hot day, get a bottle of pop from the showroom's old-style metal-maze opening cooler. We might even have a candy bar or treat like Mounds, Clark's, Lifesavers, Hershey's, and Reese's Peanut Butter Cups—my favorite—or Juicy Fruit, Beechnut, and Beemans gum.

> *summer sun*
> *splatter-paints freckles*
> *no school for months*

Although Marilyn and I grumbled a fair amount about hours of hot and tedious weeding and shelling in those early years, I now enjoy gardening very much. Howard and I have had gardens in most places we've lived—ratatouille veggies in Iowa, azaleas and night-blooming cereus in Florida, and assorted herbs, lettuce, and posies in North Carolina.

I loved looking across the fields behind The Building to see the red barn at the old Evans place that Daddy bought. He painted "Harvey F. Corson" on the barn in big white letters visible from Route 14. Sometimes when we flew into or out of the Montoursville airport we proudly saw the sign from the air. Janet made a beautiful Amish hex sign to hang on a side gable facing the road beside the Evans house, just down the road from where the new Corson Castle was built. We no longer literally own that land, yet it is an unforgettable home place.

Allis-Chalmers Orange

tractors, rakes, combines
straw hats in hot July sun:
Allis-Chalmers orange

Business at The Building was powered primarily by tractors and cars when I was growing up. These vehicles brought us many adventures, as well as our livelihood. Although my sisters and I thought the Chrysler and Plymouth cars we sold were very fine, it was the Allis-Chalmers tractors that caught our imaginations—especially that nifty orange color. Right after the war Daddy made wooden toys such as little Scotty dogs with a jigsaw. My favorite was a little wagon he made for Easter. When it arrived, Marilyn and I relished its cargo of Easter candy treats. This childhood treasure now holds a collection of stuffed animals in my study. It is, of course, painted Allis-Chalmers orange.

Marilyn, Bette, and I had zealous brand-loyalty for Allis-Chalmers. We made fun of other brand colors like red Farmalls and green John Deeres. When we went along with Daddy to the Lycoming County Fair, he sometimes gave away A-C orange straw hats that the farmers liked. Other times there were model tractors to sell or to give away to special customers. We always had an exhibit space that faced onto the backstretch of the race track. It was exciting to sit up on the tractors and watch the sleek harness racing horses and their silk-clad drivers thunder by in sulkies, not even minding the billowing dust.

We liked viewing the livestock in the barns too. Daddy knew a lot about that: he'd won first place medals at Penn State for judging cattle.

Allis-Chalmers holds such good memories for me. Howard and I display a collector's model tractor on a shelf in our living room. It represents a 1967 Allis-Chalmers Model 170, with an early advance in tractor safety known as a Roller-Over Protective Structure with seat belt. Recently, a local hardware store offered big thermometers with an Allis-Chalmers logo (made in China!), so one of them hangs on a post on our porch. I sentimentally keep one of Daddy's tan denim shop coats with its orange lapels and pockets and ALLIS-CHALMERS stitched across the back.

When I did some web-searching about A-C, I found that the Allis-Chalmers Model B was introduced at the end of the 1930s and caused "a revolution in tractor design." I love this further comment: "But the Model B had something else—sex appeal, according to its designer. The company insisted that the tractor had to be aesthetically pleasing. In an era when most tractors were painted dull grey, the B was bright orange. Farmers liked the distinctive color."[26]

In the summertime, Daddy would occasionally drive us all out into the country to visit a customer or make a sales call. We got to see a variety of home places, and sometimes there were kids to play with—we might talk shyly at first and then end up chasing fireflies. Once we were invited to try some cider in a barrel out front of a house; we were given long hollow dandelion stems to suck it up through the bunghole. Another time some rangy older kids were rolling down a hill inside a big old rear tractor tire. They invited us to join, but we didn't have the nerve for that scary-looking stunt.

Maybe the lady of the house would come to chat with Mother or take us on a tour of her garden. I'd usually take a library book along and read even by dim barnyard light until Mother insisted I quit. We'd listen to the radio and Mother would pass around Juicy Fruit gum or Lifesavers from her purse. When I got interested in playing the trumpet, the instrument Mother played in her high school orchestra, she taught me the fingerings for the scales while we waited. Occasionally, it could be tense when Daddy went out to repossess some machinery because the farmer was far behind in payments—you never knew where that might lead.

Daddy took great pleasure in driving long distances, so he and Mother took us on many road trips, mostly in the summer. What a contrast to driving jeeps, trucks, and whatever other vehicles he was called to drive and care for as a soldier in ordnance. Also, what a comfort for us to ride with a master mechanic in a nice car (usually one of the Chryslers he sold). One of my favorite trips was to the Gaspé Peninsula in Canada. We counted white work horses in the fields, chanting: "Lucky lucky white horse,/ Ding, ding, ding./Everywhere I go/ I find something." Even though we laughed and sometimes complained of Daddy's love of "covering miles" on our trips, we loved our journeys. They opened worlds to us. On this trip, Percé Rock left an indelible impression: a great stone monolith near the shore, a rookery for sea birds that swirled about it with wild, stirring cries. They circled out widely enough to include us on the cliff heights. It seemed that we could easily stretch out our arms like wings, step out into the salty air, and join them. Down on the beach, immersed in the glitter and crash of waves, I collected shells I'd never seen before, blue mussels.

> *inland autumn*
>> *empty seashells whisper*
>>> *summer*

Vue du Sud-Ouest.   View from the South-West. Percé, P.Q.—PV16

Along the Gaspé roads people sold simple handcrafts. After bargaining sprinkled with jokes and bits of French he remembered from the war, Daddy bought a well-made wooden boat from a shy little boy who probably came from a fishing family. The boat, still in my keeping, inspired this poem:

To a Gaspé Child

Your family's wooden boats
bore marks of experience
in North Atlantic waters.
When Daddy bought us this
two-master with birch bark sails
you penciled on it.
"RITH TO ME PLEASE"
I always meant to
before your name and address
blurred, gone
like white horses
we gaily counted
along Gaspé roads.
Now it's absurdly late,
impossible except for angelic

messengers to tell you
sixty years later
"Your boat is still beautiful.
Wherever you are,
I hope you are happy."

Stairs

in a door window
at the bottom of long stairs
daffodils

As I've mentioned before, I feel that I've been circumambulating sacred space as I go around The Building in my imagination. There is something akin to the mystical about reflecting on this place. I've been reading about Hindus, Buddhists, Jain, and Bon followers who undertake the pilgrimage to holy Mount Kailash, among the northernmost reaches of the Himalayas. They believe that by devoutly circling the mountain, which they associate with Mt. Meru, the axis mundi or center of the world, on foot, they will be cleansed of all earthly sins. In fact, it's thought that 108 circuits assure nirvana!

Often, circumambulations of holy places are to honor a particular saint or founder. It's not too great a creative leap for me to imaginatively walk around The Building and find somehow concretized the mysteries of beginnings, in a ritual of affirmation for me and for my family. For a while it was the center of the world for us, and Daddy was its founder, its presiding genius. (I make no claims about cleansing of sins, but it's a beguiling thought.)

Daddy's dreams and actions gave The Building its functioning shapes. I don't know exactly when Daddy drew up the plans or with whom; some parts of The Building are rather eccentric, yet they served his purposes. Judging from some photos of myself there as a baby, the basic construction was completed before the war. When he left for the Army, The Building grew in importance as it assumed for Daddy the power of a talisman of return. After the war it became the matrix for his success, the castle he'd dreamed of creating.

As I made imagined walks through The Building, I felt compelled to draw a map of the first floor, the business zone. That exercise led to my recognition of The Building's many stairs as the means of transportation between our private and public worlds. They can be viewed as symbols of emotional and spiritual development and the search for knowledge.

The Building had five sets of stairs. Each one had its particular use and its unique connections with the whole. The first and shortest set of stairs led from a little passageway wedged between the back of the first floor offices and the back wall of the shop down into the cellar with its low ceiling. These depths of The Building smelled of soil and coal dust. With hissing of steam at the valves and clanking in the pipes, the furnace sent heat into radiators in the first and second floors. There were small metal containers attached to the radiators which we filled with water to maintain a level of humidity in our apartment during the winter. (The radiators got so hot that you could dry wet socks on them; I sometimes melted old candles into Jell-O molds.)

Jutting out from the side of the cellar opposite the stairs, behind the coal bin with its deep blackness, was a root cellar. It was a musty, cobwebbed place with earth floor and a few simple shelves with Mason jars of canned fruits and vegetables. The era of canning had been mostly replaced by freezing when I first took notice, and most of the jars were dusty and old—not appetizing. This part of the cellar had a sort of primeval feeling about it, like an eerie underworld entrance.

My shiver at the cellar darkness reminds me of images of

buildings as cellar-to-attic symbols of layers of consciousness. I refer again to Bachelard's *The Poetics of Space* when he speaks of the novelist Henri Bosco's house in a cosmic daydream:

> It possesses the verticality of the tower rising from the most earthly, watery depths, to the abode of a soul that believes in heaven. Such a house, constructed by a writer, illustrates the verticality of the human being.[27]

As a writer reviewing the cosmic qualities of my childhood home, I appreciate the analogue of house to person. In the broadest sense, my own Christian tradition images life as a vertical progression from Earth up to Heaven. I think of English poet William Wordsworth famously portraying life as a cycle of heaven to earth to heaven, with each child coming forth, at birth, from the spirit world, "trailing clouds of glory."

The second and most normal set of stairs were the outside wooden ones with banisters that led up to our apartment. They began on a cement sidewalk, were open to the outside as far as the midway landing with door, then they turned half-circle to finish up on our porch. They were on the more private "home side" of the building, with its picket-fenced play yard, grassy lawn, and garden. The high porch gave great views of the surroundings, as well as a good climbing work-out, I'd guess, to the milkman in early years. When we dressed up for errands, trips, or social events, we came down these steps. Guests used these stairs. Only rarely did customers use them, after hours.

The third and least-used set of stairs led up behind a barely noticeable door in the interior hall of the second-floor apartments, to the semi-finished third floor I've already mentioned. There was a fourth set of stairs that we children avoided. Daddy constructed it later in a very basic way, with steep, widely spaced steps and no handrails; it served for business use as an interior link between the upstairs and downstairs parts storages. Definitely not kid friendly. These two sets of steps (third and fourth) are also disappointing in terms of keeping that metaphor of verticality going unless I consider them as primitive spaciousness for basic subsistence.

Our fifth set of stairs, however, richly evokes that vertical tower of lower to higher consciousness. Since the first floor had such a high ceiling, to accommodate the shop and large machinery showroom on the ground floor, these inside stairs connecting the second floor apartments and the downstairs (sharing a wall on one side with the offices and the shop on the other) were quite long. They were one straight flight with no banisters, flush with the walls on both sides. My sisters and I were lucky that none of the tumbles—which we all took down them at one time or another—hurt us badly. They were quite narrow, so although it sounds strange, Marilyn once fell and got stuck sideways— she had to be unwedged by an adult.

We hated to be sent down those long stairs at night, usually to fetch something from the big horizontal chest freezer on the far side of the showroom. We'd go as fast as we could down and back. Even with the neon Chrysler and Plymouth lights on in the showroom front windows, there were lots of spooky shadows, as well as weird sounds from the shop, from air compressors and such. There were so many doors we hoped were locked!

While it was fun to scare ourselves this way, there were times when I felt panicky, racing across the showroom, rummaging around in the freezer for the required item—a box of peas, string beans, or lima beans we'd helped to pick and prepare that summer, some of Mother's great frozen strawberry jam, some hamburger, or whatnot—then racing back, taking the stairs as fast as possible, crossing the short hall to enter the house by the laundry door and locking it behind me, just in time.

In my dreams of that space, once quite frequent, there was always something menacing just beyond the two laundry-room doors—the one to the hallway as well as the one perpendicular to it that led to that big back storage area. My heart beats fast, and I lunge to turn the keys in the locks just in time to barricade myself against whatever scary thing approaches. Was I still seeking safety from childhood fears? I've recognized that our apartment was the highly charged place where Daddy delivered frightening tirades of anger at household messes for which we girls were held responsible. Was it also a place where Mother's fears pooled when she was left alone with me in that big empty building during the war? I suppose all kids are secretly glad to have spaces like this, archetypal sites of fear and testing for bravery.

On the other hand, those long stairs afforded me a particular pleasure. On regular days, going up and down them, I recall the joy of my long legs scissoring to reach over as many steps as possible. I could do "thirds," though I don't remember doing "fourths," and certainly not *fifths.* In the same way I reached up in doorways until I was tall enough to touch the lintels and then to put my palms flat on them, pleased to have inherited good height from both parents.

Furthermore, being able to freely go up and down those stairs meant that I belonged there in that busy, productive place; I had open access to it. Daddy's castle belonged to us all, and it seemed to bestow a certain elevation of self-esteem.

"Home is the place where memories are housed." So Bachelard speaks of the intimacy that is written in our dreams and inscribed in our bodies by inhabiting unforgettable places. I remember The Building, our home, a primal place, so that my family and I will not be forgotten. To be literally obliterated, literally *un-written*, is probably the writer's, if not every human's, greatest fear. So I attend to this now-vanished place as a repository of cherished life, and I attempt to share it, not so much as a reliquary, but as a container, even a chalice. Those stairs linger as paths of memory; even in their ordinariness they bloom into lasting symbols of a castle tower rising from the depths to mysterious, wondrous heights.

Princess Dreaming

And how many dreamers look everywhere in their house,
or in their room, for the garment that suits them!
– Gaston Bachelard

As our family grew, we needed more space for bedrooms. The solution was to cut through a wall to the adjoining unused apartment and to add the front part of it (with windows facing the road) for that purpose. The back part—a kitchen, bath, and two other rooms—was still empty except for storage. One summer, at Daddy's suggestion, I painted those extra rooms and one of them became my bedroom. As I reflect on this, I appreciate his thoughtfulness in noticing that it would be good if I had my own space. Also, I imagine that my labor was welcome to spruce up those drab unused rooms.

Previously Marilyn, Bette, and I had separate beds in one big room, but now I had my very own space. It was such a pleasure to pick out and hang curtains, put up pictures, and arrange my bed, dresser, desk, and bookcase in a room with a door I could close for privacy. Now a teenager, I loved wearing the clothes in my closet. There's one special dress I used to dream about: a turquoise print sheath of polished cotton with a cowl neck and a purple leatherette belt with round buckle. It must represent something of my feelings of becoming a woman in my own right; I knew I looked good in it. There's also a circle skirt and matching blouse, the first outfit I made by myself, without my home ec teacher's finicky scrutiny. It was made of plaid-patterned pink cotton, and starched half-petticoats made the skirt stand out, the fad then. I first wore this outfit on a Corson Friday night in Williamsport—for supper, some shopping, and a movie—and some cute guy in Woolworth's gave me the eye. Through dreams of this closet I re-enter a youthful world of ideals for the future. I'm reminded of the meanings of dressing up, of being well-dressed, and the ways our clothes satisfy our desires to be seen as sexual persons, as persons of status and of style.

Our family had what you might call nice upper-middle-class clothes. Mother had her favorite stores, ones where she took us girls shopping, and I know that Daddy enjoyed going to one particular tailor for suits and slacks. As a farm kid, he grew up wearing hand-me-downs and being frugal about everything. As a soldier, he wore Uncle Sam's wardrobe. He must have greatly enjoyed being able to afford good quality clothes for himself and for his girls. I liked to explore our closets; some were filled with regular clothes, others held hunting garments and winter woolens that smelled of mothballs. In a back room of The Building there had been a closet with a box containing a leather motorcycle suit as well as some old satin gowns —romantic remnants of my parents' youthful adventures.

Bachelard's phrase "the garment that suits them"—sends me to wartime again. I remember admiring the clothes Mother and my Nanaw made for me when I found them in storage boxes, especially the pretty summer dresses—white cotton with tucks and silky pastel sashes. Mother told us that Nanaw had advanced dressmaker skills and sewed lovely clothes for *her* when she was a young woman. I am certain that Nanaw's garments gave Mother style that Grandpap couldn't have afforded if they'd been store-bought. Mother's lovely style attracted Daddy, and she carried it through the rest of her life. We girls tried to copy it, each in our own way.

When we were younger, like most young girls, we loved to dress up and be appreciated. We practiced by playing with our dolls; our paper dolls with their many outfits allowed us to play-act desired roles in society. As kids, Marilyn and I loved playing dress-up with Mother's pretty clothes and accessories. She had a jewelry box with a mirror on the inside of the lid; it was full of combs, necklaces, bracelets, and other things that we'd raid for glitter and glamour. Sometimes we sampled her lipstick and eye shadow. Then we'd take turns parading in front of the vanity with the big round mirror, pretending that we were being filmed for Hollywood.

> *Teetering*
> *on Mama's pink satin mules*
> *princess-in-waiting*

When I was in fourth grade, age ten, I got to play princess by helping to wind the Maypole on May Day. This was an annual event attended by many townspeople who gathered, with cameras ready, along the street in front of our handsome river-stone-faced school building. First the May Queen and her court, elected by seniors, processed to their thrones on the steps; there were introductions and proclamations. Then our group of fourth graders came forward to form a circle around the pole on the lawn. Picking up our long pastel ribbons, we walked rhythmically—boys in one direction and girls in the other—weaving over and under, to the recorded music of "Pomp and Circumstance." At home before the event, I was happy to pose in our rose arbor by the picket fence gate with my floaty pink organza dress and new white flats with silky socks. My hair looks recently permed, a stinky process that usually took up a whole Saturday morning at a beauty shop in town—Mother's idea of a fashion necessity then.

That same year, 1953, a real princess, Elizabeth II, was crowned as Queen of England. She was thoroughly regal, even glamorous, and I thought Mother looked like her. I cut her picture from *The Philadelphia Inquirer* Sunday magazine and pasted it in my scrapbook. My Aunt Mae, who sent me stamps for my collection, sent me an exciting first-day-of-issue envelope. It was postmarked "THE QUEEN" with a captioned photo: "Elizabeth II by the grace of God of the United Kingdom of Great Britain and Northern Ireland and of her other realms and territories Queen, Head of the Commonwealth, Defender of the Faith."

I know that Elizabeth and her family had endured the war; I wonder what stories she remembers as most poignant from those times? Did she have a sense of her father, King George VI, working hard to surmount his handicap of stuttering so that he could speak clear words of inspiration to his people? Did she have any personal feelings about the great Cunard liner, her namesake, *Queen Elizabeth*, refitted as a troop carrier? It must have been a great symbol of hope to her and other Britons as it brought American troops like Daddy to join the Allies in Europe.

One of my teaching colleagues had been among the many British children shipped away from wartime London with its bombing blitzes to places less vulnerable in the British Isles and as far away as Canada. Their experiences of displacement and disorientation surely had lifelong impact, even when they were placed with warm and loving surrogate families.

> *lonely flowers sigh*
> *hummingbirds flew south*
> *last night while we slept*

The Building and its many secret places, its storage of souvenirs, now confined to memories, is forever marked for me with deep feelings of childhood and early adulthood. One rainy summer evening, as I stood on the upstairs porch, I was particularly enchanted by the way the rose arbor leaves caught the lights of Mom's Lunch across the road and the traffic going past it. It was one of those teenage times of wishing to be elsewhere, but not knowing quite where.

> *rainy night*
> *taillights stream*
> *bright trails into dark*

Fire

When I had my "teenager's bedroom" at The Building, I sometimes worried about fire. Maybe it was because that room was partly over the shop downstairs. Maybe it had to do with feeling some unease with all the changes I was experiencing as an almost-adult and getting used to having, at last, a room of my own. I knew there were plenty of flammable materials in the shop and around the gas pumps out front that were zealously watched over. Mother taught us to be exceedingly careful about such things as unplugging irons and blowing out candles.

In 1965, about a decade later, there *was* a big fire. Five years earlier, Daddy and Mother had sold The Building and set up a smaller business in a building across the road. One of the new tenants let a curtain blow over a red-hot stove burner, and it ignited. Conditions apparently were right for the perfect blaze: the vulnerable wood frame of The Building went up quickly. It burned to the ground.

This event was a realization of the nightmares I had when we lived there. I was in graduate school in Iowa at the time of the fire, and our family had already moved in 1959 to the new Corson Castle across the fields. Still, it must have been a wrenching experience to see The Building crumple in flames. It's hard to imagine the emotions my parents must have had as they watched it helplessly from across the road—giant flames overtaking the structure and siren-blaring fire trucks arriving too late to save it.

The fact was that The Building, my cherished first home space, and that first "castle" Daddy had built, was gone. And now I finally miss it as it deserves to be missed—almost as a living presence. It was like a chambered nautilus shell that grew with us, giving a secure hold while opening wider and wider to allow us purchase into the larger world we were preparing to enter. But we never thought we'd leave one time and never see it again. The disappearance of The Building has led me to ponder what it means to lose our origin places. My husband Howard's childhood home has been leveled and made into a parking lot. One of my friends lived in a house that finally succumbed to the yearly floods of the nearby creek. The news is filled with tragedies of homes lost to such things as mud slides, tsunamis, hurricanes, and wars.

A Chance to Return

Yet once in a while we get a chance to return. When I returned to Muncy for my fiftieth high school reunion, I had an extraordinary experience. When the planned festivities had concluded, my friend Linda and I set out to find our way back to Daddy's old home, my grandparents' farm. After a series of wrong turns, we finally climbed the steep unpaved road up to that little plateau in the Muncy Hills that holds the one-room Baptist church Daddy attended as a boy, its cemetery, and the Corson family homestead. As we stood hesitating to go snooping around the house, an older lady appeared over the brow of the hill just beyond the garden. It was the wife of the couple who bought the farm after Grandpap Corson died. She was just returning from a walk.

She and I chatted about people we'd both known, and she welcomed us to walk around. The snowball bush that Grammy had planted by the outhouse was in full bloom. The barn was still there, but there were no animals; it was being used for storage and seemed small and a bit lonely. I walked out on the cement truck-greasing platform where we'd loved to call out and hear echoes back from the nearby church. I peeked into the garage where Grandpap had kept his Ford pick-up. I kept having the strangest sensations of déjà vu. Then, to top it off, we went down the hill to the church, and found it open. We walked in, and once again, I had a weird sensation of time-traveling. We'd often gone there to "play church" when we went as kids on those long-ago Sunday visits.

I picked up a card with the pastor's name and address from the visitors' table. When I got home, I wrote him a note that said in part: "After my father, Harvey F. Corson, who used to have an Allis-Chalmers and Chrysler-Plymouth dealership north of Muncy, returned from World War II in 1945, we began the ritual of driving almost every Sunday up to the farm adjoining your church and cemetery, and our visits there were highlights of my youth." He wrote back, saying that he'd read my note to the congregation and it had prompted a "great buzz of reminiscing."

What pleasure it would have given Daddy to see his old home place being so well kept. It appeared much as I remembered it many decades ago when he and Mother brought us there nearly every weekend after he returned from the war.

I had seen the farm just one other time after it was sold. One winter day, likely sometime in the 1980s, when Howard, our daughter Rebecca, and I were visiting for Christmas, Daddy wanted to drive to see his old home. At that point, I wanted to remember the place as I had known it, and I almost didn't go. It had just begun to snow, and I welcomed the veil of blurry edges that the whiteness provided.

> *summer tanager buried*
> *red flight*
> *still*

Bambi and Slaughterhouse Five

Because of the way my youthful imagination had seized upon fear of fire and because fire destroyed The Building, it is a theme that continues to draw me. Fire in violence, especially the violence inherent in war, links it with my explorations about the World War II experience.

It must also be said that fire is a source of creation as well as of destruction or punishment. There are some important examples of this positive quality of fire in mythology. In Greek myths, Prometheus is a fire-bringer; his gifts include civilization and all the powers of fire, from cooking to smithing. There is also the phoenix, which cyclically burns on its pyre-nest and is re-born. When I studied goddess traditions for my women's literature classes, the Celtic goddess of smithcraft, poetry, and healing, Brigid, became my favorite. I've woven Brigid's crosses from reeds at her feast day, February 2, Candlemas, and hung them over our front door to ward off fire. I treasure the thought that Brigid's flame of peace and unity is kept burning at her shrine in Kildare, Ireland, a symbol of the constant need in our world to counter violence.[28]

Of fires I've known in art and literature, the forest fire in "Bambi" stands out. Daddy and Mother took us to see that 1942 film when I was quite young, probably not more than nine or ten, and I was devastated when Bambi's mother was killed by hunters. The fire that Bambi and all the animals had to flee to survive was terribly frightening. In retrospect, I see this early 1940s film as a prophetic cultural artifact; a generation of children like myself was horrified to see the destructive force of a holocaust upon animals we saw as analogues of our own families. At best it was a parable about survival in spite of great loss. At worst it prefigured the cruel depredations of war as manifest so horribly in the Holocaust. Later, a graduate teacher told our American Studies colloquium that Disney films were banned in Sweden because they were too violent.

Kurt Vonnegut's novel *Slaughterhouse Five* depicts the

firestorming of Dresden, underscoring the violence of World War II and of *any* war. The author was in a group of American soldiers captured and imprisoned in what was a defenseless German city, one of the greatest cultural centers of Europe. His group survived the horrific USAF and RAF fire bombing raids of February 13, 1945, in an underground slaughterhouse, a meat locker called Schlachthof Fünf (Slaughterhouse Five).

In papers discovered by his son after his death in 2007, Vonnegut had written of his horror at the "obscene brutality" in Dresden that could never leave him:

> Dresden, a beautiful city, built in the art spirit, symbol of an admirable heritage, so anti Nazi that Hitler visited it but twice during his whole reign, food and hospital centre so bitterly needed now...

> There can be no doubt that the allies fought on the side of right and the Germans and Japanese on the side of wrong. World war two [sic] was fought for near-holy motives. But I stand convinced that the brand of justice in which we dealt, wholesale bombings of civilian populations, was blasphemous.... I felt then as I feel now that I would have given my life to save Dresden for the world's generations to come. That is how everyone should feel about every city on earth.[29]

Probably the quintessential fire image from the war, one stamped forever on our collective memory, is that of the German crematoria for their Jewish prisoners. The word *holocaust* is derived from the Greek *holo* + *kaustos*, "whole burnt." In English it has evolved from referring to biblical sacrifice of male animals in worship to referring to fires of extreme destructiveness, of humans by humans in war. Now "the Holocaust" has come to refer primarily to the murder of millions of European Jews, gypsies, homosexuals, and others vilified by the Nazis. I have told of the ways I have learned about it and have participated in educating my students about it.

A Phoenix Story

But that's not how I want to end this writing on fire and home places. There is a phoenix rebirth involved. After Howard and I married and Rebecca was born, our own family ritual became a summer drive from Florida to visit Mother and Daddy at the new Corson Castle across the fields from where The Building once stood. As I have said, this was their dream house. Daddy had assessed the land as having rich soil and good prospects. He asked the owners to contact him if they ever considered selling; they did. He and Mother built a home with a wonderful view of forested Bald Eagle Mountain with the west branch of the Susquehanna curving around it. We knew the river was there although it was invisible to us because of distance and the wooded land on its banks. On our summer visits there, Rebecca loved meeting the new beagle puppies Daddy bred to sell and to use in hunting. She and her Aunt Janet had puppy races with the sleepy little plushballs. The photo below captures the great vista that stretched all the way to Bald Eagle's dome.

look out, rabbits
come autumn, these milky puppy noses
will find you

Sometimes we had the pleasure of being there at Christmastime—for Floridians to have a white Christmas was a real treat; we never really did get used to palm trees with Christmas lights. I think of the table covered with a deep red table cloth and Christmas candle centerpiece, silver and china and special glasses, delicious food—perhaps a ringneck pheasant Daddy had shot and Mother roasted with sherry—and most of all, the family gathered around.

There's a photograph of Corson Castle in winter that looks much like the picture on that card Daddy sent to Mother and me in 1944 from "Somewhere in Belgium." Though The Building was consumed in flames, this beautiful home, the new "Corson Castle on the Susquehanna," had already taken its place by then, and we enjoyed it for many years.

What will endure, I believe, is the truth that the image of "Corson Castle on the Susquehanna" helped Daddy survive and come home to us. Viktor Frankl's work *Man's Search for Meaning* holds much wisdom on this topic. This noted psychiatrist, survivor of Auschwitz and other Nazi prisons, as well as of the loss of his entire family, brings us the message that having a goal while keeping faith in a meaningful future is a trait of those who survive. The Castle was an image of such a salvific goal for Daddy.

V

Filling in the Blanks

Bittersweet

(A Letter)

Dear Daddy,

As I write about "Filling in the Blanks," I'm aware that some of your days were not so happy, days in which the world was hard to swallow. Still, those may be the very days that take us to the necessary depths of our journeys, the places of holy discomfort that lead to hard but critical truths. There are some stories that aren't so easy to tell, but to tell the whole story honestly and authentically, I must. Some of the blanks have to do with food, with the huge contrast between the food we had in the US during and after the war and situations of hunger and even famine in Europe. Others have to do with incidents in which our relationship was confused by anger, while others, especially your saving my right arm, demonstrated your amazing generosity.

As I'm continuing my hunt for information about what it was like in the war for you, I wonder if and how you came to reconciliation with it all. I wonder if your search for your lost map is a sign that you too hunted for closure? At first, I didn't understand what "ordnance" meant, but now I know a great deal more. Even in the worst of battles—and there were awful ones—I'm sure you found ways to problem-solve, that was your genius. I just wish you could fill out these blanks with me, and most of all, that doing so would bring you a sense of healing and peacefulness.

Love,

Nancy

Feasts and Famines

Home Cooking

With large helpings of humility and gratitude, I recall always having plenty of good food in our home. We ate meals together as a family. We kids learned table etiquette and took turns saying simple graces like, "God is great, God is good, and we thank him for this food," even though we wondered why "good" and "food" didn't rhyme. Mother was a splendid cook—Daddy always said that was an important criterion for his choice of a wife. She told us that she'd learned from Nanaw to make just about everything except piecrusts since Nanaw insisted upon making those herself.

Learning to cook gave me a sense of accomplishment. The first whole meal I prepared by myself was cornbread served with milk and blueberries, a standard Saturday lunch for us. Daddy had brought the recipe from childhood at the Corson farm, so of course he was pleased.

Other Saturday lunches, typically American, were also considered a treat by us kids, and we could easily help make them: hot dogs or hamburgers with canned baked beans and potato chips; grilled cheese sandwiches with pickles and carrot sticks; and the best—BLTs with fresh garden tomatoes and lettuce. For summertime Saturdays, we might make a picnic, and take it to a shady park with a swimming area nearby. We were glad that business closed at noon that day.

While Saturdays were fun for informal meals, Daddy and Mother regularly invited guests, usually family, for more formal dinners. Daddy, like the good people shown in the famous Norman Rockwell Thanksgiving print, always believed in having generous meals for guests; he always said, "Better too much than too little." We were so proud of Mother's cooking for those feasts and of how pretty the table looked. After many failures as an apprentice *sous-chef*, I finally learned to make gravy without flour lumps.

For birthdays Mother made pink seven-minute icing that we loved to spread on cakes in grand, loopy swirls. Like most kids, we argued over who got to lick the mixer beaters. For the presentation part of our birthday ritual we got out the special cake pedestal that had a wind-up music box in its base. We sang along with its tinkly version of the "Happy Birthday Song" as it turned the cake like a merry-go-round.

> *Mixmaster swirls*
> *drops of red food coloring*
> *summer sunset*

Passing along the tradition, I made pink birthday cakes for our daughter Rebecca.

Daddy was the one to please at the dinner table: we took seriously the old adage, "The way to a man's heart is through his stomach." In our gardens, we raised his favorite vegetable, lima beans, though the pods tended to get mushy with mold in wet weather, and they attracted nasty little yellow bugs that made shelling unpleasant. Once I responded to his nostalgic mention of elderberry pie by picking some wild roadside berries in late summer and baking them up—it was a one-time event because the berries were full of big, potentially tooth-breaking seeds.

One year, I was assigned the task of getting Grammy Corson's recipe for yeast buckwheat cakes. That turned out to be a lesson in cooking as an art of improvisation. Grammy gave directions like, "I put in a little blue glass of milk, then I add flour until the batter falls in sheets from the spoon like this...." It was hard to record, but somehow we managed to make them. Mother was a great improviser too. So, for a number of years we celebrated Fourth of July, Independence Day, with a big breakfast of buckwheat cakes with real maple syrup and sage-flavored sausage outside over a wood-fired grill that Daddy had fixed up in the old spring shed at the farm up at Huntersville.

When Daddy bought the land for deer hunting, in the mid-'50s, the Huntersville farm also became a sanctuary for us, much like Grammy and Grandpap Corson's farm after Daddy returned. Some two hundred acres of lovely hilly Pennsylvania fields and woods, it was greatly enhanced with a big spring-fed farm pond he made with a bulldozer.

I remember the routine of the pond's making—we'd have a quick supper after the business closed, drive the seven or eight miles from our home to the farm, and he'd get right to work in the long summer evenings. We worried for Daddy's safety as he turned on the bulldozer's headlights and kept chugging away, carving out the pond bottom's steep slopes at the deep end as it got darker and darker. But of course, he'd had strenuous lessons in operating big machinery as an ordnance man in the war. Maybe this seemed like a positive use of that dangerously hard-won skill.

In later years, whenever we visited the Huntersville farm in the summer, we were happy to swim and canoe and to fish and fry up the bass and bluegills he stocked in the pond. I enjoyed staying there overnight in late summer, being lulled to sleep by the rhythmic singing of the katydids in the big trees around the house. In rarer winter visits, we could skate on the pond and enjoy meals by the toasty fireplace. We had lots of good family reunions there until Daddy finally felt he could no longer maintain it and sold it. We missed it as a special family place, but most of us visited only once or twice a year, not enough justification to keep it.

morning mist
lacy cakes rise
the last time

Daddy loved apples. I remember how many different varieties he could name for me when I was writing a poem about them. One of his skillful homemade machines was a cider press that he installed in the machine shed below Corson Castle. The cider press afforded the pleasure of using picked fruit and windfalls from his own small orchard. In keeping with his frugal farm husbandry he spread the "pommies" (leftover pulp) as compost on the fields.

I love this picture of Howard, Daddy, and Mother with the cider-press—it resembles one of Rube Goldberg's fantasy machines; it was a conglomeration of spare parts Daddy always kept handy that worked fine.

Apples link our diet in Pennsylvania with memory of the war in France. Once Howard and I heard Daddy mention "calvados," and we went to many a liquor store until we found for him a bottle of this potent apple brandy. We guessed it was one good taste he remembered from Normandy, perhaps paired with toasts from French farmers grateful to the Allies.

Army Chow

I could only try to imagine the contrast between the Army rations Daddy had lived on for over two years in Europe and the fresh food—from our garden or Grammy's in the summer—that Mother cooked so well. Good food, especially in Daddy's estimation, was a definite priority in our household.

To learn about Army food, I went to a "US Army Rations of WWII" website (all quotes on rations are from this site).[30] There I read about food that was decisively non-gourmet and never fresh.

The Army had two special-purpose rations, Field Ration D and Field Ration C, intended to provide "the best food available in the best and most appetizing form within the realm of reasonable possibility particularly for troops in combat." The trouble was that the meat components of the C rations had to be produced quickly, in huge volume, hence little variety. So the troops had repetitions of meat-and-hash combos in the field and the same were served when they returned to the central messes. As the site reports, "It was little wonder that there was much early denunciation of the C Ration."

Also according to this site, the C-rations commonly included a D-ration, "used throughout the war as the Army's emergency ration and as a supplement to other rations." But it too had its downsides:

> The D-ration was a 4-oz. chocolate and wafer bar that could withstand temperatures of 120°F without melting [an accommodation to troops in combat in the tropics].… It was intended to taste bad to prevent it being eaten casually.… One veteran described it as "very difficult

to eat, hard as a rock and rather bitter…I would shave it into small fragments to prevent tooth fracture." It was nicknamed "Hitler's Secret Weapon" due to its effect on some GIs' bowels.

Unfortunately, there were wartime food facts that couldn't be laughed away. Several scholarly studies of food and war in World War II demonstrate how food was used as a weapon:

> The German military cut off the food supplies to Russian cities, a million people died in the siege of Leningrad alone, and similar numbers of Soviet prisoners of war were deliberately starved to death. Another group deemed "useless eaters" were Jews, millions of whom were starved or executed. Occupied Greece proved another example of wartime famine in this period. Other millions starved to death in Japan, China, French Indochina, and Bengal in British India.[31]

Since Daddy was with the Allies in late 1944 serving somewhere in the area of the Netherlands and in Belgium, he was in the midst of the worst food crisis in Western Europe, the "Hunger Winter." The Dutch government in exile in Britain called for railway strikes. The Germans retaliated with a food embargo. The embargo, a harsh winter, fuel shortages, bombed-out farmland, and floods combined to bring about the death of more than twenty thousand people in Holland. Food rations provided fewer than a thousand calories a day. Survivors ate tulip bulbs and sugar beets. It was not until liberation of the Netherlands in May 1945 that the Hunger Winter ended.[32]

Bill Mauldin drew a cartoon in an Italian setting that could easily have been sited in the Netherlands. Captioned "The Prince and the Pauper," it shows Joe, wearily smoking a cigarette with mess kit in hand as he faces a barefoot, raggedy urchin holding her empty pail. He later wrote about this cartoon:

But there is a big difference between the ragged, miserable infantryman who waits with his mess kit, and the ragged, miserable civilian who waits with his bucket. The doggie knows where his next meal is coming from. That makes him a very rich man in this land where hunger is so fierce it makes animals out of respectable old ladies who should be wearing cameos and having tea parties instead of fighting one another savagely for a soldier's scraps.[33]

Another soldier expressed a similar statement about the much-maligned C-rations: "We hated them until we ran out and started to starve. Then the hash, wieners and beans, beef stew with a biscuit and condiment cans became winners."[34]

Today's food riches in the post-war era seem prodigious, even shaming, as I think of them, but when I was growing up, I had no idea of this stark wartime context that had surrounded our soldiers, of the cruel deprivation so many people suffered—and continued to suffer for years.

Not only food, but also the hygiene surrounding it, was linked to the war in our household. Daddy insisted that we wash dishes until they were immaculate. He said he had seen too many soldiers get sick with dysentery because they didn't keep their mess kits clean. My friend Marian P told me that her M.D. father, who'd been in the war's Pacific theater, had similar concerns. He insisted that his family always clean their tubs and sinks with disinfectant because he'd seen such awful ailments there—jungle rot, hookworm, all manner of diseases carried by mosquitoes, flies, mud, and water. His alertness to such problems led him to initiate the building of a swimming pool for children in Muncy because he'd seen too many young patients with ear fungus. They'd been exposed to it while swimming in the Susquehanna River. Several drownings in the river also prompted his action.

Food was never far from Daddy's thoughts—not only as breadwinner and one who enjoyed good eating, but also as one who thought about his daughters' vocations. He let us know that he thought it would be great if we all became home economists. His 1944 birthday letter to me said: "Mother and I are taking out some insurance for you, so that someday you can go to college if you choose and learn how to be a test kitchen expert—like your Dear Mamma."

I know it would have pleased him mightily if I had followed that program at his alma mater, Penn State, as my next two sisters did. However, winning a scholarship to Susquehanna University, a liberal arts college, took me there instead to study English literature. Daddy called in our pastor for a consultation to decide if this was an OK course for me to take. I remember a rather formal meeting of the three of us in Daddy's office. I think the two men did most of the talking, but I must have been able to make my wishes to accept the scholarship evident. Luckily our minister approved and Daddy agreed. I'm so glad I didn't take that other path. I enjoy gardening, cooking, and eating, but I'm sure I was never destined to be a professional home economist.

Red Anger

As I re-imagine the post-war years and the evolution of my relationship with my father, I find both tares and wheat. Tares and wheat can refer not only to the weeds and good crops of a culture, but also to contending parts of ourselves—that is what we humans *are:* an infuriating and lovable mixture of both. The parable (Matthew 13: 24-30) says we are not to pull up the tares lest we uproot the wheat, but to wait for the separation at the time of harvest. I interpret that to mean that we must continue to strive toward a loving life, not prematurely judging, but trusting to an over-arching wisdom to make the final sorting. When I write about home, about the Castle on the Susquehanna, and The Building, I am heaping up wheat. That affirmation comes first because gratitude edges out my hesitations, but there are some things, like tares, that I've needed to acknowledge to find wholeness and reconciliation.

When I speak about my relationship with Daddy, I know I am speaking universally about relationships, none of which are perfect. Most of us struggle to do our best. Our family life generally flowed placidly along when I was young, yet there was a kind of underground stream that occasionally flooded over and thrust up uncontained, disruptive energies. The flooding had to do with Daddy's anger.

When my sisters and I played in the early years, we sometimes had a sense of wondering if there was some task we'd overlooked and for which we might be held accountable—there was a submerged question: "Have I done *enough?*" In my case, Daddy's expectations were in fact demands for a certain level of discipline and productivity that could rattle an already hyper-responsible and conscientious kid. My internalizing of them is a blessing and a curse in my life. Daddy's rule that we should "see things to do" is now part of my modus operandi, and I do usually manage to get a lot done, but it's hard for me to stop and rest (I call this my "Energizer-bunny syndrome"). I have a tendency to keep going until I'm totally exhausted or, nowadays, to do something dumb like stretch too far and strain my back. Somehow this was what seemed expected, a sort of self-sacrificing reach for an unattainable goal.

During those first post-war years, especially that first decade, when Daddy was working to "make up for lost time," he brought a kind of military organization into our home and probably into the business too. You felt you were being watched and judged by his standards. That made it hard to have the freedom of your own pacing, to know when it made sense to work hard and when it made sense to relax and rest. Daddy was trying so hard that he pushed *himself* to the point of total exhaustion, and his nerves sometimes frayed into frustrated anger.

The anger, whatever its cause, boiled over from time to time. When it did, Daddy would come up the inside stairs to our apartment for supper as usual. But the door would *slam*, a bad omen, and then he'd march through the entry room, past the washer and gun cabinet, into the dining room.

There, in front of that big formal dining room table that became our dumping place, with its heaped up mailings, magazines, toys, and what-nots, he would explode.

"This place is a mess! Look at this pile; you can't even see the table! Dorothy, with all these girls to help, can't we even keep our house clean? *Look* at this!"

After the ranting, all the shame-blaming that may or may not have been accompanied by spankings—it certainly had the emotional equivalent of that in any case. Marilyn and I would run to get the sweeper and then push it energetically back and forth over the rugs. I think we both felt that the sweeper was sort of like a noisy shield we could put between him and us. It gave a physical outlet to the agony of emotions brought up. We frantically put toys and other stuff away, and generally attempted to appear busy while crying and hoping that this misery would soon be over.

Once, after another particularly bristling diatribe and uproar like this one, I ran off to hide in a closet, sobbing. I stood in the midst of garment bags and long coats in the dark, saying over and over "I hate you; I want to die!" I wasn't sure who the "you" I hated was. It seemed utterly blasphemous and disloyal to wish this upon my father, but was I then to become the scapegoat? I did know that I felt persecuted enough that I didn't want to be anywhere around there.

Suppers afterward were a trial. There was a pall over the table that made it all a continuation of the trial, one we hoped to soon escape by excusing ourselves, helping with cleaning up, and leaving, finding some solace in a far corner by reading or playing with a pretend-sympathetic dolly or otherwise distracting ourselves. When we got our first hound dog, Rosie, we could pour out our woes to her when we took supper outside to her in her pen. I remember delivering some long tearful soliloquies to her as she chomped away at her food.

These couldn't have been happy episodes for Mother. When I think of them now, it seems that his ire implied that she wasn't the ideal superwoman, able to simultaneously handle full-time jobs as secretary, housekeeper-cook, and mother who could marshal little girls into being live-in maids in a small apartment. After all, she'd just spent most of the day in the office downstairs and had only recently come upstairs herself, speedily making supper for us. And then there'd be this avalanche of anger that left her no room for comforting.

Can I blame these angry episodes on the war? It took me a while to understand that wartime kids often indirectly share the terrifying experiences of violence and cruelty their dads encountered in combat. Today we talk easily about Post-Traumatic Stress Disorder or PTSD, but there were no ready words for it then—it was termed ambiguously as "gross stress reaction." They named it "soldier's heart" in the Civil War and "combat fatigue" in World War I, so it was not an entirely unknown entity. Although the affected adults tried to keep those events pushed down into their psyches, they sometimes erupted. Daddy was certainly not one of those men who beat their wives and children and went into drunken rages. If indeed he did suffer what would be classified now as PTSD—which we'll never really know—the episodes we experienced were relatively mild. But for impressionable young girls, they were frightening enough.

The best mechanic in the shop at The Building was a feisty man who'd been in the war too. As his boss, Daddy was concerned that he could occasionally let loose an angry side of himself, treating customers rudely. Daddy himself never displayed his anger in public, at least not that I know of. If it did show up, I could only guess it was triggered by something like a mechanic failing to follow orders and badly screwing up in the shop or a customer turning surly or doing something such as misusing a piece of machinery, breaking it, and refusing to pay for it.

When I did some research to find Daddy's exact rank in the Army, I found another example of his anger. I always thought that he had been a sergeant. I *wanted* him to be one and loyally felt that he deserved at least this rank. But when I scrutinized the insignia in photos, I found a two-striped chevron with a "T" underneath that signified a corporal, technician fifth grade, T/5.

I asked my sisters about this, and they remembered that he had been promoted to sergeant, but then, because of a dining hall incident, Daddy was busted back to Corporal. The story goes that his unit had been served food that he considered unfit to eat. He threw it back at the server. Our daughter Rebecca, a staunch supporter, insists that it would have been in character if her grandpa did it on principle, considering not just himself but others. Daddy was not a complainer: when there was a problem, he worked to fix it. We can imagine him saying something like, "My men and I need something better than this crap to keep going—it's not even fit for the hogs!" Or maybe those C-ration stews, in their gooey monotony, had just pushed him over the edge on a particularly bad day. At any rate, he told it like he saw it and took the consequences.

Here's another anger story that's memorable for me particularly because it took so long for me to really understand it. At one point when we were probably about three and six years old, Marilyn and I picked up the habit of making a sound of gagging at the dinner table when we didn't like something—we thought it was funny. Daddy got tired of it and announced that the next person who made the sound would get paddled.

Well, not too long after that (it was winter), the furnace went out and Marilyn and I were playing in the bathroom, all warm and cozy because we had an electric heater going in there. We were sitting on the floor by the door, pretending that our dollies and teddy bears were having a nice meal together. One of the animals, however, didn't like the food we served and made *that noise*. As luck would have it, Daddy was passing by at that exact moment. He heard the gagging sound, whipped the door open, and demanded in a loud voice, "Who made that noise?" We were stunned. I said, "What noise?" and he said, "You know what noise I mean!" Marilyn gave me a questioning look, but I was absolutely certain that I was being truthful and stuck by my story. After a long moment, Daddy said gruffly, "I could have *sworn* I heard that noise!" and left. It wasn't until years after that I realized that I *had* made that noise, speaking for a teddy bear who didn't like something on his plate, and that Daddy's totally surprising entrance had shocked me into instant amnesia.

One time when I was in my early teens, Daddy got so mad at me that he grabbed me and threw me across the living room. I had (once more) forgotten the event until Marilyn reminded me of it. She remembered because it had frightened her so. I can only guess that some smart-alecky remark of mine had angered him. I know I could be sassy. When I was, he'd say in rebuke, "You know everything, right? Nobody can tell you anything, can they?" The fact that I remembered those words marked a continuing tension between us for awhile. I don't remember any other occasion of physical abuse. What happened that time didn't hurt me physically, but I was both shocked at the intensity of it and confused—was I wrong or wronged? My psyche apparently decided that since I couldn't decide, it was better hidden away.

There's a kind of body memory that stores trauma of any kind; it gets embedded and eventually is aroused and needs to be healed. That's what I keep thinking about: when I relate these stories about us as kids being bewildered by Daddy's anger, I'm not judging. Instead, I'm realizing more and more fully that the inescapable violence of war leads to a kind of infection that soldiers unintentionally carry home into their families, their workplaces, and their culture. My sisters and I are not alone in having experienced this bewildering force.

I got some help in pondering this issue from a definition of "anger" offered by the American Psychological Association: "Anger is a normal emotion with a wide range of intensity, from mild irritation and frustration to rage. It is a reaction to a perceived threat to ourselves, our loved ones, our property, our self-image, or some part of our identity. Anger is a warning bell that tells us that something is wrong."[35] What strikes me about this definition is that it sounds like the threat reaction soldiers are trained to feel so that they can be effective defenders and protectors. Once this emotion is aroused for "good cause," against enemies in warfare, it allows for violent acts that include killing. It is like a genie that won't easily go back into the bottle when soldiers return to civilian life. When stresses pile up, it's easy to see how anger can rise. What was previously a good defense tactic can be a hard-to-control and inappropriate response back home.

It's hard to assess this on the macrocosmic level. But I believe that if we lived in a culture that valued *all* bodies and considered their loving care a priority, what immense burdens of abuse—from war and other violence—might be lifted. If war can be seen as a misdirection of men's testosterone powers, then I believe that it is a culture's duty to re-channel them into ways that help persons and communities—all environments— thrive.

The relative normalcy of our life after the war—even the mundane details that I remember—had to be healing. Daddy's manual labor in the shop, the physical tasks of farming and gardening, and even the long walks and waits of his game hunting must have been part of his own healing. I hope so. I've learned a phrase that resonates with me, "embodied healing." In my understanding, that means listening to our body's wisdom and following where it leads us; we can do this alone or, often preferably, with skilled helpers.

I have had the good fortune to experience many kinds of embodied healing work, from massage to physical therapy; I count swimming, gardening cooking, singing, making love, and walking the labyrinth among them. Yet as a word-focused person and one who has benefited greatly from talk therapy as well, I regret that Daddy wasn't able to tell more of what he could remember about the war and maybe other issues. I believe that might have been a powerful mode of relieving traumatic memories for him, a way to open them up for healing.

Purple Heart

One morning in October 1958, when I was fifteen, I heard someone yell, "The bus is coming!" before I was ready. That's *still* a nightmare scenario for me: the bus comes and I cannot assemble my outfit, all the books and homework papers, gym clothes, permission slips, and whatever else I need for the day in time to run out and catch it. I dash about madly trying to organize myself, but I cannot. I wake up from the dream feeling anxious and frustrated.

But that day was no dream. I was still upstairs in our apartment in The Building when I heard the call, so I grabbed my coat and school stuff and dashed down the outside stairs, slipped on an icy patch, and fell hard, banging my right arm against the banister. As soon as it happened, I knew something was wrong: I couldn't move my arm. It was such a shock that I barely remember what happened then. I became part of an unfolding drama that took me further and further away from any ordinary morning. Mother knew I was rushing to get the bus and when she heard the sound of my fall, she came right away. Someone, likely Daddy, drove me to the hospital.

An X-ray showed that not only was the upper arm bone, the humerus, broken, but also that it was so thin, due to a congenital malformation, a bone cyst, that it might not be possible to mend it—there wasn't much bone to re-join.

An orthopedic surgeon was summoned, and he quickly came to the conclusion that the only way to save my arm from amputation was a bone graft. Since I was fifteen, he felt my bones were still growing, and therefore it would not be wise to use my own bones for a graft. Daddy had the same blood type as me, O positive, so he was identified as a good candidate, and he offered his bone without hesitation. Mother remembered that day as a heavy one; Janet was just a babe in arms, and this unusual operation would be quite risky for both Daddy and me.

It all happened quickly. Our orthopedic surgeon Dr. Francis Costello's strategy was to shave bone from Daddy's hips and then to pack the chips in around the small amount of bone I had in my arm; it was a complicated double operation. Dr. Costello's bluff manner somehow gave me confidence. I never doubted. It worked miraculously, and I must say that it amazes me more now, as I realize what a stupendous healing happened, Daddy's bones knitting to mine and growing together to save my arm. In fact, we learned later that it was a procedure so unprecedented that Dr. C presented our case at a medical conference in Europe!

For nine weeks I lived in a strange cast that looked like the top of a high fashion white gown that wrapped entirely around my torso and rested on my hips. It was sleeveless on the left side and had one "strap," over my right shoulder. From that strap, the cast continued down to my right hand like a long glove with the fingers cut out. This wrapped arm was braced up in a right-angled position at shoulder level. (I think this was to keep the muscles and other tissues stretched.) I had to sleep on my back, propped up with a pile of pillows. It's lucky that it was wintertime because hot weather would have made a misery of the itching of dried skin on my back in the last few weeks. As it was, I could take something like a ruler and reach under the cast to scratch itchy places.

Mother helped me assemble a small wardrobe that fit over this construct, and I went back to school—it just seemed to be what had to be done. I scrawled exams and did tenth-grade biology drawings as a lefty. I became fairly ambidextrous and could even tie my shoes with one hand, sort of. Once, after the cast came off, a small piece of bone worked its way out in a kind of boil. It *would* happen while Daddy and Mother were away on a short business trip, and I got to imagine all sorts of calamities, but it finally healed up OK. The bone has held well under a six-and-a-half-inch scar.

Daddy's recovery, however, was far more difficult than mine. He pretty much had to learn to walk again due to the severing of muscles and nerves over his hip joints necessary to harvest the bone. He was wonderfully non-complaining, and I had little sense then of how tough it was for him, both during recovery and ever after.

About two decades after the operation, when Howard and I made our yearly visit to Corson Castle in the summer, Mother told me privately that I should thank Daddy for his bone gift. He had obviously been thinking about this and needed acknowledgment from me. I was embarrassed that I hadn't thought to say thank you often enough and that he felt I'd taken his sacrifice for granted.

In 1984 the *St. Petersburg Times* invited readers to tell how a tissue or organ transplant had improved their lives. I saw it as an opportunity to make up for my seeming ingratitude, so I wrote, and my piece was published. I repeated an unusual story that Daddy told me: after the operation, while he and Mother were on vacation, a gentleman asked him why he was limping. Daddy told about his gift of bone to me, and the man said that he, too, once had the chance to give bone to his child for a similar operation. But, he said, "I couldn't do it. I regret so much that I didn't have enough courage to do it."[36]

I concluded my article by saying that as a right-handed writer, a swimmer, a bread baker, a sometimes calligrapher and tennis player, as a wife and mother, I was awed to think how different my life would be without two arms. Though Daddy was not wounded or killed by hostile forces as required to receive the military Purple Heart award, I think he suffered arthritis in those chiseled bones for the rest of his life. For his great gift, I unreservedly declare that he fully earned his Purple Heart of Fatherhood.

I imagine that I have messages embedded in my cells, passed on from what Daddy "knew in his bones." Even though I can't decipher them precisely, they give me strength and courage. I don't want to ever forget that they are there.

> *spring peepers down by the creek*
> *reassuring voices*

Lost Evidence

Oh, dear. I'm having another fit of "why didn't I ask before it was too late?" If I'd been a boy, would I have been more interested in war stories and all the accoutrements of war? I'll bet that if I'd had brothers instead of sisters, I'd at least have been able to eavesdrop on such conversations they would have had with Daddy.

However, I was up against something else too: that generation of soldiers was inclined not to talk about their war and tended toward stoic silence, often all the way to the grave. Terese Svoboda sums up the cultural values that served to enforce that silence: "People were not expected to express any emotion in the 1950s. The returning vets of the Greatest Generation kept quiet about the horror they witnessed, they internalized it. Any negative reaction to all the death they witnessed would sully the sacrifices of the dead."[37] Even if that doesn't exactly fit how Daddy felt, he was intent on focusing his energies on the work at hand, with that ever-present goal of "making up for lost time."

Despite the soldiers' reticence to speak, publishers have pumped out a steady flow of World War II literature. For example, *Battle Zone Normandy*, a series marking the sixtieth anniversary of D-Day, divided the events of D-Day and the Allied breakout of Normandy into fourteen volumes. Since Daddy mentioned some of the places named in their titles—St.-Lô, Utah Beach, Juno Beach, Omaha Beach, Orne Bridgehead— how much more would I understand if I read those books? Or if I went to Europe on guided war tours or followed battlefield walking guides? The fact is that I could watch a hundred war films and read libraries of books, walk miles and study maps, but I'd never be able to fill the huge gaps that remain in Daddy's unique narrative, the one I want to know about.

One of Howard's cousins asked her uncle, then in his eighties, what it had been like to fight in Italy during World War II. He said, "You don't want to know," and that was that.

box turtle on our drive
here one minute
gone...

One day in the weight room of our local YMCA, I saw a man wearing a T-shirt with ARMY written in big letters on it. Another man, probably a generation older, came up to Mr. Army-T-shirt and they began to share "Army talk." The little I heard and how they said it made me feel how alien Daddy's experience in the armed forces was to me and Mother and my sisters. I also know that once discharged, he would never have worn that T-shirt.

Perhaps unconsciously, I didn't want to know what he knew. I think that was true for Mother, who, I believe, wanted nothing more than to restore balance and peace when her husband returned; perhaps I followed her lead.

Dreams can be incisive truth-tellers. During this writing, I had a dream about my frustration over missing materials, the many gaps in my knowledge of Daddy's war and how he felt about it afterwards. In the dream I learned that he had been kidnapped by the Secret Police. Somehow this didn't seem as alarming as it should have been, and I quickly recognized it as a pun-dream. The kidnappers could better have been called The Secrets Police because they'd taken an important *part* of Daddy away from me, impounding secrets I would never know. Perhaps Daddy kept silent to protect us from the stuff of nightmares.

We did have one big chance to learn a lot about Daddy's military experience. Being the practical observer he was, he had drawn a map detailing his Army journey in Europe. It's hard to know exactly when he made it. I wonder if he kept it as a kind of journal as he went or whether he drew it after he figured the information would be de-classified, after the armistice, or even on shipboard on his way home. He knew, of course, that Mother had no record of where he'd been because of the censors' careful removal of any hint of troop locations or movements from anything he sent home. Obviously this meticulously prepared map was very special to him. Making it must have been a ritual of hope, of determination to survive, or even a celebration when peace came. However, despite our turning our living quarters and attached storage areas upside down a time or two in search of this map—he was so determined to find it—it never surfaced, a bitter disappointment. I don't know if he'd searched earlier, but I was old enough the last time, maybe seven or eight, to remember the event.

We had to settle instead for brief mentions of places he'd been. Besides big cities like Paris and Berlin, there was Saint-Lô and only one or two others. I've learned that fighting was terrible at Saint-Lô because of nearly impenetrable taller-than-a-man hedgerows enclosing the Norman farmers' fields; there was so much shelling there that the town was nearly totally wiped out. Those would be reasons to remember it.

The only image I recall that he shared of a battlefield was of some cows that had been blown up into trees and stuck there. With my child's imagination, I'd thought that was sort of funny, but I expect, from what I know now, that he saw bloated and bloody carcasses in his mind's eye instead of my cartoonish cows.

How was any soldier ever able to really relax? There must have been nearly overwhelming noise, bloodshed, death, and an unending sense of high alert. In the summer heat of France after D-Day, the stench of rotting flesh, human and animal, in the battle zones was said to have been horrendous.

Daddy did also mention Sainte-Mère-Église, the first French town liberated by the Americans; this town and Saint-Lô were both close to Utah Beach. He told me of Nancy, France, but I don't think he actually went there. If we'd found his map, I know we'd have an enormously expanded sense of where he'd been and what he'd experienced, but that was not to be.

When I investigated the Queen Mary, the ship that probably carried him, along with thousands of others, from New York to Gourock, Scotland, in late March 1944, I did locate information about this particular passage. Without Mother's memory of dates, this disclaimer (posted on ww2troopships.com) would have prevented my learning anything more on the topic:

According to our (U. S. National Archives) records, in 1951 the Department of the Army destroyed all passenger lists, manifests, logs of vessels, and troop movement files of United States Army Transports for World War II.

(Sorry, but there was no word on why the records were destroyed.) Thus there is no longer an official record of who sailed on what ship, though there are still valuable sources that can be found. So this web page is an informal collecting ground for information about troop ship crossings.[38]

When Mother took Bette and Janet on a tour to Western Europe in 1967, Daddy didn't go along. I would love to have heard the conversation between him and Mother that led to this decision. Daddy never marched in Memorial Day parades, although my sisters and I did, as members of our high school band. We wore navy blue wool uniforms with long sleeved white cotton shirts we had to iron and white bucks—suede shoes—we had to polish with soppy white liquid. We marched over a mile from the school to the cemetery. One hot Memorial Day, Marilyn, having lugged her heavy baritone horn all that way on a scant breakfast, fainted just after taps was played.

> *fresh lilacs*
> *old graves*
> *once-a-year bugle calls*

Daddy is listed along with other veterans on a plaque above a brick memorial planter on Main Street in the center of Muncy, next to where the VFW (Veterans of Foreign Wars) hall used to be. It reads, "1917–1953 In honor of the men and women who have served their country and in memory of those who made the supreme sacrifice," but I don't think he ever went to that local VFW hall to drink and "shoot the shit," as he called it, with other vets. Because Mother loved shrimp, however, I remember that we did go sometimes to the VFW hall in nearby Montgomery, just across the river, for their special all-you-can-eat shrimp dinners. That put a pleasant family focus on a place that otherwise must have been a reminder of a time Daddy preferred to forget.

bird-splattered war monuments
"better give flowers to the living"

I have heard of some World War II veterans who continued friendships with buddies in their units after the war; some of them even arranged regular reunions that continued for decades. My friend Rev. Bill Knox proudly led memorial services at the annual reunions of the "Timberwolves," the 415th of the 104th Infantry. As late as September 2012, a friend of ours celebrated that his father, then in his nineties, was well enough to be driven to a long-awaited reunion with five buddies from his Army regiment. In contrast, I don't remember Daddy ever mentioning any particular person from his ordnance depot; nor do I recall any post-war re-connections or reunions in which he participated.

I've met a number of people who share frustration of knowing so little about their veteran relatives' actual combat experience. At a 2009 dinner gathering, one of the women at our table told us that her father, a veteran of the Pacific theater, had just died. He'd been buried with full military honors. At the funeral, she learned that he had been at Iwo Jima. Furthermore, he had been the sole survivor of his unit because just as the fighting was at its worst, he had been called away as a witness in a military trial. In his case, his survivor's guilt probably compounded the generational reticence to talk about the war.

lettered olive shells
sea-script
untranslatable

During that conversation, someone mentioned the National Personnel Records Center of Military Personnel Records in St. Louis and suggested I get in touch with them. I wrote to the center and, in a few weeks, I received a form telling me that they could not respond to my request: "The record needed to answer your inquiry was lost in the July 1973 fire that destroyed millions of records here at the National Personnel Records Center. The records stored in the area which suffered the most damage in the fire were those of: Army veterans discharged or deceased between November 1, 1912 and December 31, 1959." So all of Daddy's records went up in smoke!

My next quest for information took place in London, at the Imperial War Museum, which we visited, quite by chance, in the week of Armistice Day, November 9, 2009. When I said I was searching for any information pertaining to my father, the staff kindly escorted me to their reading room where a librarian showed me books that might contain helpful information. I didn't have much time, but I skimmed through some materials about the complexities of ordnance work. They also gave me an information sheet, "Tracing American Service Personnel." It led me to the US National Archives and Records Administration. As in Saint Louis, my search was thwarted, this time by a 35 percent error rate in scans of Army Serial Number microfilm of computer punch cards to a digital format.

In 2011, I had good luck. My inquiry about whether Daddy's grave site would be honored for wartime service with an American flag for Memorial Day weekend led to a surprising discovery. I'd contacted the Department of Veteran Affairs in Lycoming County, Pennsylvania, where Daddy was registered as a veteran. They informed me that if I simply contacted the county courthouse in Williamsport, I could obtain a notarized copy of Daddy's Honorable Discharge paper. Within days I received a copy of this "testimonial of Honest and Faithful Service to this country" dated October 12, 1945 by mail from the Department of Veteran Affairs.

Daddy's "Battles and Campaigns" are listed as Normandy, Northern France, Rhineland, Ardennes, and Central Europe.

Each of these has some kind of code. After "Normandy," for example, are the letters and numbers "GO 33 WD 45" and after "Ardennes" are these: "GO 40 WD 45." When I inquired of my contact at the Department of Veteran Affairs office about this, he said "GO" stood for "Government Orders" and "WD" was for "War Department." As for the numbers, they are yet another mystery. He suggested that these could lead to manifests with troops' names on them *if* they still exist and *if* they could be found. Judging from other records either accidentally or purposely destroyed, it seems the chances of my finding any more information now are minuscule.

The most researchable new fact on the discharge paper was that Daddy's "organization" was the 182nd Ordnance Depot. Using this clue, I found a *History of the 182D* [sic] *Ordnance Depot Company,* from April 16, 1943, through May 15, 1945, listed under The Memories Project of the George C. Marshall Foundation in Virginia. (For brevity, the publication is referred to as the *182nd History* in further text mentions.) I quickly requested a copy. Their archives librarian sent a copied four-page typewritten history followed by a page of 14 names (not including Daddy's) in the "3D. SQUAD."[39] It's unclear whether these men helped to write the *182nd History* or were just members of the squad; I don't have any idea what the designation meant. I was excited to receive the *182nd History*, as I thought it would provide more pieces of the puzzle. It did jibe with some details Mother had given us, for example that Daddy's "Mobilization Training Program" began in June 1943 at Camp Breckinridge, Kentucky, and was followed by participation in desert training in California. When Daddy reached England he was stationed at Malvern Link, Worcestershire, it said. The 182nd Ordnance Depot was assigned, at first, to the Third United States Army under the command of Lt. General George S. Patton, Jr.

The *182nd History* shows the 182nd was attached to at least six different ordnance battalions. On September 11, 1944, it was "relieved from assignment to the Third US Army and assigned to the First." In mid-May 1945 it was re-assigned to the Ninth US Army. Apparently the ordnance companies were treated as highly movable units, to be sent wherever most needed. That would make sense for them as part of the Army Service Forces (ASF), responsible—along with the corps of engineers, quartermaster corps, medical corps, signal corps, chemical warfare service, and the military police—for supplying and servicing the US Army.

Unfortunately, the *182nd History* also led to more questions I have no way of answering—instead of the Queen Mary that Mother remembered, this account claimed the 182nd Depot crossed the Atlantic aboard the Queen Elizabeth. Mother confidently told us that Daddy arrived in Europe on D-Day plus five, but the *182nd History* differs. The variety of reassignments for the 182nd specified even in this one document suggests exact information would be hard to prove, but I believe that Mother would know as well as anyone such basic details as Daddy's departure ship name and the date of his arrival in Normandy.

The fluidity of ordnance depot assignments would have made it difficult to follow any section of an ordnance depot and just about impossible to follow the path of any individual soldier. Now I see how valuable Daddy's lost map was—no other person or archive in the world could have had an accurate record of the maze-like branchings of his assignments; he was the sole authority.

Obviously, there are blanks I cannot fill; there are blurs I cannot bring into focus. In the end, beyond the few verifiable facts, there is the realm of myth-making, imagining what *most likely was true*. A myth, after all, is a *story*, based on an amalgam of psychic, even archetypal, and physical facts, not just a fantasy. As Jean Houston, a great contemporary teacher on this topic says, "A myth is a story about what never was but always is."

I believe Daddy would be amused at my busy scratching for facts. But I hope he'd understand that I do it to honor his service as well as to satisfy my lasting curiosity.

In Ordnance:
Heroism and Horror

What does ordnance mean—in both a "small o" general way and a "large O" World War II Corps way? The best definition I found comes from the Army wartime newspaper that published a small booklet, *The Flaming Bomb* (named for the Ordnance Corps insignia). It covers the history of ordnance in the European theater of operations. One of the series of *G.I.*

Stories published by the *Stars & Stripes* in Paris in 1944–45, it gives a high-spirited general definition of Daddy's area of service:

> The story of Ordnance in the European Theater of Operations is the story of men as well as materiel. It's the story of maintenance crews who put damaged vehicles back into action while sniper bullets zinged nearby and 88s screamed overhead; of ammunition companies fighting off dive bombers and infiltrating attacks; of tank recovery units and contact teams, depot companies and storehouse workers. It's the story of welders, small arms mechanics, artillery technicians, instrument repairmen, bomb disposal men, foreign materiel experts and clerks. It's the story of 150,000 officers and men who not only delivered the goods but kept that equipment in fighting condition through France, Belgium, Holland, Luxembourg and Germany.[40]

In his folksy way, the famous American journalist Ernie Pyle praised ordnance for taking care of small things that matter big to keep men and materiel moving: "The gasket that leaks, the fan belt that breaks, the nut that is lost, the distributor point that fails, or the bearing that burns out, will delay GI Joe on the road to Berlin, just as much as if he didn't have a vehicle in which to start."[41] If it weren't Pyle talking about World War II, I'd recognize such particulars of vehicle repair from overhearing shoptalk at The Building.

One great problem that tested the ordnance men's mettle early in the war was the tough Norman hedgerows, the *bocage*. In *The Ordnance Department: On Beachhead and Battlefront,* Lida Mayo describes the hedgerow country where orchards and pastures were "cut into tiny fields each field fenced in by dense hedges of shrubs and small trees growing out of embankments up to ten feet high, often flanked by drainage ditches or sunken roads. The hedgerows could conceal anything from an enemy sniper to an antitank gun."[42] When tanks climbed over the hedgerows, they tilted upward and exposed their underbellies, thereby becoming easy targets. The first solution devised, an unwieldy one, was to blow openings in those living walls with TNT.

Someone told me they read that Eisenhower mentioned an "unknown sergeant" who was a hero for solving this dilemma for the Allied tanks. The "unknown sergeant" figured that the heavy scrap metal littering the Norman beaches after the D-Day invasion could be attached to the tanks; this weight would hold them level, enabling them to plow straight through the rows rather than go bucking over them or waiting for passageways to be detonated. Who knows? Daddy was a sergeant—at least for a while—and he was extraordinarily resourceful. People had confidence in his skills; his Hughesville High School yearbook blurb was, "if anyone wants a problem solved, he usually finds the correct answer." My family believed he might have been the man who figured out how to save the tanks.

But this myth-making stumbles over facts: however much we'd like to claim this accomplishment for Daddy, Mayo's history names Sgt. Curtis G. Culin, Jr., and Lt. Steve Litton as the contributors of the best solution to the tank hedgerow challenge. Their device was a strong iron fork with five straight tines attached to the front of a tank to dig its way through; from its looks it earned the name "Rhinoceros." To create it, Lt. Litton re-used the angle iron bars or tetrahedrons that the Germans had placed on the beaches to rip the bottoms out of landing boats. Mayo notes the providential timing of the invention of the hedgerow cutters—less than a week before the planned Operation Cobra.

Major General J.B. Medaris arranged a demonstration of the device at his Twenty-Fifth Battalion headquarters for the large crew of welders and skilled mechanics he'd organized from his maintenance companies and then sent tank transporters to the beaches to gather up the plentiful tetrahedrons. Supplied with the critical welding materials he had had the foresight to stockpile, they soon were at work. "In forty-eight hours First Army

Ordnance men made nearly 300 hedgerow cutters, and in a week three out of every five tanks to be used in the breakthrough were equipped with them."

Operation Cobra (July 25–31, 1944), combined with the efforts of the Second British and First Canadian, transformed the high-intensity infantry combat of Normandy—a bloody month for Americans bogged down in the "hellish war of the hedgerows"— into rapid maneuver warfare, and led to the creation of the Falaise Pocket and the loss of the German position in northwestern France. Since the *182nd History* says Daddy's "company began operating as a forward armored depot on July 23, 1944, and accompanied the Third Army spearhead across France," I can visualize Daddy among those crafty welders. Clearly, this was a crucial victory in which ordnance played a key role.

Here's another story from Lida Mayo's *The Ordnance Department*, from the Ardennes. We know that Daddy was involved in the Battle of the Bulge there in the winter of 1944–45:

> Some of the combat organizations were badly crippled, not only from battle losses but from accidents on the icy roads. One observer in the Ardennes reported that "you would have thought an armored column had gone mad to watch its vehicles careening off trees, crashing through the corners of houses on turns.... To provide better traction [for tanks], the maintenance companies welded steel "tacks" or cleats to the tracks, scrounging welding equipment from the neighborhood when they lacked it, improvising the cleats, and working night and day. One unit, by cutting steel cubes from the side of the track itself and welding them on the track face, was able to report: "Within a few days every tank on our schedule was equipped and clopping across the ice like a mountain goat."[43]

Again, I believe that Daddy could have been there, problem-solving with the best.

———— ◦ ————

The Battle of the Falaise Pocket (August 12–21, 1944), named for the town of Falaise, France, is described as the decisive battle engagement of the Battle of Normandy. Daddy's discharge document lists "Normandy" under "Battles and Campaigns." I have a small collection of postcards, his souvenirs from Belgium, from the quarries of la Falize, the town of Acosse, and of Aywaille, south of Liège, all towns in this area. I keep remembering his mention of Saint-Lô, France; on 26 July 1944, US forces broke through near that town, forcing a German withdrawal from the Normandy region.

One account, in the *World War II Database, Normandy Campaign, Phase 2, 25 July–22 August 1944,* describes the Battle of the Falaise Pocket as epitomizing the horrors of war:

The battlefield at Falaise was unquestionably one of the greatest "killing fields of any of the war areas," Eisenhower noted in his memoirs. "Forty-eight hours after the closing of the gap I was conducted through it on foot, to encounter scenes that could be described only by Dante. It was literally possible to walk for hundreds of yards at a time, stepping on nothing but dead and decaying flesh."

Robert Rogge, who fought with the Canadian Army in Falaise, recalled the destruction:

"It reeked of the destroyed [German] army. Burned-out tanks, lorries, motorcycles, and carts were in ruinous heaps. Bloated, black-faced corpses lay everywhere, and the summer stench was overpowering. Dead, grossly swollen horses were carelessly mingled with human corpses and savaged equipment.

"The men held dirty handkerchiefs over their faces,

but nothing could keep out the smell. It got into their clothes and remained with them for days."

Pilots reported that the terrible odor was evident hundreds of feet above the battlefield.[44]

Mother said that, from what she knew, the worst was the Breakthrough of the Normandy Campaign, four months after Falaise, just before Christmas 1944, when the Germans made a surprise attack on the Allies: "I was in Altoona at that time, for Christmas (the year that Nancy got the little pink wicker doll buggy), and it wasn't a happy time, I can tell you that!"

W.C. Heinz, war correspondent for the *New York Sun*, vividly describes that attack:

Shortly before six a.m. on December 16, 1944, 17 German divisions, moving through the rain and the fog in the wood hills of southern Belgium, suddenly struck at four American divisions along an 80-mile front. Here in the mysterious frozen darkness of the Ardennes Forests, the Wehrmacht monster turned on its pursuers in one last death struggle. For days the outcome of the fighting was in doubt. [The *182nd History* says, "When the enemy broke though our lines in the Ardennes a few miles from the depot, the company was forced to make a 48-mile retrograde movement, leaving Dieuport (Belgium) at 1600 hours and arriving at Acosse, Belgium at 2030 (without exact date, sometime between 14 December and 11 January)."] Then after six weeks, this "Battle of the Bulge" was over. It cost 158,000 casualties on both sides. It was the beginning of the end of Hitler's "thousand-year" Reich.[45]

Again, the *182nd History* says: "On 10 March 1945 the company moved into Germany, leaving Acosse, Belgium, at 0925 hours and arriving at Aachen, Germany at 1330." The company left Aachen on March 30 and moved to Bonn, Germany. Two clues to Daddy's whereabouts after the Ardennes suggest that he was in Aachen then. The first is the photo frame for Mother's portrait labeled "Aachen, Germany/March, 1945," one of the few treasures he carried, and the second is a photo of him, identified on the back as taken in Aachen. In this photo, he relaxes with other soldiers, presumably after they had entered the thoroughly conquered city.

W.C. Heinz wrote of chaos in Aachen, presumably about the same time. It was the spring of 1945, after the infantry had taken Aachen the previous autumn:

> Eighty-three percent of the houses were destroyed or damaged in Aachen and 70 churches and 50 schools. In what was left of the houses there were canaries dead in their cages and rubber plants turning yellow and, in the kitchens and dining rooms, where the chairs had been pushed away from the tables in haste, the food had turned to mold on the plates. At the foot of a child's bed, sitting so that it faced toward the pillow at the other end, was a doll with its arms outstretched. There were also the Nazi propaganda books and swastika armbands and swastika pins.[46]

To think that this city, known in English by its French name, Aix-la-Chapelle, was once a favored residence of the Emperor Charlemagne and the coronation site for the kings of Germany.

If Daddy experienced *anything* like what Eisenhower and others described about the Falaise Pocket or what W.C. Heinz wrote about Aachen, it's not surprising that he had no wish to re-visit those places, either literally or in stories.

One of the most read and most often taught books for the generations right after the war in the US was J. D. Salinger's novel *The Catcher in the Rye* (1951). No other book affected me so strongly when I was in high school. As an Army sergeant, Salinger carried pages of that novel-in-progress with him through the war. His biographer, Kenneth Slawenski, writes: "It is difficult to overstate the impact of D-Day and the 11 months of combat that followed. The war, its horrors and lessons, would brand itself upon every aspect of Salinger's personality and reverberate through his work."[47] Protagonist Holden Caulfield's struggle for meaning in a bittersweet world gave me and my contemporaries a vicarious initiation into the destructive aftermath of war. Later in life Salinger told his daughter, in regard to his being among those who marched into the concentration camps at war's end: "You could live a lifetime and never really get the smell of burning flesh out of your nose."[48]

What terrible energies were unleashed on those killing fields, in those ruined cities, in those cruel camps. How much love and care can it take to restore what they damaged or destroyed? Is that even possible?

Because those who died so often died absurdly, I've had trouble using the word "grace" or "blessing" for those who survived. What *can* be said is that war is like a mad beast killing randomly, and that we humans are idiotic to continue engaging in it.

VI

What If I'd Been a Son?

The Tangle of Gender
(A Letter)

Dear Daddy,

Here's a big question for us to ponder: "What if I'd been a son?" It's something my sisters and I wondered about. We knew that you loved us, your four daughters, but we also knew that you were disappointed that there was no male heir.

It's tough to discuss the issues of gender and sexuality, but they have affected me so much that I need to untangle some of the worrisome ones between us. Born in 1943, I inherited a conventional first half of the twentieth-century American understanding of men-women relationships and evolved to become part of the feminist movement seeking equality between the sexes. What I felt increasingly as I grew up, Daddy, was that values were changing, and I needed space to reflect and to choose ones that most nourished my life.

You ran the Men's World of the shop at The Building, as I've guessed, much like the Army hierarchy, with its strictly ordered connections of technology and personnel. This worked well on many levels, but it was hard for your daughters to find a place there. You and Mother gave us educational opportunities to follow our own paths, but the playing field is still uneven. Our culture still can't even pay women equal pay for equal work. Some sources report that at the current rate, women won't close the gap until 2059.

I'm not ungrateful. I just want to clear away the discouraging idea that girls aren't as important as boys. We need each other as equals to be our wisest, kindest, free-to-be selves!

Love,
Nancy

Men's World

When I came down the wooden outside stairs from our apartment at The Building to the ground level sidewalk, if I kept walking straight ahead to go to the front of The Building, I'd pass two big showroom windows on my left. They were set back just enough to make a small ledge where we sometimes put tomatoes to ripen in the summer. (If forgotten, they left brown acid stains we had to scrub off.)

We used the small wedge under the stairs as storage for a few wagons, sprinkling cans, and garden tools. We could play in the wider area there when it rained. Beside that cement slab were two doors. The first opened into a small outside bathroom which was usually locked. It was only for family outdoor use. We kids loved to use the conical paper cups dispenser by the sink, and on hot summer days the smooth cement floor felt smooth and cool to bare feet.

The other door led into The Building itself—you'd walk right into rows of parts bins behind the showroom parts counter. I was so proud of the few times when I helped farmers find a part by matching their broken one with the picture in the parts book and then searching it out from the carefully labeled bins.

> *machine transplant:*
> *with this part you can finish plowing*
> *tomorrow*

If you went back outside that door and headed toward the back of The Building, you'd go by two folding garage doors, kept closed because the old grease pit bays behind them were now used only for storage. The last room on this side was piled high with tires. We thought we'd found a grand place to play until Daddy warned us to stay out.

> *the tire room was not safe*
> *remember the garbage crusher*
> *in "Star Wars"?*

A gravel driveway circled The Building. As kids, we loved the vacant lot feel of the area where the Army trucks and some other used machines were parked out back. There were empty oil barrels and tall weeds and even a few wild red raspberry bushes on the far property line with the next door neighbor, a trucking company.

The driveway continued around to the repair shop, on the far side, 180 degrees around the circle from where we started under the stairs; it had folding doors large enough to allow bulky farm machines entrance. These doors are visible on the left side of the shop photo, with three men between the foreground tractor and a harvester in the background.

This was mostly *terra incognita* for me and my sisters; we didn't understand the tools and equipment there or how they were used to service cars and farm machinery. We only scampered through on some particular errand during work hours, for example, delivering a message Mother sent. This was Daddy's area of operations. We knew some of the mechanics, had occasional crushes on some of the young ones, but it wasn't any place we belonged. In fact, it could be dangerous. We had to be careful outside the shop too, especially around the loading platform and in the open space where sometimes the big car transporters noisily unloaded their deliveries of the new season's vehicles, shiny Chryslers and Plymouths.

Some of the youngest mechanics must have seemed like sons or like the younger soldiers Daddy had been with during the war. He taught some boys' 4-H classes on topics like contour plowing and other agricultural practices in special night classes in the shop. I remember watching him teach on at least one occasion, and it seemed to me that he was good at it and that he enjoyed it.

The shop was definitely Men's World, and that posed a series of questions that grew larger over time for me. My sisters and I speculated about what it would have been like if we had been sons instead of daughters. Although we thought that Daddy and sons would have had alpha male conflicts, we also thought he would have loved teaching them about all sorts of things, from repairing machines to hunting. Early on, we accepted the conventional roles of men and women, but as we grew older, it seemed that boys got so many unfair advantages. We didn't call it "patriarchy" then. It wasn't until decades later that the women's liberation movement brought that word and what it represented resoundingly into consciousness, especially for me.

As in the feudal world, at the castle there apparently needed to be a male heir for things to be right, for the rules of succession to be properly honored. Mother wanted so badly to have a son that she cried when she learned that she had given birth to a third daughter. Daddy said that was never to happen again, that he loved us no matter what sex we were. The topic had enough emotional currency for me that when we studied genetics in high school biology, I brashly told him that it was *his* fault we didn't have boys since his XY chromosomes were responsible for selecting girls.

Janet was born, the fourth and last child, nine years after Bette. She and Daddy became good buddies even though she senses that she was conceived in a final effort to have a son. Somehow the idea of having a son was ingrained in his psyche, and it continued to bother him even though he said it did not.

I think that Daddy liked having girls, but he wasn't always sure about how to go about raising us and left that largely to Mother. He generally gave good advice and supported us in our projects and enthusiasms. When I showed interest in art, he arranged for me to take oil painting from a lady in town. He helped me get started in photography, one of his hobbies, with a film developing kit for Christmas one year. But when it came to more intimate things, I wish he'd allowed himself to trust his feelings. Once when I was about eight or nine, I had a bad dream and woke up crying. He kept asking me over and over to explain what was wrong. I'm sure that if he had just taken me in his arms and hugged me, assuring me that I was OK, it would have been so much more effective than a grilling for a rational explanation I didn't have. Here, I have to say that I doubt that *his* dad had this warm personal touch with him either. I guess it's hard to learn different ways after being immersed in a macho culture from birth.

Of all the awkward conversations we had, "the talk" about sexual responsibility was one of the most uncomfortable. We were riding together to an eye appointment I had in Williamsport, a rare happening since Mother usually took me. At the Montoursville light, waiting for it to turn green, Daddy asked if I'd had any sex education classes at school. I said "Yes," hoping he'd drop the subject immediately. But he went on to say a few things and then delivered this zinger: "If you get pregnant, don't come home." Wow. Now *there's* a message to ponder for a shy teenaged girl who didn't even date. Did he really mean that he would put me out on the street? I had never envisioned such bitter consequences, being ostracized by my family, if I should transgress the code laid down for "good girls." It was harsh, though probably a fairly typical welcome to sex for girls in patriarchal households of that time. Clearly sowing wild oats wasn't for us, on pain of being shunned.

I always wanted an older brother. When I was in grade school, one of my friends had two brothers in high school, and I thought that would be so wonderful—they could give me piggyback rides and all sorts of big-brotherly advice and protection. I envied my cousins who were lucky enough to have older brothers. But I didn't think of the negatives. An older brother and I might not have liked each other; we might have been jealous of each other as strong-willed individuals; he might not have wanted to give me the attention that I imagined other girls with big brothers received. Would Daddy have encouraged him to go to war? (I've read that many World War II vets, especially Midwesterners, did exactly that.) In the '60s, he might have run away to Haight-Ashbury or been a draft dodger; or he might have gone to Vietnam and come back terribly changed, with lasting PTSD or Agent Orange maladies; he might have been killed. He might have come out as gay.

Or this older brother might have been an ideal "red-blooded American boy" who survived the gauntlet of cultural expectations, from sports to warfare, and then gone into the farming and machinery business with Daddy and accompanied him on hunting trips. If the latter had happened, my pipe dream is that we'd still have a place in Pennsylvania to return to, and a comforting sense of continuity with that land and that community we knew as children. I'd have liked that. But we also might have kept our place if one of the sisters had stayed in Pennsylvania and showed an interest in maintaining the land. None of us did. From another perspective, our hypothetical brother might not have shared Daddy's interests at all. They may have quarreled and become estranged.

When I try to think about what my life would have been like if I'd been a son, I'm aware of many challenges. It would have been an honored position in our family. I would have had access to things I never learned about as a girl, but I would have had much to live up to in the Men's World. If I'd kept my interests in literature and writing, where would they have fit? What about my later progressive politics and my lack of interest—even dislike—for hunting?

Daddy did have four sons-in-law. He put them to work when they visited. Whenever we came to Corson Castle, Howard bravely asked if he could help with any of his projects. I say "bravely" because he never knew if he'd find himself doing something like stacking lumber, digging potatoes, or being hung by a harness while he tarred a steep roof. It was always a boss-to-laborer situation except for that one rare time Howard remembers, when Daddy acknowledged that his way of shoveling away a large pile of seed hulls, starting at the *top* rather than at the bottom, was better than his own.

A few times Howard was given jobs with the tractor. I take special note of that because none of us girls ever were. It's true that Daddy taught all of us to drive a car. I learned with a manual transmission and have always been grateful for this skill. But I did no tractor-driving. I occasionally steered a big truck for hay baling with Daddy and men from the shop loading.

Instead, my sisters and I were assigned the job of mowing our huge front and back lawns with the riding mower. That took at least an hour. One compensation for the tedium was that we got some tanning time in. When we helped with projects, we ended up handing Daddy tools and holding things. In our household, that's just how it was: jobs were divided by sex and that was that. I remember being astonished when one of

Marilyn's friends got special permission to take shop class with the boys instead of the usual home economics with the girls at school—who knew this was possible? In retrospect, I'm not sure if I or my sisters even knew how to change a tire when we left home. I wonder now why I didn't ask and why I didn't have more curiosity about such matters? The gulf between men's and women's work was one I only questioned later. My sisters and I do seem to have learned principles of management—I guess that came to us by osmosis from our parents and from our own practiced work ethic.

The sons-in-law, however, got to do large muscle tasks, part of designated men's work. They all enjoyed the camaraderie of their Corson Castle work-crewing on the occasions they visited at the same time, and they later laughed at stories about them. Any time they tried to cut corners or sneak a beer, they were found out.

I spent my first years in a "Women's World" with Mother, her mother, my Nanaw, some women friends, and few men. When my father returned from war, I was overwhelmed by his man's world, his dominant character, and by a culture that placed highest value on rationality, progress, and productivity. All of these were focused on competition and taught to boys in sports and elsewhere.

When I was already teaching, I celebrated the 1972 passage of the landmark Title IX and its significance for women in education, including sports. It stated in part that "No person in the United States shall, on the basis of sex, be excluded from participation in, be denied the benefits of, or be subjected to discrimination under any education program or activity receiving federal financial assistance." I didn't directly feel the impact of this, but I knew how important it was to my friend and colleague on the faculty who coached the women's volleyball team. At last she could apply for decent funding and claim institutional respect for her teams.

Senator Birch Bayh introduced Title IX in Congress and was its author and chief Senate sponsor. He spoke out in the

Senate against cultural values that had oppressed generations of women. Many schools held that it was foolish to waste a man's place on a woman because most women used college as a husband-hunting ground and went on to marry, have kids, and never work again. Title IX gave us at least a beginning to challenge such stereotypical notions that worked against women with professional ambition, including me.

I was born into an era ripe to question these lingering views of women's roles. In my scrapbook, a valentine from one of my second-grade classmates illustrates an early '50s conventional male-female roles portrayal, still embedded in familiar war imagery:

When "Rosie the Riveter" stepped forward during World War II to "wo-man" all those tough jobs, that was OK, but after the war she was sent home where she allegedly *really* belonged. The War Advertising Council cunningly wove slogans and visuals that propagandized working women—portrayed as all white, middle-class, patriotic housewives—as being welcome in the workforce only as long as there were no men to fill jobs.[49]

Rosie and her sisters were to follow the genteel dictates so conspicuously portrayed by then-popular women's magazines like *Ladies' Home Journal*, *Woman's Day*, or *McCall's*. Mother subscribed to those magazines, and I diligently read their recipes, style pointers, and hints about how to make a stylish comfortable home and how to please your man. They tended to tout a stereotypical happy homemaker focused on the traditional European *Kinder, Küche, Kirche* (children, cooking, church). For a while I fell under their sway; I spent many summer vacation hours making recipe files and absorbing their advice on make-up and proper feminine behavior. If a woman did have interests beyond that, such magazines told her that she needed to stay subordinate to men or else risk being an "old maid."

I know that the old stereotypes provided a comfortable way to organize the world for many, women as well as men, but I believe that the waste of talented women who were stymied by them was criminal.

Many of the litmus tests of feminine quality promoted in that time were enacted publicly in the Miss America pageant. Daddy liked to watch it and select his favorites. I watched it too and was somewhat interested, though I always felt I'd never be one of *those girls*. I could see by the judging, Daddy's and theirs, that that kind of beauty wasn't what I had. But that observation came with a kind of self-deprecation—I might have been really special if I looked like that and attracted the kind of attention those girls obviously did. I might be someone less glamorous, but still worthy, I hoped. The adage "beauty is more than skin deep" intrigued me, even though I wasn't sure I understood it then.

If we could use a magnifying glass on the wall to the back right in the photo of the shop at The Building, we might see that one of the posters featured an Alberto Vargas pin-up girl. America's entrance into the war in 1941 had set off a golden age of pin-ups. Racy photos adorned lonely soldiers' lockers and barracks walls. Lusty drawings embellished the fuselage of bombers and fighter planes—the posters were often considered mascots or good luck charms for safe missions. Vargas was joined by other highly successful commercial artists like Gil Elvgren and Zoe Mozert, a rare woman pinup artist. Real life models included

Rita Hayworth, Ava Gardner, Veronica Lake, Bettie Page, and, most famous of all, Betty Grable of the million-dollar legs. The US military unofficially sanctioned this kind of art and even paid for it as a morale-booster. I suppose it had its place during combat, but it persisted in the post-war world, so that my sisters and I and our contemporaries were confronted by this art. We might have asked ourselves why such obviously intimate images were displayed in public places. Were these images of some ideal we were to strive to attain, even though we knew they were sort of sleazy?

Daddy had a school-girlish photo of Mother he carried to war with him, the same photo of Mother that I pasted next to his when I made my scrapbook as a teen. I liked it that Mother was *his* beauty queen, and that was always true. Our daughter Rebecca remembers a time, late in his life, when he asked her to bring Mother's photo from his office; he held it up for her, saying, "Did you ever see anyone so beautiful?"

I distinctly remember a sunny day in early autumn when I wasn't quite old enough to go to school yet. I was in the graveled driveway at The Building riding my tricycle, and I heard the school bus leave from the bus stop just beyond our mailbox. I told Mother, who happened to be nearby hanging out laundry, "I can't *wait* until I can go to school!" She said cheerily, "Next year!" As it turned out, my schooling helped me find ways to develop my own unique talents, to find my own path through the mazes of patriarchy. I wasn't a pin-up type and I wouldn't win beauty contests. I chose my own category instead. My "A" report cards and honor rolls were my prizes to bring home. Daddy told me he was pleased and proud of them, and so was I.

My sisters and I mostly enjoyed catering to Daddy's likes, and Mother encouraged us to do so. When we set the table, we were to be sure not to give him anything cracked or "not best"—we'd give those to ourselves. The line between humble service and self-deprecation can be hard to discern. What does it mean to be someone who is encouraged to make a habit of taking second best, even in "small things"?

As girls, my sisters and I generally had a good life at home and at school. I have the sense that it might have been harder for a brother to break out of the expected mold there in our castle on the Susquehanna than it was for us. None of us had a sense of obligation to inherit the business or show our loyalty by being a hunter or land manager; those expectations might have imprisoned a son. But this does not mean that misogyny was a lesser evil.

I greatly admire Denise Levertov's poem "Prayer for Revolutionary Love." The prayer envisions men and women loyally giving mutual support to each other's "meaningful work," asserting the desire that "our love for each other's work give us love for one another."

I believe that such hopeful words can help us stretch into wider, kinder definitions of selfhood and relationship.

Wanting an Heir

Not long after Howard and I were married, we made what became our annual summer trek up the coast from St. Petersburg, Florida, to visit with Mother and Daddy in Pennsylvania at Corson Castle. One evening after supper, Mother drew me aside and confided that Daddy had told her that he had an idea to have sex with another woman so that there could be a Corson son.

I was shocked. I remembered the story we'd all heard, many times, that Mother had cried at the birth of a third daughter because she knew how much Daddy wanted a son. She was sad to learn that this matter still persisted and that he'd considered such an upsetting idea. I felt sadness, anger, and confusion—for Mother and for myself. It seemed such a shameful matter to me that I couldn't even tell Howard right away, and later, when we went to bed, I silently cried myself to sleep.

I think of the young woman I was then, the one who had made, not so long ago, that scrapbook page celebrating what I saw as my parents' ideal marriage. I carried those same wishes for my own marriage. This news hit me like a broken promise. Even though the thought was not carried out, it was unfaithful and demeaning of Mother. Further, it carried the barbed message that neither she nor I nor any of my sisters measured up to patriarchal requirements. Only the production and presence of a *male heir* would satisfy—it seemed downright feudal.

Daddy may have thought of this as a kind of clinical solution, but to me and obviously to Mother, it was an interpersonal and moral matter. I remember also what he often said, in complete honesty about his love and admiration for Mother: "I could have searched the whole world over and not found a better wife!" Still, it was clear that no "happy housekeeping" could stave off the chill of men's world when it asserted its right to break rules (or should I say unwritten relationship agreements?) in its own interests.

As I contemplate that event now, decades later, I try to understand. On one side were centuries of patriarchal culture and its persistent grip; the man's world of the war reinforced this too. The post-war US, even with its just-rising feminism, still remained a patriarchal stronghold. Daddy was indeed a patriarch in being the head of his family. He faithfully assumed full responsibility for being our breadwinner, our guide and organizer, and our protector. Risking his life in war was part of his duty as a man, a father, a citizen, *and a Corson*. So it would follow that leaving a legacy, a son, was a *sine qua non*. There may have been not only determination, but also desperation as he aged, that caused him to consider breaking with his general good sense and propriety. I do not know; I'm trying hard to understand.

There have been many surrogate mothers in history, in many religions and civilizations; there is the famous Biblical instance of infertile Sarah offering her servant woman Hagar to her husband Abraham to pass on his bloodline. But the modern concept of surrogacy didn't really begin until the mid-1970s when the first "official" legal surrogacy agreement was enacted, opening the way to many kinds of accepted surrogacy. The crucial point is that Daddy's idea broke a marital norm then. It might have worked as a mutual decision, but it obviously was not right for Mother.

I'm still left with the facts of patriarchy's influence on Mother, myself, my sisters, women of the past, and our daughters, who were and are still—to often infuriating and humiliating degrees—considered lesser because of our sex. Intelligent, capable women of Mother's generation were kept from furthering their educations because of reasons that now seem archaic and absurd—they didn't have the right wardrobes for college; "women can't be art historians" (the reason given to thwart my mother-in-law's ambition) or any number of vocations arbitrarily marked "for men only"; women "aren't safe in the city" (the reason Mother was forbidden to accept a scholarship to Temple University in Philadelphia and briefly attended instead what she considered a mediocre teachers' college). Some were told, "We don't want housewives in our program" (an insult to a friend of mine who later achieved her Ph.D. *and* was a wife and mother), and so on, *ad nauseum.*

I was fortunate. I earned a Ph.D. and taught as a college professor. It was only when I began teaching that I learned about the feminist revolution. My students asked me to sponsor an independent study, "Women in the Arts," and this led to my offering other courses for a newly forming women's studies program. I learned that I had more sister-mentors—both contemporaries and predecessors—than I'd ever guessed. My education continued as I studied and taught works by Betty Friedan, Simone de Beauvoir, Adrienne Rich, Audre Lorde, Maya Angelou, Elizabeth Gould Davis, Charlene Spretnak, Robin Morgan, Margaret Atwood, Riane Eisler, Nelle Morton, Alice Walker, Deena Metzger (I love her title *The Woman Who Slept with Men to Take the War Out of Them*), and many others. There were also artists like Louise Nevelson, Judy Chicago, Faith Ringgold, and Käthe Kollwitz. All of these assured me of women's power and beauty by their rich (although often ignored or trivialized) "herstory." Earlier, "Anonymous was a woman," but no longer!

The German artist Käthe Kollwitz's work especially moves me; the death of her younger son Peter in World War I roused her "implacable opposition to war," and she continued to produce posters, sculptures, and drawings that make us see the horrors of hunger, poverty, and war even after she was threatened by the Gestapo. She also lost her grandson in World War II.

These women, in their art and in their lives, provide us with a brave heritage, a basis for me to give myself, my students, and others the freedom to shine our talents into the world. I also knew that I would never come home and harangue Daddy and Mother about their marriage in the light of feminism. I was the one who needed to change, and these women helped me gather courage to do so, to assert the value of my own achievements, of my own talents and temperament, even when it took extra gumption.

The patriarchy clearly asserted its powerful claims (I was to learn that they were centuries old) as the men in our family yearned to have sons "to carry on the family name." I remember overhearing that term being bandied about in conversation by Daddy and his brothers during a holiday at my grandparents' farm. Of the three, only one had a son, and they all thought that it was a shame there weren't more Corson men of the next generation. As the eldest child, a daughter among daughters, I found it strange that because of my sex alone, I lacked the credentials, was not worthy, to "carry on the family name." I think this realization contributed to my having an odd mixture of determination to succeed along with a lack of self-confidence.

I do, however, have the small triumph of carrying the family name in my legal signature—Nancy Corson Carter—since in grad school, after I was married, the registrar claimed they couldn't fit "Nancy Virginia Corson Carter" on my student I.D. card—too many letters. I made a quick decision to drop "Virginia," which was both Mother's middle name and mine. I regret that I wasn't liberated enough then to insist upon keeping it. Now it's clear that I too operated within the patriarchal mindset, and in so doing, disregarded Mother's intended gift of connection with her. I love that our daughter had the wit to hyphenate her middle and maiden name and add her married name onto that to make the requisite three names, first, middle, and last as required on a California marriage certificate—*she* got it!

Many studies show a direct link between a country's attitude toward women and its social and economic progress. A phrase new to me, "pink tax," names the ways women are even charged more than men for the same mundane items—things like dry cleaning, personal products, and vehicle maintenance. The disgraceful wage disparity of women and men has remained in place for at least twenty-five years. I had to fight for equal wages in my own career. The Equal Rights Amendment, first introduced into Congress by Alice Paul in 1923, and which I kept taped up over my office desk, still has not been ratified by all states.

One sign of hopefulness is the decision to place black abolitionist leader Harriet Tubman on the front of the US $20 bill, moving slaveholding former president Andrew Jackson to the rear. We did achieve the goal to accomplish this before 2020, the hundredth anniversary of the Nineteenth Amendment giving women the right to vote.

Despite my feminist ideals, Howard and I began working in conventional roles. When we were both young Ph.D.s, we assumed he'd be the first to work, and I would follow his jobs. I defended my dissertation when I was seven months pregnant, and Rebecca was born several months before I was awarded my degree. When he found a job, and I wanted to go from part-time to full-time at the same institution he taught at, I ran into anti-nepotism policies; these disproportionately affect women. Under a benign dispensation, I worked as a continuing part-time non-tenured faculty member. I had an interesting career, managing to teach innovative courses and contribute to the school on various committees and projects, but I never had access to tenure. I was fortunate to find ways to exercise my leadership skills outside of academia, as moderator of a national environmental non-profit, as board chair of a local camp and conference center, and facilitator of several church earth care committees.

It's not that Daddy wasn't sympathetic with the dilemma, for example, of my being burdened by nepotism at my work. But the truth was that feminism made everything more complex for me as I puzzled over navigating the territory of patriarchy, especially as I'd grown up with it. But that was how things were then, and our father was our mostly benevolent ruler. My sisters and I found it nearly impossible to avoid reverting to that order when we returned home as adults. Yet Corson Castle was a citadel, a sanctuary for us and for our families for a good long reign. I never considered allowing the issues of feminism to change my family story into one of alienation.

Living in a patriarchy leaves me with continuing questions: how to be humble and offer skilled service without being self-denigrating or falsely modest *and* how not to become secretly derisive and arrogant? At the same time, how to deal with obvious prejudice in issues such as lower pay and nepotism, without becoming bitter or resigned to the role of victim? How to be an activist without burning out in anger at injustices or becoming, finally, cynically indifferent, or just plain exhausted? In terms of a spiritual journey, how does one perform as servant, even a servant-leader, without being servile? Also, how to persuade others that men and women both lose when women are considered *per se* lesser?

In the best of all possible worlds, all of us would have had better earlier role models and lived in a world of equality throughout our lives. My father and I were never estranged, only distanced. With the belief that death does not end a relationship, I trust that Daddy and I both, as mature persons meeting each other as equals, now can love each other into reconciliation for all time.

Girls Reign

Our high school history teacher, Mr. H, unlike most of his contemporaries who served, relished telling of his World War II exploits. We suspected they were largely embellished. Later I heard that among vets there was a strict code: "You don't talk about it—anybody who did wasn't there." Mr. H barely got us as far as the Civil War in our studies. On the other hand, the Revolutionary War directly touched Muncy and surroundings, so we learned about it in grade school.

An exciting twelve-by-six-foot mural in the post office celebrates a local heroine of that period. "Rachel Silverthorne's Ride"

(1938) was painted by John W. Beauchamp as a New Deal project.

Rachel Silverthorne

British-allied Indians had raised fear in the region because England paid gold for each settler's scalp—men, women, and children too—that the Indians turned in. In early August of 1778, a band of about thirty Indians, operating under the cover of fog, attacked a group of settlers harvesting their grain on rich land along Loyalsock Creek. When Captain John Brady, the commander of militia stationed at Fort Brady in Muncy, received the news from a runner, he ordered his mare saddled. When he asked for a volunteer to warn others of the danger, Rachel Silverthorne was the one who responded. She rode out on horseback to reach local settlers in time for them to take refuge in Fort Brady before sunset. The next morning pillars of smoke rose from enemy campfires up Muncy Creek.[50]

I liked looking at the mural; it made an ordinary errand to the post office special. Rachel Silverthorne astride her galloping horse made a powerful impression upon me. Could I do something that brave? It's been suggested that she may have been particularly interested in saving the farming parties because the man she loved was among them. I've also learned that the appearance of a woman as the central heroic figure was rare in the New Deal murals in Pennsylvania post offices. I like to think of Rachel as a "fore-sister," an answer to the paucity of images in the 1950s that encouraged girls to aspire beyond conventional homemaking. I feel a connection with her because my portrait was hung on another public wall in Muncy, at Muncy High School, after I was inducted as the seventh alum elected to its Scholastic Hall of Fame at the graduation ceremonies in June 1993. Mother nominated me for this award, and I am embarrassed to say that it took me a while to understand what an honor it was. I wasn't sure I wanted to spend time and money at the busy end of the school year to fly from St. Petersburg to Muncy for this humble event. When I arrived, I was met by my proud parents and then the hospitable folks at the high school. They had appropriately rented a University of Iowa doctoral gown and hood for me. I'd always worn a borrowed gown with a hood from another school—a frugal, slightly self-denying gesture—in academic rituals at Eckerd, so this was special; the new home economics teacher had pressed it beautifully. That afternoon, the principal gave me a generous introduction, including Proverbs 31:10: *Who can find a virtuous woman? for her price is far above rubies*. Oh, my.

My brief speech allowed me to say thank you to the school and its teachers, to the people of the town, including my parents, of course, and even to the valley, all part of "the community it takes to raise a child." My final words conveyed that gratitude:

> I feel blessed by this community for giving me a solid foundation for living in an ever-expanding community of body, mind, and spirit. I'd like to think that the Muncy Indians had a saying like that of the Iroquois, that we must make all our decisions being mindful of the seven generations before and after us. I wish each of you 1993 graduates of Muncy High School the blessing of finding a joyous and productive place in a community that old and that large!

It was a great privilege to give that speech outside in that elegant green semi circular courtyard of my old school before those gathered for graduation. Though I hadn't been able to foresee it, it completed one of those great circles of return with which we are sometimes gifted.

So I claim Rachel Silverthorne as part of my community heritage. Her image belongs with many from my growing up time. In my imagination, that world is still a sanctuary, even as I try to understand how the maps of previous generations, especially that of World War II, underlie my own. How can I best build upon these foundations?

Girls and Horses

Thinking of the Rachel Silverthorne mural has led me to consider in a wider way the image of the girl on horseback. It is especially beguiling for young women. There's an allure that's hard to explain, although it includes a collaborative relationship with a large, beautiful, and powerful animal. Think of the whole genre of horse stories going back to Anna Sewell's 1877 novel *Black Beauty* and epitomized on film by the young Elizabeth Taylor starring in *National Velvet* (1944).

Dale Evans rode her trusty buckskin horse, Buttermilk, in the highly successful TV program *The Roy Rogers Show* (1951-57) which we *must* have seen on early TV. I know Daddy liked Roy Rogers's films and Dale was naturally in them with her husband. In her exhibit at the National Cowgirl Museum and Hall of Fame in Fort Worth, she defined "cowgirl" like a feisty pre-feminist: "'Cowgirl' is an attitude really. A pioneer spirit, a special American brand of courage. The cowgirl faces life head-on, lives by her own lights, and makes no excuses. Cowgirls take stands; they speak up. They defend things they hold dear." Whoo-hoo for cowgirls!

Marilyn and I loved the metal horse statuettes we got at one county fair. We often played games in which we pretended we were on horseback, making whinnying sounds and holding the reins to guide our imaginary steeds. We thought that to own and ride a horse would be the pinnacle of glory.

When the Star*Lite Drive-In Theatre became our next-door neighbor across that wide field toward Williamsport, we got to indulge our love of things western even more. Daddy drove us over to see Audie Murphy films. He'd been a soldier, a war hero. In the course of his World War II service he became the most decorated American soldier of all time. Afterward, he played in cowboy movies Daddy liked.

For a while, Daddy and Mother held annual open houses for our customers. They invariably featured a country-western music group. We usually had to stay upstairs during these mostly-adult events, as they went past our bedtimes, but we still could hear their cowboy-western music and maybe have some of the dough-nuts and sandwiches for breakfast, if any were left over.

We had crushes on cowboy actors, like Audie Murphy and John Wayne, and we were thrilled to receive cowgirl outfits with cap guns in white holsters for Christmas one year.

> *fall round-up*
> *Bang! Bang!*
> *caps pistols' smoky coils*

No matter how much we begged, we never got a horse of our own. In the era of tractors and self-propelled combines, they were no longer considered a functional part of farming, and Daddy didn't want to be bothered with the upkeep of one just for kids' play. Janet did have a pony for a short time, one he trad-ed for some machinery, I think, but by then, Marilyn, Bette, and I were either in high school or in college; we were well beyond the stage of begging for horses.

When we *were* in that stage, Daddy said that we couldn't even keep goldfish from Kresge's Five and Dime Store alive for more than a few weeks, so how would we take care of a horse? That wasn't a fair argument, but we didn't have a convincing rejoinder. So we had to be satisfied with some county fair rides on gentle nags going round and round in tethered circles. Later in life, when I rode a horse at a central Florida ranch where I was helping to chaperone a youth group, it was enough to quash any of my equestrienne dreams.

> *Triple A Ranch*
> *saddle sore*
> *it looked so easy*

Although Rachel Silverthorne's warning of Indian danger played into the stereotype of the bloodthirsty Indian of mid-twentieth-century western films, there was much to be learned about these First Peoples, as I discovered when I later taught "Introduction to Native American Literature."

Farmers working the fertile land on the floodplain of the Susquehanna River often found Indian artifacts. A farmer who Daddy did business with showed us some fine arrowheads that he'd found in one of his fields; another had uncovered an ax head in a field near the river. The local tribe was the Muncy, the source of our town name. English spellings of the name differ: there's a Muncie, Indiana, too, and that led to our high school band's being mistakenly announced as being from there when we proudly marched one year in the Cherry Blossom Parade in Washington, D.C. There's even a Monsey, New York, and there may be more.

> *muddy fields*
> *plowed for spring planting*
> *arrowheads sprout*

Our school athletic teams were called the "Muncy Indians." We weren't yet to the age of political correctness about indigenous people.

There are so many secrets in our buried multi-layered past. Girls, boys—we have our special dreams with images that match our times. Some disappear, some hang on, and some evolve. The image of Rachel Silverthorne, a woman involved in dangerous colonists-vs.-natives conflicts rife in America in the eighteenth and nineteenth centuries, leads me to the theme of an evolving sub-genre of books about women and warfare.

Women Write on War

I've found that there are now more and more war memoirs by women, especially by daughters, as they remember fathers who brought the war home. C. Tyler created a moving graphic memoir about her father, a World War II veteran, in three volumes, *You'll Never Know: A Graphic Memoir*. The work began when her dad, after sixty years of silence, decided to tell his story of service to his artist daughter.[51] In Book One, she sets forth a common theme. She depicts Hitler as the demon of war still affecting her father and actively shaping her family's life. Making his stiff-armed salute beneath a blood-stained sign in one of her drawings, the Führer gloats to her father: "That your children suffer because I've damaged you fills me with pride!"

Souvenirs: Healing After War, is a film written and directed by the daughter of a Vietnam War veteran, a long-embattled sufferer of Post-Traumatic Stress Disorder. It probes Mara Pelecis's question after her father's unexpected suicide in 2002: "How could my father survive the war, but not the peace?"[52] She offers these thoughts about the complexities involved: "I really wish people had a better sense of empathy for what our veterans are going through, and, on a larger level, a better understanding of the experience of anyone who's gone through a trauma. It's not something you just 'get over.' The effects can take years to show up. That kind of experience changes a whole life, whole families' lives."[53]

My guess is that daughters' memories or souvenirs are generally different in kind from those of most sons. I suspect that sons are more likely to remember the public faces and facts of war along with Big Drama while daughters feel the undercurrents of relationships. The three of us, Pelecis, Tyler, and I, have this in common. We don't ignore the guns, guts, and heroics, but what has especially moved us to tell our stories is the human struggle to deal with the aftermath of war's trauma. We are exploring how soldiers' families, friends, and societies write about waiting out a war and what happens when the combatants come home. Our stories may portray people who carry a burden of psychic wounds that may not ever be healed.

Obviously, whoever waits at home, regardless of gender, has a far different perspective on a war than those who serve and return. George Packer wrote a 2014 review essay in *The New Yorker*, "Home Fires: How soldiers write their wars." He finds that, for various reasons, the "new war literature [of Iraq and Afghanistan] is intensely interested in the return home."[54] Yet not one of the books Packer reviews is written by a woman, though he does say that he sees a change as women like Kayla Williams, the author of two Iraq memoirs, serve in combat.

In a 2015 book, *Ashley's War: The Untold Story of a Team of Women Soldiers on the Special Ops Battlefield*, Gayle Tzemach Lemmon tells of little-known women's service. She focuses on a woman who died while serving alongside Army Rangers Special Operations Forces in Afghanistan, as part of a Cultural Support Team. These women soldiers provided support for Afghan women and gathered information from them as well, an enormously useful, though highly dangerous, service. In yet another category of women and war, *We Served Too*, a 2013 film, tells of the late-recognized Women Air Force Service Pilots (WASPs) of World War II. Between 1942 and 1944, eleven hundred WASP pilots proved they could fly every type of aircraft in the US military arsenal at the time, including the heaviest bombers and fastest fighters. They freed men for combat duty by ferrying planes around the US, delivering overhauled ones, and towing targets for live ammunition practice. Thirty-eight women died in this service. The efforts to grant them military status, which would have provided fair salaries and repayment of expenses, failed in 1944 when arguments arose that they were taking men's jobs. They were forgotten, their records classified and sealed until the late '70s and early '80s, when they were granted veteran status with limited benefits and received World War II Victory Medals. In 2010, the fewer than three hundred WASPs still alive received the Congressional Gold Medal.

Women journalists broke still other barriers. Penny Colman's *Where the Action Was: Women War Correspondents in World War II* tells the story of 127 women who managed to obtain official accreditation from the US War Department as war correspondents. In spite of US military regulations that forbade women to cover combat, they found ways, often quite creative and brave, to get their stories where the action was.

It wasn't until 2015 that Elizabeth P. McIntosh's first-hand account of the Pearl Harbor attack was published. Filed as a report for the *Honolulu Star-Bulletin*, her story of the attack and aftermath was deemed too graphic to run in 1941. Such irony. Her waylaid intent had been to help women in Hawaii cope with the death and destruction they witnessed, and to prepare them for a future of war.

In 2016 our nation wrestled with the possibility of trusting a woman with the presidency—Hillary Clinton, the Democratic candidate, a woman extraordinarily well-prepared for the office. After a nasty race that included blatant misogyny, she was defeated. We might read WWII stories of competent, trustworthy women dealing previously with critical national issues to eliminate the argument that women aren't suited for the presidency. A recent example: *The New York Times* of August 22, 2016, ran the obituary "Doris Bohrer, World War II Spy for Allies, Dies at 93" by Williams Grimes. Working first at clerical work for

US intelligence in the Office of Strategic Services (OSS), where nearly all women hired were consigned as "the invisible apron strings" of the agency, Bohrer was sent to photo reconnaissance school. She helped plan the Allied invasion of Sicily and gathered intelligence about German military movements and locations of arms factories. Her work remained secret until 2011 when *The Washington Post* ran an article of her friendship with Elizabeth P. McIntosh, the author of *Sisterhood of Spies: The Women of the OSS*. As Grimes writes, "In their day, they had encountered condescension and naked hostility from male agents." In Ms. Bohrer's experience, "Everybody else was 'Lieutenant So-and-So,' or 'Captain This'; we were 'the girls.' I was doing the exact same thing as majors and lieutenant colonels, but I was [just one of] 'the girls.'"[55]

Clearly we have many strong, gutsy women in our past. They give us a foundation for progress. The truth, however, is that we still have plenty of work to do. In a January 2015 collaborative article, Sheryl Sandberg, chief operating officer of Facebook, and Adam Grant, professor at the Wharton School at the University of Pennsylvania wrote on "Speaking While Female." I can vouch for all they say based on my own experience. They cite a Yale psychologist's study of executives who voiced opinions more or less frequently: "Male executives who spoke more often than their peers were rewarded with 10 percent higher ratings of competence. When female executives spoke more than their peers, both men and women punished them with 14 percent lower ratings."[56] They conclude with this story: "When President Barack Obama held his last news conference of 2014, he called on eight reporters—all women. It made headlines worldwide. Had a politician given only men a chance to ask questions, it would not have been news; it would have been a regular day."

The "unending war," in its aspect of combating misogyny, continues, with some extraordinary breakthroughs. I was thrilled to read the story of pilot Elaine Harmon buried with full honors at Arlington National Cemetery on September 7, 2016.

The Washington Post carried the story online reported by Petula Dvorak:

> Harmon defied the chauvinists and misogynists when she flew P-51 Mustangs during World War II as one of the Women Airforce Service Pilots (WASPs).
>
> Then, she showed Congress that women should be treated as proper veterans when she testified for the recognition of the WASPs and finally got what she was seeking in 1977. And finally, after her death at 95 last year, she brought down one more barrier when an act of Congress made it legal for her and the approximately 100 surviving WASPs to be buried at Arlington with full military honors.[57]

Another extraordinary breakthrough: in May 2017, the first group of women graduated from US Army infantry training.

I wish that all of these advances for women would be in peacemaking rather than in war-making. But in the matter of equality, this seems right. I think of Rachel Silverthorne and smile.

VII

Seeking Healing, Unearthing Secrets

Disagreements

(A Letter)

Dear Daddy,

As I look ahead to the topics in "Seeking Healing, Unearthing Secrets," I'm feeling the weight of things that we disagreed about. You gave me the gift of reading (and listening) with books you sent home from Europe that Mother read to me, with books you and Mother bought later for all our family, and with the joys of reading everything from "Sunday funnies" to adventure novels. However, my own life of reading led me into political views that didn't agree with yours. When Howard and I visited, you often lectured us on our mistaken ideas. We felt your mistrust of our lives as academics. That was hard.

I hope that if we had the chance now, we could meet with loving attention, Daddy, and really listen to each other. I know the topic of Japan hit a sore spot that never healed. While you considered Japan as a vicious enemy, we found it a fascinating nation when we visited there.

We had the good fortune to travel to Japan with friends and colleagues, Gil and Sheila J, who had lived and studied there. Their companionship, as well as the hospitality of Tim T in Kobe, gave us wonderful insights into Japanese culture.

Still, hoping to find a bridge between you and the Japanese, Daddy, I explore the idea of nature as balm. I compare your joys in the natural world, in places like the spring in the woods at the

Huntersville farm, which you carefully tended, with the joy in nature expressed by the Japanese poet Matsuo Bashō.

> *Cuckoo's cry—*
> *moonlight seeps*
> *through the thicket of bamboo*[58]

Secrets keep popping up about the war. I think you'd be fascinated by the diversity in the ones I've found so far—from crickets to bombsights. Of course, I keep pondering the German man's revelation to you in Sudan. I also wonder about the meaning for you of all those hunts you took around the world. You had so many adventures in your life, Daddy. I'm glad you got to choose some of them for your pleasure!

Love,
Nancy

Reading and Misreading

My sisters and I loved sitting together on the couch with Daddy while he read the Sunday funnies to us from the Williamsport *Grit* and *The Philadelphia Inquirer*. He liked comic action heroes like Joe Palooka, Dick Tracy, and Steve Canyon. My favorite was Mandrake the Magician. I wanted to be his girlfriend Narda, especially when she won the Queen of the Universe contest. She was picked for beauty *and* for brains.

But there came a fateful Sunday when I was in second grade: Daddy told me I could read the comics well enough on my own. Once I got over feeling that I had been cast out from the warm circle of intimacy his reading created, I realized that I could find my own way into the worlds of words.

sapsucker
pecks "delicious"
in birch bark Braille

I quickly became the family bookworm, but I had to learn balance in reading and the rest of my life. Sometimes I had to be reminded not to neglect chores. An early lesson came when I thought I'd easily combine frying bacon for supper with doing just a little more homework in the study. I left the bacon to sizzle and returned to my book. It didn't take too long for burning smells to let me know that these two activities didn't mesh, at least not with the heat too high and me obliviously occupied in another room.

When I went to school, it became evident that I needed glasses for reading, as well as for seeing far—I was tested as near-sighted. I got glasses when I was in second grade. When we arrived home from the optometrist's with my first pair, I exclaimed in delight to Mother that now I could see the *tops* of trees.

> *first glasses:*
> *stars crowd nighttime sky*
> *yes, there really is a Big Dipper!*

If I'd been male and of age, I would have had trouble getting in the Army during the war before they overturned their rule of rejection for near-sightedness. Certainly I never would have qualified as a sharpshooter like Daddy. What if I lost my glasses? What if they'd gotten mud-smeared or broken?

In high school I was inspired by Thor Hyerdahl's *Kon-Tiki*. The marching band gave me a copy of his *Aku-Aku* when I was recuperating from my arm bone transplant. I admired Dr. Tom Dooley's adventures as a Navy doctor who helped evacuate thousands from North to South Vietnam in the mid-1950s. Through Dooley's work, I became aware that in some times and places, wearing glasses marked you for death—as a member of an educated and therefore politically devious elite. As it turned out, I was training to be a member of just such a group. Reading and teaching became my life work.

Mother and Daddy both prized education. In his school days Daddy loved spelling. His tales of triumph in country school spelling bees so beguiled me that I begged to learn hard words, and he'd come up with ones like *Czechoslovakia, Susquehanna,* and *Mississippi*. And there was *depot*, one that he told us he'd been miffed to miss in a spelling bee. When the teacher corrected him, he felt he'd been wronged and protested: "That's not *de-poe* (rhyming with *hoe*); that's *de-pot* (rhyming with *hot*)!" I wonder if Daddy thought of this when he was assigned to the 182nd Army Ordnance Depot Company.

When the mechanics in the shop misspelled things like "weal" for "wheel" or "baring" for "bearing," Daddy said he worried that he'd get mixed up and start misspelling them himself. Mother's spelling was excellent too, though her city schools didn't have spelling bees. I have a book, *King Arthur and His Knights* by Mary MacLeod that bears this inscription on the flyleaf: "To Nancy Corson for attaining *First* place in Spelling Contest given April 15, 1954, Grade 5." That day I was a proud "chip off the old block."

Both our parents were extremely practical people with an admirable diversity of capabilities. Daddy's skills—gathered from his farm boy youth, his degree in Agricultural Engineering, as well as what he called the "school of hard knocks"—ranged from chairing a local bank board to building a farm pond, from fixing a carburetor to calming an angry client. He created a machine designed to clean the unusually-shaped seed from crown vetch, a crop he raised and sold to the state of Pennsylvania. Mother's skills ranged from keeping the books for the family business to Red Cross lifesaving, from baking bread to sewing without a pattern, from hunting with Daddy, to playing a Chopin "Polonaise" on the piano or show tunes on the electric organ.

I've mentioned that both Mother and Daddy were good about bringing books into our home. We had encyclopedias and lots of magazines too, from *LIFE* to *Farm Journal*. When we went for our family night out on Fridays to Williamsport, we often visited Otto's Book Store where Daddy bought books I wanted even when they must have seemed odd to him, like J.M. Déchanet's *Christian Yoga* and Kahlil Gibran's *The Prophet*.

Until his younger sister Pauline got her degree, Daddy was the only college graduate in his family. He supported himself at Penn State with many odd jobs to supplement his steady job as a waiter in one of the women's dining halls. With his modest country schooling background, he had to work hard to catch up to his roommates who had more advanced urban high school educations. Despite his own academic pioneering, he was suspicious about academia. Once when I was studying for my Ph.D. in American Studies he asked, "Why don't you become a *real* doctor?"

Mother told me that Daddy suspected that as academics Howard and I lived an unsavory lifestyle. He'd made some disturbing allegations that sounded almost like the red scare propaganda of the McCarthy era. I was in counseling then to untangle some relational things and had to have many talks with my therapist to get the courage to confront him. My opportunity arrived the next time he and Mother came from Pennsylvania to visit us in Florida. It's a very vivid memory to me. I was hanging out wash on our space-saving umbrella clothesline. It stood in a green corner of the backyard by the Valencia orange tree and I always found the activity relaxing. But on this occasion I knew Daddy was reading alone in our spare room and that this was my chance to speak out. My hands were clammy, and I felt nauseous.

A little voice in my head said, "You know you promised your therapist that you'd do it. This is the moment; go and say what you need to say."

I went inside the house, and, standing just inside the door of the room where he was reading, I said, "Daddy, I'd like to talk with you. I think you have some wrong ideas about us. Howard and I are *not* communists, we do *not* practice wife-swapping, and we try to live solid, moral lives. I really have to insist that you don't keep harboring these suspicions about me and my family."

He listened in silence for a few long moments, and then he said, "Well, I'm glad you told me."

I guess it was OK after that.

But I have to say that I yearned for the time when we might talk more comfortably as equals, when Howard and I were not viewed as kids who needed to be set straight. The same kind of concern about our training and beliefs triggered lectures when we visited Corson Castle. They were generally given when everyone else had left the dinner table, and only Howard and I were left, a captive audience. Daddy seemed firmly convinced that we were naïfs about politics and topics like racism. Any defending responses on our parts only launched further instruction. Howard did try once or twice to ask for equal time, but that didn't work out very well. This uncomfortable ritual generally was the topic of discussion, in order to decompress from it, for a hefty portion of our long drive back home to Florida.

The topic of racism was a thorny one. We knew that he had had one memorably bad experience in the Army when a black soldier freaked out in the midst of fighting. The man ran across a field, thus betraying his unit's position. His comrades, Daddy included, were exposed to enemy fire. Even one incident of such life-endangering behavior in those circumstances could have bled over into general distrust; there may have been others. How could we judge?

I know that at least on one occasion General Eisenhower called black soldiers into the fight, though we still had a racially segregated Army until after the war, in 1948. I'm grateful that George Lucas made the film *Red Tails*, inspired by the Tuskegee Airmen and their significant combat service over Italy and Germany. It took sixty-five years for the story of their valor to reach American public media, and that is shameful.

In March 2014, twenty-four ethnic or other minority US soldiers, who performed bravely under fire in World War II, Korea, or Vietnam, but were prejudicially bypassed, finally received the Medal of Honor. Only three men, soldiers in South Vietnam, survived to attend the White House ceremony with President Obama. My optimistic thought is that if only we'd practiced more give-and-take about this and other topics of friction, Daddy, Howard, and I would have been able to hear each other out, not to see who was right, but to understand each other's experiences and how they had formed us.

I did vote for Barry Goldwater in my first presidential election, a good Republican vote from our Republican house. From there on, however, probably all my votes did indeed prove Daddy right when he said, "It's a shame that your votes cancel mine."

My writing also puzzled him. When I wrote about the New Testament's Martha, Mary, and Jesus stories, he said, incredulously, "You wrote a *whole book* about just those few verses?" That was all he ever said about it.

Daddy didn't write that much himself after the war, and I was always pleased to find something he'd hand-written to me. Mother took dictation for business letters, and he seldom wrote more than postcards. I treasure his note in a dictionary he and Mother gave to me: "Nancy—Make good use of this book. Sincerely, Dad."

It's my guess that slight hand tremors presaging his later Parkinson's were at least partially responsible for his not writing more. Besides, being a salesman was his métier. He was a maestro of the oral tradition. Nevertheless, I also remember him as a dedicated reader, sitting in his favorite rocking chair with books, articles, and *The Wall Street Journal.*

I'm grateful for both Mother and Daddy launching me on my life of books. As for the ways our readings led to divergent points of view, in later years that mattered much less. I would hope that, given time, we'd have come to amicably disagree on some issues.

Japan: Anger and Art

Anger: Coming to Terms

When, some fifty years after Pearl Harbor, Howard and I announced that we were going to travel to Japan with friends, Daddy said, "Why would you want to go *there*?"

Every August on the commemorative days for the bombing of Hiroshima, the sixth, and Nagasaki, the ninth, we ponder again the events that made them infamous. The effects, militarily and humanly, were strategically calculated. Secretary of War Henry Stimson's staff estimated that an invasion of Japan would have cost more than 1.7 million American lives and more than 5 million Japanese lives. Instead, 140,000 Japanese, mostly civilians, died at Hiroshima, and the number at Nagasaki was around 80,000—a comparatively large reduction in numbers, though still severe losses. Since then many others have died from leukemia and solid cancers attributed to radiation exposure. War brings us to calculations like these.

At home, on the other side of the world, Mother felt that the A-bombs in Hiroshima and Nagasaki kept Daddy from having to go to the Pacific directly after his two and a half years in the war in Europe. For her, it would have been like starting all over again with the excruciating anxiety of his absence. Instead, six days after the detonation over Nagasaki, on August 15, Japan surrendered to the Allied Powers, signing the Instrument of Surrender on September 2, 1945, to end the Pacific War, and therefore—since the war in Europe ended May 7—officially concluding World War II.

It was only in 2010, during the sixty-fifth commemoration of the bombing of Hiroshima, that the US and other major nuclear powers first attended the rites of this occasion. Altogether, seventy-four nations were represented. UN Secretary-General Ban Ki-moon presented flowers at the Eternal Flame in Hiroshima's Peace Memorial Park. He said that the time had come to move from "Ground Zero, to Global Zero"—a world without any nuclear arms. Katsuko Nishibe, a Japanese peace activist, spoke for those who still found the bombing unjustified. "We have a very different interpretation of history. But we can disagree about history and still agree that peace is what is important. That is the real lesson of Hiroshima."[59]

> *tea ceremony*
>
> *even chipped cups*
>
> *can serve peace*

Howard and I visited Kyoto as well as Hiroshima. We learned that this beautiful city had been first on the list to be bombed, ahead of Hiroshima. However, War Secretary Henry L. Stimson had admired Kyoto, where he and his wife had honeymooned, and he ordered that it be spared. This fateful decision exemplified such quirks of luck/fate/grace—call it what you will—that happen more often than we'd ever guess during war.

On our trip, I was inspired to write *Near the End of the Rainy Season: Poems from Japan*, a chapbook. I wish my parents had lived to see it published. We might have talked about it. These three stanzas from my poem "**Hiroshima: A Children's Commemoration**" convey my lasting sense of connection with those events:

> Decades later, I am in Hiroshima
> and my heart is sad.
> Rain, no longer black and blistering,
> falls in grey and stoic lines.
>
> In the Peace Museum, a mangled
> Japanese boy's tricycle
> reminds me of the one I loved at home
> (painted orange, it had a noisy silver bell).
>
> In the Peace Park, bouquets
> of origami cranes wreathe
> Sadako Sasaki's memorial
> (she died of leukemia
> when we both were twelve).[60]

From Daddy's negative response to our plans to travel in

Japan, I guessed that the old animosity never really disappeared. I felt sorry that was so. It made me feel a distance between us that I didn't know how to bridge. When I read Laura Hillenbrand's 2010 book, about the world-class US runner Louis Zamperini, *Unbroken: A World War II Story of Survival, Resilience, and Redemption,* it gave me glimpses of reasons Daddy still harbored resentment toward the Japanese. When Zamperini's Air Force plane crashed into the Pacific on May 27, 1943, he spent forty-seven days on a raft only to be captured by the Japanese Navy and held in captivity and severely tortured until the end of the war, some two years later. His terrible experience was unfortunately common among the Allied POWs in Japanese hands.

Zamperini eventually achieved redemption through extraordinary courage and strength of will. After the war, PTSD and alcoholism nearly defeated him; then a Billy Graham revival meeting brought him miraculous healing. Hillenbrand notes that many were not so fortunate: "As of January 1953, one-third of former Pacific POWs were categorized as 50- to 100-percent disabled, nearly eight years after the war's end."[61] Would I have ever wanted to go to Japan if Daddy had been one of those disabled veterans? Would our family have been able to work though anger and pain to peaceful compassion?

Yet the US also inflicted suffering on many Japanese-Americans. When my dad was in California undergoing desert training at Fort Ord in 1943, already between 110,000 and 120,000 people of Japanese ancestry who lived along the West Coast had been removed from their homes; the exclusion area included the entire state of California. They were sent, with scant belongings ordered to be packed quickly, to one of ten inland US internment camps where, without due process, they were imprisoned behind barbed wire.

The average enforced stay in the camps was two and a half years, time enough for most to lose their homes and valuables. One researcher reported that "Pilfering and vandalism often began before they were hardly out of their homes. A postwar survey revealed that 80 percent of goods privately stored were 'rifled, stolen or sold during absence.'"[62] These Japanese-Americans suffered not only intense weather in undesirable places with minimal comfort, but, worse, the grave humiliation of being miscast as enemies. As soon as the young men of the camps could, they seized the opportunity to join the US military. In her memoir *Farewell to Manzanar*, Jeanne Wakatsuki Houston tells of her brother Woody's eagerness to join. He was in the 442nd Combat Regiment that was "full of heroes, fighting in Europe to help the Allies win the war."[63] The 442nd became the most highly decorated regiment in Army history. President Harry Truman honored them saying, "You fought not only your enemy; you fought prejudice, and you won."

Not until 1952 did Congress pass a law to grant Japanese aliens the right to become naturalized US citizens, and not until 1988 did Congress pass the Civil Liberties Act, which called for the government to issue individual apologies for all violations of civil liberties and constitutional rights, awarding $20,000 tax-free payments to each internment survivor. I wonder how it feels to receive such belated apologies and awards. As for the surviving Nisei veterans of the 442nd, the 100th Infantry Battalion, and the Military Intelligence Service, on November 3, 2011, they received the Congressional Gold Medal, considered, along with the Presidential Medal of Freedom, to be the highest civilian award in the US.[64]

———— ◦ ————

In the mid-'90s I visited the Japanese American Historical Plaza in Portland, Oregon. My co-leaders and I had arranged to spend time here for our "Poetry, Dance, and Healing" group in the annual Society for Values in Higher Education meeting. We wandered meditatively among the twelve huge granite stones that rise from a low wall of basalt stones curving gently along the Willamette River.

At a midpoint break in the wall is a tall stone within a circle of granite pavers. On the face of this stone are the names of the ten internment camps: Gila, Granada, Heart Mountain, Jerome, Manzanar, Minidoka, Poston, Rohwer, Topaz, and Tule Lake. Each of the twelve granite monoliths in the wall bears a poem. I choose this one for its bright, forgiving spirit:

> With new hope
> We build new lives.
> Why complain when it rains?
> This is what it means to be free.[65]

Art: Haibun

I first began to explore the memories and feelings that became this memoir by adding haiku to my prose, in a kind of hybrid form called *haibun*. My parents would probably find it ironic that I owe so much to Japanese literature. When I re-discovered *haibun*, the evocative interlinking of short autobiographical prose narratives about a journey with *haiku* (short poems), it helped me start on this writing. I hadn't thought of using the form when I first met it in the late 1980s or early 1990s, but the formlessness of the first memoir notes seemed overwhelming to me until I thought of trying to use it. When I did, it seemed like I became a gardener who, overcome by large unruly patches of mixed-up plants, found order by using a small bed for each plant instead. Besides that, I welcomed the suggestions of healing relationships with nature at the heart of haiku itself.

I was first introduced to *haibun* by the work of the seventeenth-century Japanese poet and diarist, Matsuo Bashō. His classic work *The Narrow Road to the Deep North* drew on journal, travel, and landscape genres as he visited special places hallowed by tradition, seeking to understand the mysteries of life and death. I felt I'd found a kindred spirit. I also appreciated learning that there was a form that consists of calligraphing haiku on an art piece. It's called *haiga*, and I adapted it by combining a typed haiku on a photograph. My Hiroshima photo with text on the first page of this chapter is an example.

There's another irony in my use of Japanese forms. I think that some people in the US in the '40s and '50s would have rejected them outright simply because of their origin. Indeed, when I was young, we considered Japan an alien place where they made "junk"—a judgment founded on cheap and poorly constructed "Made in Japan" plastic toys and paper party favors that crowded counters at five-and-dime stores like the Kresge's in Muncy. But my story involves efforts toward reconciliation, and the forms, *because* they are Japanese, play a symbolic role.

> *tulip petals fall*
> *bold colors lose hard edges*
> *shadows shrink and fade*

I like David Rosen's words about haiku in the preface to his book *The Healing Spirit of Haiku*: "Creative haiku represent a healing union of intuition and sensation, past and present, self and other; ordinary and extraordinary, as well as current and ancient memories."[66]

Haiku lends itself to the peace-making theme that keeps evolving for me in this project. One soldier wrote:

When I returned from military duty in 1970 as a US Air Force historian in northern Thailand, I no longer believed in myself, my country, or my idea of God. I had come to understand how war, so closely entwined with power, corrupts countries, cultures, and people. And, I had become deeply ashamed of my participation in that war. Thankfully, finding the world of haiku, and the honesty inherent in the form, has helped my long road back to belief.[67]

Not to be forgotten: haiku often brings laughter, and that too has peace-making powers even in small things. For example, I felt more kindly toward our pesky spring visitor when I wrote:

> *Bluebird pecks windows,*
> *taunts mirrored foe:*
> *"Come out, fight,*
> *you handsome coward!"*

Except for a few fragile Japanese teacups, perhaps *imari* porcelain, and a large vase that Mother kept behind a chair in the living room, my sisters and I knew little of beauty or wisdom from the East as we grew up. I guess that vase was a wedding gift that didn't fit with our décor, yet it intrigued me; sometimes I'd stop to trace its low relief patterns with their bright colors. There were special occasions when Mother arranged tea parties for us girls with those beautifully painted and gilded cups and saucers. When I got older, I liked to clamber up on the kitchen counter and reach into the dark and dusty recesses of the top shelf to bring out these treasures. In retrospect, I compare my bringing them out into the light with the Japanese ceremony of launching paper lanterns (*tōrō nagashi*) toward the sea to commemorate those lost in the bombing of Hiroshima.

> *tea sparkles in the cup*
> *the river glitters with lanterns*

May this haiku of renewal bless us all:

> *Two herons soar high*
> *white wings flush pink with dawn*
> *winter fades to spring*[68]

Nature as Balm

I've mentioned Bashō's *The Narrow Road to the Deep North* (*Oku no Hosomichi*) as a treasured model. Perhaps our Pennsylvania and mid-Atlantic seaboard was not so layered with centuries of cultural, religious, and political landmarks as his Japanese terrain, but we too made pilgrimages to such places as family homesteads and sometimes a cemetery or historic site. For example, Daddy and Mother took us to see Plymouth Rock. The Rock itself was in a covered pavilion, sunk down below the visitors' level and fenced-in, not too interesting. What I liked best was the wonderful scent of pine pillows and leather goods that permeated a gift store on a hill behind the Rock. Marilyn and I got little leather coin purses that we used for our school lunch money. We also visited Revolutionary War sites such as Valley Forge in Pennsylvania and Fort Ticonderoga in New York—the latter notable to me as the site where I was greatly embarrassed by mistaking a cigar store Indian for the real thing.

lichens etch stone buddhas and cherubs—
I forget whether I am East or West

At home, our family's gardening, farming, and hunting brought us close to the mysteries of the natural world that Bashō wrote about. He tells of wonderful trees he visited in his journey, like the willow tree "near the village of Ashino on the bank of a rice-field," a tree described as "Spreading its shade over a crystal stream" by the poet Saigyō. Bashō also celebrates a huge chestnut tree with a priest living in seclusion under its shade on the outskirts of Shirakawa; he is so moved by the feeling of being in "the midst of the deep mountains where the Poet Saigyō had picked nuts" that he wrote on a piece of paper: "The chestnut is a holy tree, for the Chinese ideograph for chestnut is Tree placed directly below West, the direction of the holy land."[69]

I know that Daddy also had deep admiration for trees; he loved a particular stately oak in the woods at the farm in Huntersville with a spring at its base. He was certain that the spring was on a path the Native Americans had used a century or so before, so it had, to my mind, a special aura. Whenever we rode out into those woods in the back of the pickup—always a treat—we stopped there while he cleared the spring for us all to drink the cool clear water. It seems now, in retrospect, a holy place, and Daddy's care of it not unlike the care that a priest might give to a sacred well. I wonder if the water still flows, if the people who now own the forest know about it and take care to keep it running clear?

a gold leaf falls
bright rings ripple

Thinking back to our pleasure in that woodland spring, I acknowledge that one of the greatest gifts of working with haiku is the quiet healing of its focus on nature. In his book *Seeds from a Birch Tree*, Clark Strand writes, "haiku is the one poetic form in all world literature that concerns itself primarily with nature, the one form of poetry that makes nature a spiritual path."[70]

Daddy also spoke of the great chestnut trees in his childhood landscape and how he missed them since the great chestnut blight of the first half of the twentieth century made them nearly extinct. David Vandermast describes how these nuts came to be so cherished:

The loss of the chestnut was most acutely felt by rural Americans whose stories were oral rather than written.

The nuts were an important cash crop for them, and they found many uses for its timber and bark. The chestnut's former importance in the southern Appalachian Mountains, where it grew to its greatest size, lives on in place names such as Chestnut Ridge and Yellow Mountain (referring to the splash of color when the chestnuts were in bloom).[71]

As a craftsman, Daddy admired the chestnuts' fine strong grain and was proud to find an antique table at an auction of this lovely, now rare wood. He gave it to Howard and me and we enjoy its beauty as it still serves as our dining room table.

> *chestnut table*
> *sun, wind, rain, soil*
> *in grained blessings*

White birch and blue spruce were also trees Daddy loved; he planted both in our spacious front yard at the new Corson Castle; they grew into magnificent mature specimens—you can see one of each in the background of this photo. Daddy planted fruit trees around the garden and behind the big back lawn where he is taking a water break on the last of his Allis-Chalmers tractors, a small "G" he used for mowing and other gardening jobs.

Daddy taught me the names of crops that he and local farmers grew; there were familiar ones like corn, soybeans, wheat, rye, alfalfa, sorghum, and potatoes—and occasionally the rarer ones like buckwheat, sunflowers, and red clover, which makes me think of Bashō's frequent mention of bush clover. Daddy and Grandpap Corson always walked the fields during our Sunday visits to the grandparents' farm, and they watched the weather closely. A long while back I had fun writing a paper about weather sayings for a folklore class:

> *mares' tails   mackerel cloud   sun dogs...*
> *I turn off the weather channel*

One summer day when I was in my early teens, I led the neighborhood children on a maze walk as I did my chore of mowing our lawn with the gas-powered push mower. Instead of making the usual outside-to-inside spiraling path, I made random lines. Daddy was not amused by the inefficiency of my game. Years later I mentioned the incident, and neither he nor Mother remembered it. I was amazed that our family memories differed. I'm reminded that even though I try to be fair and truthful in my storytelling, I must acknowledge that memories of certain incidents can vary widely or disappear altogether.

> *Pied Piper lawn mowing game*
> *I got rats*
> *for wasting gas*

Another time, Daddy called us out to the yard to look at a huge light green luna moth on the picket fence around our play yard. We'd never seen anything like it before. It was like something out of the Lycoming County Fair freak show. I wanted to capture it for my bug collection, but it squirted out a stream of clear liquid that effectively repulsed me. Instead, I dreamed about it—that it was kite-size, got caught in the rain, and began to shrink, a sad mess.

> *luna moth*
> *spellbinds*
> *an August day*

Besides the beauty in the natural world of Pennsylvania there were some dangers too. We were taught to be careful to watch for snakes, particularly in dark or high grass places. Once Daddy almost bought a little country house as part of a hunting retreat, but when he went up in the attic and found snakeskins, the deal was off. We'd all heard the scary story about a local boy who died after being bitten by copperheads—during fall harvest he'd had the misfortune to reach into a nest of them hidden in the center of a corn shock. Another danger, though not mortal, was poison ivy. Daddy was quite susceptible to it, and I was too. During one nasty case, I went to school with bandages, wearing a long-sleeved white blouse to cover my oozy arms. But this was nothing compared to the suffering of a friend who had blisters all over her body, even in her eyes and mouth!

When I reflect on the fact that Daddy had been a farm child and then made agriculture a strong foundation of his life, it must have grieved him to see how the well-tended French, Dutch, Belgian, and German fields, forests, and vineyards were devastated in the war. The violence that ignored such love as Daddy had for tending trees, vines, and crops suggests the fragility of the human enterprise. Yet the resilience of recovery efforts showed a counter-balancing strength. He told us that even as he was marching east toward Berlin with the US troops near the end of the war, he admired how the Germans were already tending their window boxes in the rubble-strewn cities.

> *war-ravaged earth*
> *blood red*
> *geraniums*

So, I've found that the Japanese poets, especially Bashō, can bring us back to the land we cherish. The reminders of beauty even in the midst of great ugliness give us courage to heal the land and ourselves.

When Howard and I visited the USS Arizona Memorial in Pearl Harbor, I found it especially moving that the US flag flies from a flagpole attached to the severed mainmast of the sunken battleship. I wrote this poem:

Pearl Harbor: Four Birthday Scenes

I

At the USS Arizona Memorial,
a father points over the rail
to show his son a bubble of oil
risen from the engine room below.
Like an iridescent dragon released
from guarding rusted ruins
beneath this bone-white shrine,
it slithers seaward.

II

Because we share last names, I notice
Paxton Carter among the listed dead.
His marriage photo in the museum is
rouged and touched up like my parents' own.
In another photo with those
40s Kodak deckle edges,
he could be my Uncle Jimmy posing
with my cousins in his Navy blues.

III

Around my neck a birthday lei—
orchid, carnation, and plumeria—
wafts perfumed hints of carpe diem.
My life's already twice as long
as most of theirs who fell below.
Earlier, at the museum café in Honolulu
I watched clouds flowing overhead…
Ars longa, vita brevis…

IV

Every US Navy, Coast Guard, and
Merchant Marine entering port
"mans the rails" as they glide past.
I imagine sharing my birthday
with each brave soul lost here:
I offer a giant cake aglow
with candles, wish for peace,
and blow them out.

In the week of December 7, 2016, the US marked the seventy-fifth anniversary of the surprise attack on Pearl Harbor. After decades of lobbying by family members and POW advocates, as well as great progress in forensic science, more and more of the 2,403 Americans who died that day without formal burial are being brought home. Their remains, once buried as unknowns in the National Memorial Cemetery of the Pacific, are being disinterred and sorted with the help of DNA testing. In 2016 alone, twenty sailors from the USS Oklahoma have been identified and reburied with full military honors—some at Arlington National Cemetery and others at their hometowns.[72]

Crickets, Codes, and Crosshairs

I loved the "Henry" cartoon character ring I'd found in a breakfast cereal box. But I lost it in our garden at The Building one summer. I looked and looked, but I never could find it. As I recall this cereal box gewgaw, the prizes in Cracker Jack boxes, and other trinkets that we collected as youngsters, I remember little metal noise-makers called crickets. Originally designed as a timekeeping device for band and orchestra leaders in the 1920s, they were a common giveaway at county fair exhibits in the '50s; we kids liked the chirping sound they made when we squeezed to click them.

But they had a special use on D-Day when the 101st airborne landed in Normandy during Operation Overlord. A member of the division must have seen their potential as a signaling device. Since they sound like something in nature, like an insect or bird, they were used to locate buddies and to group up after a parachute drop without alerting Germans. The rules were these: "First man cricks once. If the second man cricks back twice, he's an American. If he doesn't crick, somebody's in trouble, you or him."

Bill Priest, a paratrooper who had played dead to stay alive when he first came down, reported that, "The system worked until the Germans caught on, captured some crickets and used them to kill or capture scores of American airborne troops."[73]

Still, they served their purpose well in many instances and became iconic symbols to the men of the US airborne and to the memory of D-Day. (Crickets are featured in Darryl F. Zanuck's famous 1962 D-Day film, *The Longest Day*.)

> *post-war crickets*
> *de-commissioned:*
> *we're all buddies here*

When we played word games like pig Latin—cousin Ann Louise and her girlfriends loved trying to confuse us with this—or made up secret words, we unwittingly participated in games that became deadly serious in wartime. The most critical, complex word game, especially in the European theater, was played by the Enigma machine. This was an advanced electro-mechanical rotor machine used for the sending of secret messages that was invented in Germany at the end of World War I.[74] By mid-1940, thanks to Polish mathematician-cryptographers who'd deciphered pre-war type Enigma messages in the 1930s and the work of British code breakers, some of the German army Enigma messages could be read within twenty-four hours.

Several movies have focused on the critical work of deciphering codes, with the Enigma machine often playing a starring role. In 2014 the historical thriller *The Imitation Game*, about British mathematician, logician, cryptanalyst, and pioneering computer scientist Alan Turing, appeared. Turing led the British group that succeeded in breaking the Enigma code with ULTRA, the Allied intelligence project that tapped the very highest level of encrypted communications of the German armed forces, as well as those of the Italian and Japanese armed forces.

The deciphering of Enigma's "word game" contributed to Allied victory; it probably saved thousands of mariners' and soldiers' lives, perhaps including Daddy's. The exact influence of ULTRA is debated, but it's often said that decryption of German ciphers hastened the end of the European war by two years. I saw an Enigma machine at the Imperial War Museum in London, and I thought this hugely important piece of World War II seemed inappropriately small—like an old-fashioned typewriter.

When Howard and I traveled to the canyon lands of Utah one summer, we crossed into Arizona and visited the Navajo Code Talkers exhibit in the Burger King in Kayenta (part of the Navajo Nation). This extraordinary display contains artifacts belonging mostly to a man named King Mike, one of the 400 young Navajo servicemen who were trained and then deployed to the Pacific from 1942 until the end of the war. They used their native tongue as the basis for a complex code used to transmit information on tactics and troop movements so skillfully that the Japanese never deciphered a single message they sent. Code Talkers participated in some of the fiercest battles of the war, including at Bougainville in Papua New Guinea, Kwajalein Island, Saipan, Guam, and Iwo Jima; they were instrumental in winning several battles.[75]

King Mike was at Okinawa where more than seventy-five hundred servicemen died. He refused to talk about the matter even after the Code Talkers' role in the war effort was declassified in 1968, after he'd maintained twenty-three years of silence. He and his colleagues had been sworn to secrecy because the language was considered potentially valuable as a code even after the war. At last, his son Richard gained permission to display some of King Mike's service artifacts in the restaurant as a tribute. An Act of Congress in 2001 awarded Congressional Medals of Honor to those Code Talkers still alive. It was too late for King Mike. He had died on Christmas Day 1996.

We read the stories and studied the exhibits in the Burger King, and we were moved by the courage and sacrifice of these men. Many of them were handicapped in job searching after the war due to their oath of secrecy; their discharge documents gave no indication of any special skill or service. Because the armed forces didn't think to provide them with a simple cover story, they couldn't even get jobs with the Bureau of Indian Affairs.

Apparently the 2002 film *Windtalkers* didn't give them justice either. It's been panned for showing the white guys as the true heroes. It's hard to imagine such ahistorical disrespect.

> *Code Talkers' ideal menu:*
> *hero sandwiches*
> *& a fair shake*

Howard's father was part of a US code-breaking team attached to the Army Signal Corps in Washington, D.C., that worked around the clock. Like the Navajo Code Talkers, he couldn't speak of his war contributions for many years; indeed, his team's work wasn't declared declassified until after his death. Howard remembers quizzing his dad about his job and his dad's response that he couldn't tell anything because the information might still need to be kept secret for national security.

Another war secret later revealed involved a woman who contributed her below-knee-length hair to the government when it called for women to contribute hair twenty-two inches and longer to the war effort; hers was thirty-four inches long. Mary Babick Brown only learned forty-eight years later, at age eighty-three, when she was given a special achievement award in 1990 at the US Air Force Academy, that her hair had been used to form the crosshairs in the top secret Norden bombsight. Bill Feder, founder of the International B-24 Memorial Museum in Pueblo, Colorado, said that the Norden bombsight was so secret that it was equipped with explosives, and crews were ordered to destroy it if their bomber ran the risk of falling into enemy hands. Black widow spider webs, originally used for the cross hairs, contracted and expanded on scale in high altitude conditions that the bombers experienced, but they were fragile and hard to come by. Brown's fine blonde hair, never bleached or ironed, was unusual and shared many of the qualities valued in the spider's web. Tom Ferebee, the bombardier aboard the Enola Gay, used a Norden bombsight to drop the atomic bomb on Hiroshima; we'll never know whether or not the crosshairs were Ms. Brown's.[76]

grey fox

blurs secrets

across the lawn

Other war secrets, embedded in particular languages, were *shibboleths*, words that could be correctly pronounced only by native speakers. These words were used to ferret out foreign enemies; a famous one was the French word for "frog," *grenouille.*

There's another huge secret, one that must be particularly chilling to learn about for anyone involved with the D-Day invasion. It involved rehearsals by the US Army at Slapton Sands, a shallow lagoon backed by bluffs on England's south coast. The site was chosen because it closely resembled Utah Beach on the Normandy coast.

On April 27, 1944, an American convoy gathered there for Operation Tiger, an exercise intended to be as realistic as possible. It went horribly awry. Nine German torpedo boats attacked; many of the US troops were trapped below decks. Others drowned because they hadn't been instructed on the right way to wear their inflatable life belts. The numbers of the dead, missing, or wounded exceeded those suffered by American troops during the actual assault on Utah Beach a few weeks later.

Ten US officers with detailed knowledge of the upcoming Normandy invasion were among the missing. Until all their bodies were recovered (and finally they all were), scrapping Operation Overlord was a real possibility, since the fear was that they had been taken prisoner and would be forced to talk.

The survivors were threatened with court-martial if they ever discussed what had occurred. There is little documentation in official histories about this tragedy. In his book *The Forgotten Dead: Why 946 American Servicemen Died Off the Coast of Devon in 1944— And the Man Who Discovered Their True Story,* published in 1988, Ken Small declares that the event "was never covered up; it was 'conveniently forgotten.'"[77]

Many secrets were kept for decades under official secrets acts and such. They are both startling and fascinating. They make us wonder how many more are hidden and how many are yet to surface.

———— ◦ ————

The story behind Daddy's being the only person not crossed off the German man's hit list is one secret that I'd wager will never be revealed to us—unless the woman who invited him to a boar hunt at a chateau or that man with a list are miraculously still alive, read this book, and come forward.

> *copperheads*
> *in the wood pile*
> *better wear gloves*

Here's one more story that Daddy told us. General George Patton had asked him to be his driver when he was training for war in the desert in California, before being posted. But Daddy had observed Patton's temperament and decided that job wasn't right for him. Ironically, Daddy's company, according to the *History of the 182D* [sic] *Ordnance Depot Company*, was assigned on April 15, 1944, to Lt. General George S. Patton Jr.'s Third United States Army in England. After crossing to Normandy, they were part of the Third Army move across France, late July through August, until relieved to join the First US Army on September 11, 1944.

Hunting and Being Hunted

NRA dad with peacenik kid
"the lion and the lamb"?

Guns were a big part of my dad's life; I seldom entered except as an onlooker. I always knew he was an excellent shot, with skill first honed when he was a kid by shooting small game like rabbits, pheasant, and squirrels. Many of them ended up on his family's dinner table. I loved his bringing us ringed neck pheasant from a hunt—we plucked and prepared them as he taught us to and I collected their long, exotic tail feathers. Mother roasted them with sherry, a delicacy. Sometimes we ate squirrel, duck, or goose he'd bagged.

Once, when he and Mother returned from a hunt out West, they visited us in Iowa City, where Howard and I were in grad school. They gave us enough elk baloney to make lunch sandwiches for at least a month. (It was delicious with mustard and parsley on whole wheat bread.)

In the Army, Daddy easily won his sharpshooter rank. He told us that he'd won it for the guys on both sides of him on the firing range by acing their targets as well. In later years the deer hunt, early in December in Pennsylvania when the season opened, was a big event. We have photos of Daddy, Uncle Harold, Uncle Roscoe, and sometimes Mother and Aunt Jessie, in full hunting regalia, standing together in the snow at the farm with their trophies. One time Uncle Gordon, a non-hunter, and I helped as drivers, hallooing, gunless, through the woods.

white owl's shadow
glides through snowy trees

Reading through his hunting records accompanied by Mother's meticulous notes, I've learned that Daddy spent roughly the first two decades of his retirement (c.1968–88)) hunting big game, averaging a hunt a year. He traveled to such places as Canada, Iran, Africa, Spain, Australia and New Guinea, Colombia, South America, and the American Southwest and brought back a roomful of taxidermied creatures that Howard and I secretly called "the hall of snouts."

Though hunting wasn't our sport, we understood that it was a highly-valued recreation for Daddy. We guessed that hunting may have been a redemption of sorts for him. He had been a soldier who'd been under orders to kill other humans branded as "enemy." Later, he forged a persona as a skilled hunter of big game in rugged landscapes where he chose to travel and to test himself; he studied hard to understand animals and places he'd never before encountered. Daddy's trophies *were* impressive—they ranged from Cape buffalo to mountain goats. A photo that appeared on the front page of our local town paper, *The Luminary*, shows him with an African elephant. Although we are now worried that poachers and over-population are threatening the entire population of Africa's elephants, he was conscientious then about getting the right licenses and shooting only those trophy animals allowed. That was another era.

I've wondered if it was an advantage or disadvantage in dealing with war's carnage to be a farm boy who was skilled at hunting and butchering. I'm guessing it made it harder. If you knew how to honorably treat animals as food, the wasting slaughter of humans along with their animals must have seemed horrible in contrast. I'm sure this was deeply disturbing, something preferably never mentioned.

In a lighter vein, I smile to think that there were touches of the old Teddy Roosevelt swagger to the whole enterprise of Daddy's game hunting, a release from normal life into a realm of heroism, into places with possibilities of extraordinary adventure. Like-wise, I wonder if hunting may have provided a legitimate way to recapture some of the high drama in strange and exciting plac-es that lingered as part of the war experience. I think of a song popular in both World War I and World War II, "How Ya Gonna Keep 'em Down on the Farm (After They've Seen Paree?)."

These hunting trips abroad were solo events, at least initially. Janet was still at home going to school during most of this time, so she and Mother kept each other company. I think Mother understood that he needed to take these trips, though I know she wasn't thrilled about those long absences of her husband hunting in faraway dangerous places.

However, a dramatic event during one hunt changed this. Daddy had been hunting in Angola, and he was on his way home. Mother went to the small airport in nearby Montours-ville early, in anticipation, I'm sure, on the day when his plane was to arrive. Daddy was not on it; nor was he on any other plane that landed that day. Mother called Marilyn and sobbed out to her what had happened. She begged her to see if there was something she could do. Mother seldom cried, so you can guess Marilyn's alarm. As soon as she put down the phone, Mar-ilyn contacted a friend who had some savvy in foreign travel. He contacted the American Red Cross. They took on the task with alacrity, and, assuming that he would have sent some word if plans were changed, they were able to trace the mail from where Mother figured he'd last been. They found that it had been im-pounded for some reason in a postal station in Angola. They even found the letter Daddy had sent to Mother telling her that he'd be a week longer on the hunt, going for some trophies that had so far eluded him. In any case, Mother had to endure some terribly stressful hours before she received this news.

After that, Mother determined to accompany him on more of the trips, even to Iran and New Guinea. She mainly went as photographer and companion, though she carried a gun and bagged some game of her own. I'd wager that that one occasion when Daddy was incommunicado in Angola was quite enough to convince her that she'd rather be with him, even navigating crocodile-filled rivers in narrow wooden canoes—a later African experience—than worrying alone at home. She'd had enough anxious waiting for her husband during the war to last a lifetime.

Never one to do things in a small way, Daddy had trophy kills that set records. For example, Daddy's photo appears three times with prized animals in the January 1978 Post Season Report of Safari Outfitters, Inc., of Chicago; one of them shows him with his gold-medal tur, a wild goat with huge horns, from the Russian Caucasus. Some of his trophies are displayed at his alma mater, Penn State, including a mountain lion, the school's totem animal.

Daddy and Mother gave all four of us sisters gifts from his hunts. Our family had a zebra rug in our Florida room for a good long while, until we wore off much of the hair in daily use; Daddy said we should have hung it on the wall (as Bette did). Marilyn has an elephant footstool. The only trophies I have now are a set of seven-point white-tailed deer antlers from Pennsylvania and a hyena rug from Botswana. Mother was along when that hyena met its Waterloo (one of Mother's colorful expressions) in 1970. She wrote about it in her June 16 journal entry from their camp in Okavango Swamp:

> Harvey shot a large spotted hyena, considered vermin here—and we were amazed at the size of this vicious animal—nearly 120 lbs. with large clawed feet. Hyena are greatly feared by animals of the jungle—except the lion,

and have been known to attack men. While Jack—our professional hunter's head spotter and tracker, and Guinea Farol (Kanga) are skinning the hyena and impala, early morning game bag for today, the vultures constantly circle over head, ever watchful, patiently waiting.

I've since seen a *National Geographic* report citing the intelligence of the hyena, but its nasty reputation is apparently well-earned.

hyena rug in my study
wildness gone soft

In *The Greatest Generation*, Tom Brokaw speaks of farm boys like Daddy who "were inventive and good with their hands. They were accustomed to finding solutions to mechanical and design problems on their own. There was no one else to ask when the tractor broke down or the threshing machine fouled...."[78] Furthermore, Andy Rooney credited American can-do and fearlessness in questioning authority as keys to winning the war. He claimed that the men and officers "often improvised, they came up with their own plan, they reacted to what was happening in the field instead of just blindly following orders like the Germans. That's one of the reasons the Germans lost."[79]

An entry from one of Daddy's little spiral-bound record books, from a 1975 hunt in Sudan, exemplifies the kind of resourcefulness Rooney recognized: "Had a flat tire 61 km. from camp. With no lug wrench or any tools. Phillip [hunt leader? a man described a few pages later as "the world's poorest driver"] and a local native started to walk back. It would have taken them all afternoon and night. The skinner and I remained behind with no lunch or food. I found a tube that was OK under the seat. I found a pair of pliers and end wrench. With these crude tools we changed the tube and made it back to camp." Daddy's skills in problem solving could save lives.

VIII
What Endures

Gratitude

(A Letter)

Dear Daddy,

Here in the material world, I interweave time and eternity as best as I can. I'm increasingly aware of many circles that link us with World War II.

As you'd guess, the yearly commemorations of D-Day and other critical dates of the war bring forth stories mixing the grim and the glorious. In 2009, our local newspaper's June 6 front page included an article titled "A Sailor's Grisly D-Day Visions." An inside photo showed President Barack Obama walking with concentration camp survivor Elie Wiesel through the Buchenwald camp near Weimar, Germany. Six years later, in 2015, a former Auschwitz guard was on trial in Lueneburg, Germany, for 300,000 counts of accessory to murder.

It is a never-quite-ending war. Yet many positive acts shine out to warm our hearts. Sometimes it's just one child determined to see that her Grandpa received his medals. I read about a North Carolina man whose granddaughter's persistence led to his receiving long-overdue medals for remarkable World War II service in the Army Air Corps.[80]

Sometimes it's the whole nation expressing gratitude. The World War II Memorial in Washington, D.C., opened in 2004. It honors you, Daddy, among the 16 million men and women who served in the armed forces, the more than 400,000 who died, and all who supported the war effort at home—Mother and me included! In many states there are Honor Flight chapters which are racing against time to get every willing and able service person to visit the memorial in Washington, D.C. As a Pennsylvania man, you'd have been invited by Honor Flight Philadelphia for their Tour of Honor in May 2015. John Matthis, a submariner who went on one of the flights, said of the memorial: "The beauty of the place and the realization that what we had done had changed the world was almost incomprehensible."[81]

When I was in Europe in the summer of 1965, I heard the testimonials of grateful people who owed their lives to the Allies. I overhear them now in the US. Another vet on a Flight of Honor told of being approached near the memorial in D.C. by an elderly couple from the Netherlands. When they found out that he was a veteran, they said they owed him and others (like you) eternal gratitude for saving their country during the war. An American pilgrim to Normandy was stopped by a German woman who said, "Go home and thank your grandfathers for saving Germany, as well as the rest of Europe."[82]

I wish so much that you had been able to hear these expressions of gratitude directly. They are part of national and world history. And still they continue. In mid-December 2014, Americans and Belgians gathered in the Ardennes region of Belgium to mark the seventieth anniversary of what historians label as one of the biggest and bloodiest US battles of the war, the Battle of the Bulge. It was snowing, as it was seventy years ago—I know you'd remember. A few of the soldiers were there, with their children, grandchildren, greats, and great-greats—their gratitude endures as does the gratitude of a wider world. I saw that during Veterans Day in London in 2009.

As I think more about what endures, Daddy, I consider material things like the wooden shoes you brought back from the Netherlands, your keys, and the Leica camera you and I both used. These material things are rich symbols of spiritual realities that do not fade. I had a dream of finding you, after fearing you were lost, and it assures me of our reconciliation through even the most difficult of our differences.

Veterans who speak out against wars provide hope that we humans might stop the destruction we continue to wreak upon our world. Finally, I elaborate upon the rose as a symbol of the brave way you and Mother intentionally lived toward love and order in a time of threatening chaos. There is a saying that "the gift must move." So your gift inspires me and urges me to share.

Love,
Nancy

Good Housekeeping

Memorial Day
decorations of flowers
empty shoes

For some reason, I thought of a phrase from a poem I'd memorized a long while ago, "homely flowers in brown sod." It's in the final stanzas of Florence Bone's "A Prayer for a Little Home":

God send us a little ground—
Tall trees standing round,
Homely flowers in brown sod,
Overhead, the stars, O God!
God bless, when winds blow,
Our home and all we know.

Though the lines sound pretty sentimental now, I like the old-fashioned meaning of "homely," as simple and unpretentious, expressing the warmth of familiarity. My quest to understand my life with my family has sometimes focused on homely physical objects like Daddy's Heart Shield Bible, Mother's heart locket, or the swing set at The Building. Now I'm thinking of some other special touchstones of memory like a pair of Dutch shoes, Daddy's keys, and the Leica M3 camera. These are all souvenirs of special persons, places, and events in this storytelling.

I associate "homely" with "housekeeping." As children, we all helped with chores like dishwashing, emptying the garbage, feeding the dog, vacuuming, gardening, and lawn mowing. I remember dusting the keys of the piano, the globe in Daddy's office, and the grooved curves of the dining room table legs hidden by a draping cotton lace cloth. I liked standing on a chair to dust some war souvenirs on a high interior window ledge— little painted wooden shoe replicas, rough and splintery inside, a handsomely decorated ceramic beer stein with hinged pewter lid, and a glass with a popular German folk song stenciled on it, "The Schnitzelbank Song," a humorous paean to "my pretty little woodworking bench." There was also the lidded candy dish on the buffet that no one could close after candy snitching without a giveaway *clank*.

Later in life, I've found poetic and philosophical allies who show me other perspectives on housekeeping. They help me deal with the tediousness that sometimes invades these tasks.

The French philosopher Gaston Bachelard, once again helpful in my writing, suggests that we may make even the simple task of polishing a piece of furniture a revelation:

And so when a poet rubs a piece of furniture—even vicariously—when [s]he puts a little fragrant wax on [her] table with the woolen cloth that lends warmth to everything it touches,... [s]he registers this object officially as a member of the human household.[83]

Bachelard reassures me that a poet's consciousness, if we can develop such sensitivity to the inwardness of things, can transform our mundane realities. Otherwise boring tasks may lead to new vision:

> Objects that are cherished in this way really are born of an intimate light…they produce a new reality of being, and they take their place not only in an order but in a community of order. From one object in a room to another, housewifely care weaves the ties that unite a very ancient past to the new epoch.[84]

This special interweaving of past and present is something I understood anew when a friend laughingly told me this story: when quizzed about "what makes your heart sing" at a women's retreat, she surprised us, even herself, by replying "house cleaning." She was engaged in preparing a family home for sale; window cleaning especially pleased her as she meticulously polished until the glass shone clear to reveal the beauty inside and out. Her work was an homage to a cherished place where she and her husband had reared their children.

Upon reflection, the homely details of our life together in The Building and Corson Castle keep morphing in different directions—into psychological, poetic, and now, into spiritual realms. Touching familiar objects once in the hands of Daddy, of Mother, and of others I've loved, I am mysteriously connected with them.

Henry David Thoreau, a trusted housekeeping friend, shares his ordinary practice of keeping house in "Sounds," the fourth chapter of *Walden*. He tells us of the simple joy of cleaning his house early in the morning by taking all his furniture outside on the grass, flushing the floor with water, sprinkling white sand from the pond on it, and using a broom to scrub it clean. When the sun has dried it, he moves back in, pleased that his "meditations were almost uninterrupted." He notes:

> It was pleasant to see my whole household effects out on the grass, making a little pile like a gypsy's pack, and my three-legged table, from which I did not remove the books and pen and ink, standing amid the pines and hickories.[85]

For him, all our furniture, including our tools for writing and creativity, may be enhanced as we place it "out of doors on the grass" amidst all the sounds and sensations of nature. I think of this deepening of our connections with the Earth as a holy housekeeping I try to practice. I wish I could talk with Daddy about this. Though he'd probably choose different words, I'm sure he'd feel a kinship with Thoreau; both of them worked in the garden and in the fields and found deep roots of solace and contentment there.

Wendell Berry, always a mentor, adds an insight about materialism that goes to the heart of holy housekeeping. In *Home Economics* he lauds the Shakers as "the true materialists." He sees their careful workmanship as an honoring of materials in contrast to our contemporary desecrations of the material world.[86]

The careful stewarding Daddy modeled of things material helps me understand what Berry affirms: the spiritual and the practical must be connected. If they are not, the sloppy or indifferent workmanship that marks an unenlightened "materialism" is both an insult and a danger. I imagine that as a former ordnance man and as a careful keeper of cars, guns, ammunition, and all manner of machinery, not to mention buildings and land, Daddy would heartily agree with this view.

The *materiel* of war, however, is quite a different matter. War turns reverence for the material upside down. What was once cherished for householding and for public beauty is now profaned by destruction. Bombs wipe out flora and fauna; they destroy the lower layers of soil, which can take thousands of years to regenerate. Unexploded mines keep fear alive and land unused; the effects of radiation devastate lives. Toxins contaminate water supplies.

As a house/home keeper striving to be mindful, I've kept and cared for a pair of wooden shoes that Daddy brought back from the Netherlands. I wore them in a grade school Halloween parade as an authentic part of a Dutch girl's costume Mother made; she sewed a starched white Dutch cap to go with a long skirt and apron. But the shoes gave me blisters, so we retired them as souvenirs only.

Contemporary Crocs are quite similar in shape, but in contrast to their machine-molded plastic resin, you can see and feel the woodworker's tool marks in the wooden shoes. These testify to the work of skilled crafters who made ordinary things with integrity. They also remind me of Daddy and others who fought to protect the Netherlands and all those persecuted there by the Nazis, like the families of Anne Frank, Etty Hillesum, and so many others. For those reasons, it is a pleasure to me to dust them and to keep them on the table in our entrance hall, often accompanied with flowers in a vase beside them.

When the Florida Holocaust Museum opened in St. Petersburg, I went with my students; we had just read Anne Frank's *The Diary of a Young Girl*. I saw a ring displayed there that had been found in a box car used in death camp transport.

Souvenirs

Item 1: a silver engraved ring,
possibly a young girl's,
found embedded in
splintering floorboards…

> Item 2: a pair of wooden shoes
> mailed from Holland by my Dad
> sometime after his landing with
> the Allies on D-Day plus five…

This small circlet's enshrined now
in a glassed jeweler's box
beside an Auschwitz box car
in a holocaust museum.

> They rest at the bottom of
> my Irish great-grandmother's
> time-darkened cedar chest
> full of family relics.

The ring's sweet twining flowers
evoke lost innocence—
rosebuds scythed then burned
to smoke and ashes.

> I wear the shoes with a snowsuit
> in Mother's photo of her toddler;
> safe at home in the US,
> we're still shadowed by the war.

> Perhaps my Dad marched
> to liberate the same streets
> where the ring's owner walked,
> but, for her, not soon enough?

> After blistering my heels in a
> grade school parade, the shoes
> were stored away, outgrown except
> for writing and remembrance.

As I explore the theme of housekeeping and the ripening of relationship to treasured, ordinary things, the souvenirs of our lives, I stop a moment to honor those who do not have this privilege. The devastation of war often rips away layer upon layer of security and comfort, of treasures that hold revered memories and traditions. If we are refugees or exiles, ones whose homes have been occupied or destroyed, then we are bereft of these consolations. We wait in hope for allies of bodymindspirit to help us create our household and its furnishings anew although that may not, unfortunately, be possible. We can aim, monk-like, to be "always at home everywhere," but some losses are beyond recouping—consider the "soul loss" of the Laotian Hmong people described in Anne Fadiman's *The Spirit Catches You and You Fall Down* or the losses of others whose communities have been utterly smashed and poisoned.

The German poet Rainer Maria Rilke expands the homely celebration of place and things to include relationship with the sacred cosmos. Here is a consolation for what has been cherished but cannot last: his poem asserts that it always exists in the spiritual realm, in our own souls.

> Through the empty branches the sky remains.
> It is what you have.
> Be earth now, and evensong.
> Be the ground lying under that sky.

Be modest now, like a thing
ripened until it is real,
so that he who began it all
can feel you when he reaches for you.[87]

Keys

Beside me on my desk are two bunches of Daddy's keys. I am amazed to see the variety of them—everything from big skeleton keys to winding keys—mostly from The Building. They feel greasy with years of use; some are a bit rusty. They have "mana" for me, the kind of supernatural energy that Pacific Islanders found in persons or sacred objects of power, authority, and honor. I sense my own fingerprints on some of them, along with those of my family and maybe a few trusted others. For many years these keys to The Building, our sanctuary, our home and business place, marked ownership and security. They seem too alive to be non-functioning, yet I'd wager that almost every single door, car, or tractor, every cabinet, shed, or safe they once opened no longer exists. Holding them, I ask, "Am I awake or dreaming?" If I imagined myself at a particular door, could I find the right key, turn it in the lock, push the door open, and walk in?

Keys are richly metaphoric, of course; there are keys to understanding, keys to secrets, keys to our hearts, keys to puzzles and problems, keys to whatever is lost, keys to Alice-in-Wonderland doors. A lost key in a household or a communal place is a threat to security from many perspectives, depending on the perceived value of what it was intended to hold safe.

In a program for our local C.G. Jung Society entitled "Searching for Home," the psychoanalyst Dee Follin asserted that the outer home is often a symbol of the Self, with its archetypal intent toward wholeness; it yearns to be connected to a center that anchors us in our inner home.[88] She cited the importance of the key to the temple of the Roman vestal virgins. Their sacred charge was to maintain a fire that was considered to be a hearth for the whole city. It had to be kept continuously burning, or Rome would be considered endangered. If they lost the key, the fire would be at risk from outside enemies or internal neglect, and the virgins would be severely punished. Follin suggested that the key is symbolic of maintaining possession of our own inner home; it is crucial to remaining faithful to the Self, which Jung saw as the highest and best manifestation of our potential. So, she asserted, we must be holy housekeepers, diligent guards of our inner hearth/hearts.

Once, my sisters and I lost a key to an outside door at The Building. We were playing with it, and one of us hid it in a jar on an old set of shelves laden with many, many containers—too many to distinguish. There were lots of Mason jars for canning to add to the confusion. We searched several very long hours, under duress since Daddy was upset when he learned what had happened and demanded that we keep on until we found the key. At last to our immense relief, it turned up in one of the jars. We escaped with a stern warning not to play with any more house keys. Our citadel, our hearth, was once more deemed inviolable.

My photo of the keys shows venetian blind shadows—we had horizontal blinds on all the apartment windows of The Building. I remember how the light slanted through their wide wooden slats during the day when they were open, the way the striped shadows moved over the furniture and floors defining or obscuring shapes, and how, when the wind was strong enough, they clattered against the window frames or rippled against each other. That rippling sound meant summer to me—in that pre-air-conditioning era the windows were opened wide but the blinds were set to keep out sun.

When I went off to college soon after we moved across the fields to the new Corson Castle, I was given a key to the house. For many years, no matter where I was, I was comforted to see it on the key ring in my purse. It symbolized the abiding accessibility of that secure place where my parents kept the hearth alight.

A friend, retiring as an Episcopal vicar, recently participated in a church ritual that involved handing over his keys to the newly appointed vicar. In the Christian tradition, the Keys of Heaven were given by Jesus to Peter, marking his ability to take binding actions, in heaven as on earth. The Keys continue to be the symbol of papal authority; the Keys and the Pope's triple crown are the images on the Vatican City's coat of arms.

When we retired from college teaching, Howard and I had to turn in our office keys, less ceremoniously, to the registrar instead of a vicar, but nevertheless with momentous impact. Turning in our keys meant that we no longer had tasks to perform there, that we forfeited the use of space in our offices and classrooms and the utilities we had once freely used. Without our keys we became outsiders, stripped of our former status. As to relinquishing keys to others, many of us keep a hidden extra key to have a sense of not being totally exiled from the places once open to us, even though we would not think of trespassing to surreptitiously use our rogue key again. Once given a ceremonial key to the city, who wants to give it up?

I know that if Daddy picked up these keys I am looking at, he'd know what every one of them was for. They were so much a part of him that when I sent this photo to Marilyn, her husband David, who'd seen Daddy only about once a year, immediately identified the keys as his.

I wonder what keys were entrusted to Daddy during the war? Surely he had keys for whatever vehicles he drove or maintained. The more keys, the more status?

Then there is the relativity of what can be safely secured. Soldiers, police, and intruders can bypass keys by kicking in doors and shooting off locks. That's another level of violence we don't immediately think about when we lock up our domestic possessions, but it's part of the vulnerability of a citizenry menaced by war and lawlessness.

Everyone in our family would have different memories of these keys, where they led, what they accessed, or what they kept protected. They could evoke many moods and meanings; they carried that much energy. In a continuing process of discernment, keys signify knowing what to close and what to open, especially in the realm of spirit. Here is a "key" passage I love, from the "O Antiphons" of the Christian Advent season, just before Christmas:

> O Key of David,
> Scepter over the house of Israel,
> you open and no one can close,
> you close and no one can open:
> Come to set free the prisoners
> who live in darkness and the shadow of death.

War brings us enormously difficult tasks of transformation—*if* that is ever truly possible. In her 2003 book, *Dangerous Peacemaking,* Helena Meyer-Knapp, writes of grave difficulties in setting World War II prisoners of war free:

> It took decades for significant joint progress towards harmony in Germany's relations with the countries against which she fought, and also with the terrorized groups—Jews, Communists, the mentally disabled and homosexuals—so many of whom were exterminated. The Japanese government, in relation to South Koreans and to the Chinese in particular, is still not entirely over the bridge to peace. Too many apologies remain unsaid. Too little history has been accounted for fully.[89]

I would simply mention the role of truth and reconciliation commissions in finding and revealing past wrongdoing with the hope of resolving conflict left over from the past. The most famous of these is the Truth and Reconciliation Commission formed in South Africa in 1995. There are others, and all are founded upon willingness to work through pain toward hope and forgiveness, a boon for our world.

The finding of a key, says J. E. Cirlot, "signifies the stage prior to the actual discovery of the treasure, found only after great difficulties."[90] I'd like to think of Daddy's keys as being a sign of a phoenix transformation. I'm still thinking of that image for The Building fire. We can choose to consider that its destruction signals our intent to move on, renewed and re-placed, with Light-filled spirits wherever our journeys take us.

Pilgrim Photographer

I took this photo of a German pillbox above Utah Beach on the Normandy Coast of France long after Daddy landed there in 1944. By then, the terrible guns had long been disabled and the beaches cleared and reclaimed for swimmers, boaters, fisherfolk, and tourists like myself. In the fields above the cliffs, cows grazed placidly and orchards bloomed.

My photography was enhanced by the use of a special camera, Daddy's Leica M3, a premier 35mm rangefinder. In the

1950s, when he bought it, it was the standard for photojournalism. It introduced the new technology of a bayonet lens mount instead of a screw thread type that enabled photographers to change lenses quickly. Its viewfinder's magnification was much higher than that of other cameras, which allowed for clearer vision. Besides all these excellent qualities, it was famed for being quiet, solid, and precise with smoothly operating mechanics.

Daddy used the camera for about a decade for family photos and to document his big game hunting around the world. I felt extraordinarily privileged and trusted when Daddy lent me the Leica to take on a nine-week European study tour. This tour, focused on art, faith, and contemporary philosophy, was the gift he and Mother gave me when I graduated from Susquehanna University in 1965. I was so careful of the camera that I slept with it under my pillow.

Everywhere we went on that tour, I encountered people and places that US soldiers had helped to protect and defend in the war. I saw cemeteries full of white crosses and Stars of David stretching row on row in acres of neatly mown grass. I climbed the twisty narrow stairs to see Anne Frank's secret hiding place. In Berlin we went behind the Wall to visit with a church group gathered there in spite of all odds; they knew there was a communist informer in their midst, but they testified that that person's presence somehow enlivened their faith. The texts we studied were as diverse as *Letters and Papers from Prison* by Dietrich Bonhoeffer, the Lutheran pastor who was executed for his part in a stymied plot to kill Hitler, and Pierre Teilhard de Chardin's *The Phenomenon of Man,* pointing toward the mystical triumph of love. I saw original art in famous museums that I'd only seen before in my art history text. When I tried to imagine Daddy being on this land in the utterly different circumstances of wartime, it was very hard to do.

We traveled mostly by train, with Eurail passes, and the train tracks passed by small family gardens behind nearly every housing place in the cities—all that love and care for gardening, with no wasted space; it was a heartening sight I felt that Daddy would have appreciated.

It's hard to say all that I learned on that journey through Europe, but it has served as valuable background for the rest of my life. I do know that being able to take beautiful slides with such a fine instrument initiated my lifelong love of photography. I've used photographs, especially slides, in much of my teaching and lecturing. I'm our family snapshot-taker, like Daddy was, and, like Mother, I help keep the family archives.

sharpshooter
Leica M3
trophy images

When Daddy switched to a single lens reflex camera after Howard and I married, he sold us the Leica at a generous discount. It went with us to Europe in our dissertation years, 1969–70. During that time, we went to a Leicaschule at the Leica factory in Wetzlar, West Germany, spending several wintry days learning about the latest Leica equipment and practicing with it in the streets of Wetzlar. As an avid photographer and an engineer, Daddy appreciated the excellence of the German Leica camera. It's only now that I reflect on the contrast between the Germans as enemies in war and as partners in fine quality manufacturing in peacetime.

After fruitful years of photography with the Leica M3, we now use only digital cameras. As Howard and I grow older and contemplate moving into smaller quarters, we've begun to clear away our stuff. I found the Leica and saw that after being stored unused for several decades, it was in sad shape. The leather Leica case with "Harvey F. Corson" emblazoned on its lid in gold letters was mildewed and all the leather straps were stiff. The camera itself seemed in good shape, but we'd learned years ago that at least one of the lenses had some mold; we deemed it too expensive for us to replace. The other lenses probably were not in tip-top condition either. But I determined to get it all cleaned up as well as I could.

With saddle soap, Q-tips, lens paper, and a lot of elbow grease, I managed to transform the bag. The equipment appeared better too. All the time I was doing this cleaning, I had a strong feeling that I was paying homage to Daddy. I thought of his love of fine instruments and of all the places he had taken this equipment around the world to hunt big game. I know that he packed it with the same care and skills he gave to managing guns and ammunition, choosing clothes for different climates, establishing relationships with hunt organizers and native people, and paying attention to languages, currencies, and local customs. Somehow my careful cleaning seemed like an ordnance exercise I was completing under his guidance.

I'd checked with our local camera store and found that there was still a market for Leica M3s as collectibles, so we sold it. I hope the camera's new owner keeps it with pride and care.

———— ～ ————

As for World War II documentation, I think of great photographers like Robert Capa who landed in the first wave on Omaha Beach on D-Day and gave us a world famous photo sequence of its drama. Amazing photos that remain forever enshrined in US history range from Joe Rosenthal's flag raising at Iwo Jima to Alfred Eisenstaedt's famous photo of a sailor kissing a girl in Times Square on V-J Day, August 14, 1945.

Surely one of the most extraordinary photographic documentations of WWII, though, is the collection Howard and I saw at the Boston Museum of Fine Arts in July 2017, "Memory Unearthed: The Lodz Ghetto Photographs of Henryk Ross." This Polish Jewish photographer was confined to the ghetto in 1940 and assigned by the Nazi regime to take Jewish ID photos and propaganda shots to show the efficiency of the ghetto's laborers. But he also risked torture and death for himself and his family by taking illegal photographs documenting the horrific realities of the Lodz Ghetto. When he feared discovery, he hid his negatives and prints in the ground in the ghetto in 1944. He returned for them, as one of the few survivors, after the ghetto's liberation in 1945. Later, he said "I was anticipating the total destruction of Polish Jewry. I wanted to leave a historical record of our martyrdom."[91]

Compact cameras like those pioneered by Leitz (subsequently re-named Leica), were considered critical to the German propaganda effort. Joseph Goebbels as Minister of Propaganda, even ordered photojournalists to use such small easily wielded modern cameras. I could find no evidence of the type of camera Henryk Ross used, but it could have been a Leica. Its ultra-quiet shutter sound would have been an additional boon for his secret photographing.

Another story of brave resistance in the world of photography has recently emerged during the Leica company's centennial. Leitz lens and camera manufacturing, founded in 1914, maintained progressive labor policies. These encouraged the retention of skilled workers, many of whom were Jewish. Ernst Leitz II, who took over the company in 1920, helped hundreds of Jews to leave Germany after Hitler's 1933 election. Wetzlar's vast system of tunnels, originally dug to support iron ore mining, were used for a Leica Freedom Train. This effort intensified after Kristallnacht in 1938, until borders were closed in September 1939. After that, the company operated mainly from its cover position, supplying German government production orders.

What remains for me is the pleasure of having used a fine camera (I'm using our Leica M3 in the photo above), thus sharing Daddy's life, and the joy of learning much about the skills of good picture-taking with it. I also learned to develop and print film, exploring other aspects of photographic art. My Ph.D. thesis, *The Inner Circle: Portraits in Alfred Stieglitz's Camera Work,* is a study of photographs as cultural artifacts.

Photography continues to be a valuable tool for me in documenting and in finding meaning. No matter what camera is in my hands, when I hold it up to my eyes, I am engaging with some part of a fascinating world, trying to capture something of its essence.

As Wendell Berry says in "How to Be a Poet,"

There are no unsacred places;
There are only sacred places
And desecrated places.[92]

I have realized more and more that I am on pilgrimage, honoring all of Earth as sacred. Photography invites me into a guild of those whose art gives witness.

Veterans Day in London

*What is the use of living, if it be not to strive for noble causes
and to make this muddled world a better place for those
who will live in it after we are gone?*
– Winston Churchill

Without planning this—although I do believe in synchronicity—Howard and I traveled to visit with our friend and colleague, George M, in London for a week, arriving on Veterans Day, November 11, 2009. That year marked the seventieth anniversary of the start of World War II in Europe as well as the 64th sixty-fourth anniversary of its conclusion.

Veterans are honored on November 11 not only in Britain and in the US but also in many of the Allied nations. The armistice marking the cessation of hostilities on the Western Front at the end of World War II was signed on the eleventh hour of the eleventh day of the eleventh month. Whether it's called Veterans Day, Armistice Day, Remembrance Day, or Poppy Day, it's a day set aside to memorialize the sacrifices made by those in the armed forces and their families.

All over London we saw red paper poppies, usually in wreaths, at commemorative sites. I photographed three bright red wreaths laid around a tablet in the floor of the Temple Church built by the Knights Templar. The tablet read, "Remember in your prayers those who died in the Second World War,

1939–1945." On the grounds of Westminster Abbey, a huge "Field of Remembrance" had been set up so families and friends could place crosses in areas designated for particular services and particular years when veterans served. Late autumn winds scattered sycamore leaves over thousands of little poppy-twined white crosses. One rain-streaked cross read, "I didn't get to know you."

There's a tradition of white poppies too, though it's controversial for taking the spotlight away from the usual war-memorializing. The Peace Pledge Union of the UK website explains: "The idea for a white poppy arose from the concerns of the wives, mothers, sisters and lovers of the men who had died and been injured in World War One. Increasingly aware of the likelihood of another war, they chose this symbol 'as a pledge to Peace that war must not happen again.'"

At the Imperial War Museum, I found many broad clues to Daddy's experience, though not, as I've mentioned, any individual records. Besides an Enigma machine, there is a life-size model of the casing for the atom bomb "Little Boy" dropped on Hiroshima and V-1 and V-2 rockets. The V-2, the one Daddy said he especially hated, was huge—two stories high. With some slightly different details than I'd found earlier, the information here said that the Germans purportedly named them V or "vengeance" weapons to retaliate for tremendous losses to the *Luftwaffe* during the "Battle of Britain," the German air campaign against the UK in the summer and fall of 1940. I felt as though I was dutifully reviewing the machinery of disaster—even though I consider that war to be a just war, I could not imagine the horrible deaths, with all their pain and absurdity that resonated in some way around each piece.

Along one corridor in the museum are photos with famous quotations. George, a former US naval officer, pointed out his favorite: after the defeat of Napoleon at Waterloo in 1815, a battle which easily could have gone the other way, the Duke of Wellington said, "Nothing except a battle lost can be half as melancholy as a battle won." The melancholy of war was graphically represented by a large wall clock that continues counting war dead. The caption beside it read "200 million died as a result of conflict in the 20th century; if that rate were to continue in the 21st century, two people would die every minute." It was numbing to stand and watch the numbers keep passing (as they undoubtedly are at this very minute).

In the gift shop, I bought a copy of a pamphlet entitled *Instructions for American Servicemen in Britain 1942,* reproduced from the original seven-page typescript issued by the US War Department. This was part of the effort to prepare US troops for encountering the different cultures of Europe. The foreword explains that "Many [American servicemen] had never been abroad before, and this pamphlet's avowed aim was to prepare these young American GIs for life in a very different country and to try and prevent any friction between them and the local populace."[93] Topics include "No time to Fight Old Wars," "British Reserved, not Unfriendly," "Don't be a Show Off" [particularly about American wages being higher than British—that was a sore point emphasized in the British joke about Americans as "over-sexed, over-paid, and over here"] and "The British are Tough." Language and currency differences are discussed, and a list of "Some Important Do's and Don'ts" include: "If you are invited to eat with a family don't eat too much. Otherwise you may eat up their weekly rations." and "NEVER criticize the King or Queen." The pamphlet advice concludes with a slogan recommended for all dealings with the British (in bold): **"It is always impolite to criticize your hosts; it is militarily stupid to criticize your allies."**

A similar pamphlet was distributed to Allied servicemen about France—its list of "Some Important Do's and Don'ts" include "Remember the intense sufferings of the French since 1940. Make allowances for this" and "Be patient if you find a Frenchman hard to understand—he is having difficulty too."

About languages, I can only guess what it was like for Daddy, an immensely resourceful person who nevertheless had never traveled abroad and had only studied a little Latin in school. But he was skilled at pantomime and wouldn't let a language barrier stop him. He once told us, with great good humor, of an incident that took place in a Roman pharmacy years later. By making flatulent sounds and pointing to the affected area of his anatomy, he quickly ordered and received an anti-diarrheal medicine in a pharmacy.

I wondered if Daddy was ever able to travel to London on leave from where he was stationed in the Midlands. I'd guess not, given the strictures of travel from camp as well as the very present dangers of bombing there, but I wish he'd heard the chiming of the magnificent clock tower, Big Ben, at Westminster Abbey. When the nearby House of Commons chamber was destroyed by bombing, the clock, known for its reliability, kept on tolling. The broadcast sounds of Big Ben assumed great significance during the war, when its chimes became a symbol of hope to BBC listeners around the world. I liked hearing them and thinking of that when we were there.

For a while after we came home, we heard the chimes sound hourly, recorded on the computer in Howard's office and adjusted to US Eastern time. Another reminder of our visit is a small replica of the now-famous KEEP CALM AND CARRY ON poster designed by the British Government Ministry of Information during the war to keep up morale. This was the third and final poster in a series, marked by the symbolic crown of King George VI. The plan was to issue this one only if Germany invaded Britain. Most of these happily unused posters were destroyed at war's end, but a bookseller found one in a pile of old books and began to make and sell copies. Somehow it's touched a chord in our time with its appealing reassurance. I keep a copy on my desk, hung over a photo of the Earth as seen from space.

Vets as Peacemakers, East and West

Although very different in culture, Harry Patch and Kaname Harada were both soldiers who became known to us in the early twenty-first century as peacemakers. Patch served in World War I, and Karada in World War II. I rejoice that they are part of a growing number of men and women who served in the armed forces and are now speaking out for peace.

In 2009, Britain honored their last World War I infantryman, Harry Patch, who died at age 111. As I read the newspaper story about him, I felt I'd encountered a bright spirit. Patch hadn't spoken about the war until he turned 100; like Daddy and most of his soldier contemporaries, he had tried to suppress war memories and to live as normally as possible. The culture of his time also said that he was fortunate to survive and that he should get on with his life. But with encouragement, Patch eventually overcame his reticence in order to share his experience. He became a spokesman for his generation, acting as a peacemaker who fostered reconciliation. His wish that former comrades from Belgium, France, and even Germany, would serve as his coffin bearers was honored. A close friend, Jim Ross, said that Patch "used his great age and fame as the last survivor of the trenches to communicate two simple messages: Remember with gratitude and respect those who served on all sides, [and] settle disputes by discussion, not war."[94]

The representative peacemaker I've found from the East, is Kaname Harada, who died at age 99 in May 2016. In an article in *The New York Times*, "Retired Japanese Fighter Pilot Sees an Old Danger on the Horizon," Martin Fackler wrote, "Once a feared samurai of the sky, shooting down 19 Allied aircraft as a pilot of Japan's legendary Zero fighter plane during WWII, he used his dwindling energies to warn his nation against ever again going to war."[95] Kaname Harada feared that Japan's renunciation of war and its accomplishment of a long postwar period of peace would be discontinued by current politicians, ones who have had no experience of war. For example, Shinzo Abe, Japan's conservative prime minister, called for revising Japan's pacifist constitution. Kaname Harada told of seeing the terrified faces of the men whose planes he shot down in close combat. Though contemporary pilots may not have such close-up views of their victims, he warned that they cannot escape the horror of murdering humans who have children and families like their own.

After the war, he had nightmares, feeling he'd become someone he never intended to be—a killer of men. He founded a kindergarten in Nagano in 1965. Only then, by dedicating himself to teaching young people to value peace, did the nightmares disappear. After even more years he could finally talk about the war itself. He resolved to break his silence and speak out after he'd been shocked to overhear young Japanese describe the combat of the 1991 Persian Gulf War as though it were a harmless video game.

This former fighter ace was sought after as a speaker, and he made as many speeches as he could manage. He said, "Until I die, I will tell about what I saw.... Never forgetting is the best way to protect our children and our children's children from the horrors of war."[96] He visited the school he founded every day he was able until his death so he could see the children's smiling faces.

If Kaname Harada had lived just a few weeks longer, until May 27, 2016, he would have seen his Japanese President Shinzo Abe and American President Barack Obama placing wreaths for the victims of the atomic bombing at Hiroshima Peace Memorial Park together. He surely would have resonated with their words about that event seventy-one years earlier. President Abe said, "This tragedy must not be allowed to occur again…. We are determined to realize a world free of nuclear weapons." President Obama remembered the children:

> The world was forever changed here, but today the children of this city will go through their day in peace. What a precious thing that is. It is worth protecting, and then extending to every child. That is a future we can choose, a future in which Hiroshima and Nagasaki are known not as the dawn of atomic warfare but as the start of our own moral awakening.[97]

A moving front-page photo in *The News & Observer* (Raleigh, North Carolina) that day by Carolyn Kaster shows President Obama hugging Shigeaki Mori, an atomic bomb survivor and a creator of the memorial for American WWII POWs also killed in the bombing of Hiroshima—a long-hidden story of at least a dozen men held there.

Six months after President Obama visited Hiroshima, Prime Minister Abe told him that he wanted to visit Pearl Harbor. So, seventy-five years after Imperial Japanese warplanes destroyed the Pacific fleet there and drew the US into World War II, the two leaders stood together on December 27, 2016, at the site of the attack. As Obama had done at Hiroshima, Abe offered repentance but not apologies. Mr. Abe said, "We must never repeat the horrors of war again." President Obama, after a detailed description of the events of the day of the attack, highlighting acts of heroism by American service members, added: "The sacrifice made here, the angst of war, reminds us to seek the divine spark that is common to all humanity."[98]

All who yearn for peace realize that words must be followed by positive actions. That is the challenge, and I honor all who take it up—nations as well as individuals like Harry Patch and Kaname Harada. I like to think of these two men as part of a global network of wounded healers, ones who awaken us to compassion for all life, life without war.

Time and the Labyrinth

This poignant photo of Daddy speaks to me of his being alone for a meditative moment in a magnificent but remote place. The image suggests time's passage through our generations.

I think of one of the last times Daddy and Mother visited us at our home in St. Petersburg, Florida. We went for a walk one early autumn day in a local nature park. Daddy said that it reminded him that we all are part of the seasonal cycles, that someday we all return to the earth. I felt he was sharing a prophetic good-bye with wisdom that I should remember.

I believe that the photo was taken while Daddy was hunting in the northern Rockies, in the region of the ancestral lands of the Oglala Sioux. A passage from the life story of one of their elders, a holy man named Black Elk is often quoted. This profound vision of the unity of all creation is written down in *Black Elk Speaks*:

> You have noticed that everything an Indian does is in a circle, and that is because the Power of the World always works in circles, and everything tries to be round…. Even the seasons form a great circle in their changing, and always come back again to where they were. The life of a [hu]man is a circle from childhood to childhood, and so it is in everything where power moves.[99]

Because the war profoundly changed Daddy's life, I've been researching and pondering dimensions of that truth. I too have been changed, and now that I am an elder, I also wonder what wisdom I have to impart. What is the great circle I have noticed of my own seasons?

While there have been other wars since World War II, neither our daughter Rebecca nor any of our nieces and nephews have experienced the anxiety-filled interim of waiting for a parent to return from war. I believe that I am the only one of Grammy and Grandpap Corson's eleven grandchildren for whom this is true.

When I watched some of the fiftieth anniversary of D-Day specials on TV with Daddy in 1994, the tight hold of Parkinson's was quite evident. He said, "Having Parkinson's is the hardest thing I've ever had to endure." No wonder that someone so active and able hated this disease; it stripped away more than balance and ease in speaking—it took away his enthusiastic vigor and liveliness. In spite of that, Daddy still had his sense of humor. Even the hospice care workers remarked on that. Such utter unfairness! He did everything he could to take good care of himself and to stay in shape. He believed "Better wear out than rust out," but this disease betrayed his great will.

> *on one tree*
>
> *four kinds of apples grafted*
>
> *work done well should last*

One of the disturbing things about Parkinson's disease is that recent studies, since about 2009, connect it with pesticides. One of the chemicals they mention is Rotenone, which we used routinely in the garden at The Building; it is singled out as a very hazardous insecticide.[100] Could Daddy's illness be traced to agricultural practices that he and his farming contemporaries thought were safe?

When he was an invalid (terrible word—*in-valid*), soon to be in hospice care, we moved Daddy and Mother to a smaller home in a town near Bette and her family. But he lasted only four more months away from Corson Castle, his dream home and the foundation of a life shared generously on land he loved.

My husband and I inherited from Daddy and Mother a powerful symbol of time's passing that now stands in our home; it's a beautiful grandfather clock that Daddy selected years ago for Corson Castle. It stood stately and tall in the front entry hall. I remember the pleasure he took in winding it once every week; he also loved to demonstrate the three separate chimes that it could play: Westminster (the one he kept it on), Canterbury, and Whittington.

As long as we keep our clock wound and occasionally serviced, it faithfully keeps time. I find it's true that time seems to move faster when you grow older, so in the mood I attribute to Daddy in that photo, I too have moments of reflection on questions of the ultimates of my life.

The clock is tied for me to yet another symbol of time's passage, this one in the landscape of Corson Castle. From the front door windows beside the clock where it once stood, you could look out across the flagstone entranceway and low hedge to the wide lawn with magnificent blue spruce and white birch trees. Farther, across the two-lane country road, were fields and a small wood lot. Then in the far distance you could see the rough outline of a limestone quarry. I suppose you might say it was my Rock of Gibraltar, a sign of permanence, the way it is commercially represented in those Prudential Insurance ads. Like Bald Eagle Mountain to the southwest, the quarry rock in the northeast made me feel oriented at home. Sometimes, especially in dry weather, there was a plume of dust rising from it as machines ground away at the stone; to me it seemed a companion business to Daddy's nearby.

What I appreciated most was that it was very beautiful in the evenings, after work hours. Then the sun made the quarry rock look like a Claude Monet painting—one of those exquisite celebrations of light in his haystack or cathedral series.

So I was astonished to see, the last time we visited Corson Castle, that the quarry men had chewed away at the rock with their machines until it was only a nub. When the very geography of our lives is taken away, it is hard to find comforting reflection about it.

Late in life, we search for context and meaning. Whether it is videographer Ken Burns, cartoonist Bill Maulden, Tom Brokaw writing of *The Greatest Generation,* or an ordinary memoirist like myself, all of us participate in the myth-making of our own time.

For me, a literary person, the hero myths come to mind; they also include heroines. In this pattern, a hero/heroine chooses (or is forced) to depart from his/her secure home place to undertake a journey of initiation. If s/he can successfully deal with the challenges s/he encounters, s/he can return to his/her former home, enriched by a gift or boon to share. The men and women who participated with the Allies in World War II, to rid our Earth home of the plague of Nazism, were heroic. In mythic language, they entered the unknown and conquered a beast that mercilessly sullied the land and its people.

From what I know of Daddy's story, I understand that there was pride and quiet bravado that all engaged in the war must have felt in some way, unless they went AWOL or otherwise forfeited their integrity. But some had been wounded both physically and psychically. The healing needed was sometimes available and other times not. The fortunate ones followed a cord of loyal love back from the war's darkness to the light of day in their own homes and family relationships in their own country; they also had good medical and psychiatric care.

Even though Daddy knew he'd been in a war that nearly everyone acknowledged as just and necessary, there must have been moments when its resonances brought disquiet. That photo of him in the mountains may capture a moment of rest and satisfaction, but it also may evoke nostalgia, a yearning for the past. This was the lifelong work, even if only on a subliminal level, of all those who fought and returned. The hero's boon may be an outward bringing of peace to the realm which has, nevertheless, an inner cost for him or her.

During this writing I had a dream. I entered a busy, rather noisy, and dimly lit restaurant searching for Daddy. As Howard and I went in, I saw someone who looked a lot like him, but, looking again, I decided it was someone else. We went all around the premises, hunting for Daddy but not finding him. At last, not wanting to give up, I scrutinized the person I'd first thought was him for one more time and decided to speak to him. I did, and it suddenly became clear to me that it *was* Daddy, eating alone. He stood up and we threw our arms around each other; we both began to sob. I felt so grateful to have found him, and the tears we shared felt deeply cathartic. Upon waking, I felt that in this dream we'd expressed the gift we'd been given to have shared our lives as well as our grief in being separated by death.

Mother's Music

After Daddy's death, Mother's piano playing became more and more her refuge. When other things seemed confusing or uninteresting, or when she was lonely, she could always play—either from her extensive collection of books and sheets of music or from an amazing diversity of songs, classical as well as popular, which she knew by heart. I'm sure a lot of the old songs reminded her of Harvey, her forever sweetheart.

I enjoy having some of the sheet music Daddy bought for Mother during their courtship and in the early years of their marriage. He always said he'd hunted for a girl who could play the piano as well as be a good cook. We'd gather around the piano to sing songs like "Bell Bottom Trousers," "The Caissons Go Rolling Along," and "Deep Purple." Mother's grandfather, a Pennsylvania railroad engineer, gave her a piano when she was young; her diligence in practice paid off.

When we Corson girls began to leave home for our own separate lives, Mother initiated Corson Castle Newsletters. They were the fruit of so much she had learned in her work life—as a court stenographer and secretary and also as a teacher of stenotypy at the high school in State College for a while. Although her plans to study business in college were thwarted, she nevertheless used her skill with words and accounts as administrative secretary in the family business. In the newsletters, her reportorial skills kept her and Daddy connected with their four daughters after we went to college, worked, and married. She typed and copied this homely record week by week, sending it to us as long as she was able. She and I were faithful correspondents; I like to think I'm honoring her writing in my own.

After Daddy's death, Mother gamely kept house, played her piano and organ, worked on the daily crossword puzzle, and went to church, sometimes playing the piano there for Sunday School. We had a wonderful eightieth-birthday celebration with her in Florida, but soon after that she began to fade in health, manifesting early stages of dementia.

One of the hardest things Howard and I ever had to do was to take her to a special place for dementia patients. Even there, she continued to play beautifully on a baby grand in the public area near her room. Other people loved to hear her play; they were sure she'd been a concert pianist! Through it all, she never lost her sweet spirit; whenever we asked her how she was, she answered, "Every day is a good day." She told me that she had prayed for peace every day since World War II began.

In the days right before Mother died, I had the distinct sense that my keeping vigil with her completed the circle of vigil she had kept so faithfully with me, her first child, while Daddy was serving in the war.

at her bedside
blessing her death
as she blessed my life

When Mother, in the last few days of her life, was no longer able to speak except for a few words at a time, we said the Lord's Prayer and the Twenty-Third Psalm for her. I named all her family—Daddy, all her children, grandchildren, and great-grandchildren, saying for each one: "[name] loves you." It was a litany of love that we hoped would bear her up and surround her with light. Clearly she was dying—she was unable to eat and could barely drink anything. Our job seemed to be to help her let go.

I caressed her hair with a child's soft bristle brush; she said, "It feels so good." At the same time I thought of how tenderly she brushed, combed, and curled her four little girls' hair. I found this "Joyous Easter" postcard Daddy had sent to us from France during the war. Its sense of joyful, child-like faithfulness represents to me the great loving care that Mother gave us. We wish its pure-hearted delight to accompany her always.

> *Easter sky*
> *rains sweet music*
> *every child beloved*

Mother always took great delight in swimming; she did it with such grace. She had begun swimming as a child in Altoona when she walked to a nearby community pool. How she loved the pool Daddy built for her at Corson Castle! She swam daily in the summer, until, in the fall, it had to be drained and covered for the winter; she always reported that event with regret in the Corson Castle Newsletter. So I asked her to think of images of floating in refreshing, cool water, in light, of floating with sweet relaxation to help her make the transition from life to death to new life.

> *dive into spring pool*
> *clean breathtaking entry*
> *into forever*

Right after her death it occurred to me that I should open the window, to let her soul fly free. Where had I heard of this? I don't know, but I did it anyway, in respect and in hope. In the courtyard right outside her room windows were two pear trees in full blossom. I thought of Mother reunited with Daddy.

> *two flowering trees*
> *embrace*
> *radiance*

The One Rose

My favorite picture of Daddy and Mother together is a photo I took one summer as they stood behind a rose bush with its single deep pink blossom on the lawn of Corson Castle. There they are, in the shadows of well-tended orchard trees, with grass neatly mowed and with golden grain fields and woods in the background—in the world they both loved so deeply and diligently.

Even from the time when, as a teenager, I made that scrapbook page with a paper rose pasted between their two photos,

I have associated them with the rose. In the Gothic cathedrals of medieval Europe, the beautiful stained glass rose windows—traditionally in the west entry wall facing toward the altar in the east of the basic cruciform pattern—were earthly symbols of the enlightenment of the human spirit. The morning light streamed through the rose windows making enlightenment visible in jeweled colors. In mystical terms the rose is equated with the soul perfected through toil; the rose represents union and love, both worldly and heavenly.

When I visited Chartres Cathedral in France, I learned about a special relationship between the west rose window and a labyrinth on the floor. If you were to lay the rose window wall down over the labyrinth, the center of the window would almost exactly cover the six-petaled rosette in the center of the labyrinth. It's said that this rosette was formerly a metal plate with an image of a Minotaur, alluding to the half-bull, half-man beast at the center of the Cretan labyrinth.

I've envisioned the Minotaur myth as a story paralleling the wartime experience of meeting evil and engaging it in battle. The great west rose at Chartres portrays Christ at the Last Judgment. It implies that the powers of the rose are, by grace, destined through the heavenly light to overcome the Minotaur, as Theseus was able to slay the beast and escape the labyrinth by following Ariadne's cord. An authority on rose windows, Painton Cowen, extends this insight of merging the two myths: "In Christian terms, it is the Holy Spirit that acts as Ariadne's thread in the labyrinth of life."[101]

Though she wasn't included in my protestant upbringing, the Virgin Mary now seems to me a beautiful reminder of the spirit of healing love. She *is* the Rose so full of glory in the great Gothic cathedral windows; moreover, she *is* the "dame" for whom "Notre Dame de Chartres" and other cathedrals are named. With this rose-Minotaur overlay story in mind, I view the rose as a powerful symbol of Daddy and Mother intentionally living through a time of chaos toward love.

The labyrinth itself may be seen as a metaphor for life's journey understood as a pilgrimage; once entered, we are never lost. It has a meandering but purposeful path into the center and back out again; unlike a maze, it has no puzzles or dead ends. Overall, walking the labyrinth invites healing, spiritual and emotional growth, and a sense of the wholeness of creation. It is a tool for restoration of our wounded world. For these reasons, I am always glad to walk the labyrinth, especially one that Howard and I helped to construct in the woods of a nearby camp and conference center. Its pattern is marked with white quartz stones; the walkways are covered by green glass mixed with a few other colors, all sparkling like jewels—a sort of Holy City radiance!

As I've continued collecting reviews and news articles about World War II, I've seen over and over again how deep and lasting the wounds of war can be. I've also seen that there have been great deeds of self-sacrifice and friendship, of heroism and phenomenal willpower to survive and heal. Some of the war's heroes and heroines have been honored at last, late in their lives while many others receive due recognition only after death. The Tomb of the Unknown Soldier (or Tomb of the Unknowns) at Arlington stands for so many here in the US; there are many other such memorials around the world.

After the war, the Marshall Plan of US humanitarian aid to Western Europe for recovery helped both individuals and cultures to heal. The Japanese government's 1997 voluntary agreement with China to destroy the stock of known chemical weapons they left scattered across northeastern China in the waning days of the war may have come fifty years late but it *did* come.[102] Some raw edges of that war do get softened while, alas, new wars erupt and bleed.

World War II's literal and metaphoric poisons still leach into Earth. The eco-philosopher Joanna Macy urges us to let wisdom guide us in changing the sicknesses caused by them into health:

> When we look at the pain, when we take it in our hands, when we can just be with it and keep breathing, then it turns. It turns to reveal its other face, and the other face of our pain for the world is our love for the world, our absolutely inseparable connectedness with all life.[103]

In 2005 I published an article with a title that names my widest concerns: "*War and Environment: Breaking Covenant with God, Earth, Ourselves, and Our Children.*"[104] Its biblical theme is epitomized in 1 Corinthians 12:26: "If one member suffers, all suffer together with it; if one member is honored, all rejoice together with it." Similarly, Chris Hedges, an award-winning journalist experienced in battle zones, writes: "The only force that is powerful enough to subvert the force of war is love."[105]

I find that the rose and the labyrinth are powerful symbols of encouragement. They awaken attention to the presence of a spirit that transcends any particular faith tradition, binding together all who dedicate themselves to striving for peace, guarding against the fears and angers that war and violence stir up.

Daddy felt called to use the resources of his own faith in his sixty-ninth year; he decided to be baptized. He persuaded his younger brother to join him, and the two of them went together to receive the sacrament from Daddy's pastor at the local Lutheran church where he was a member. I trust he felt that whatever detritus of the war years remained was ritually dispersed, opening the way to peaceful reconciliations, whatever they needed to be.

A hard truth of my journey is that I absorbed many emotional burdens of the war, but it is my parents' and others' enduring sense of the gift of survival and its opportunities that I choose to carry forward. Daddy and I have had our differences, and I have spoken of them as fairly and honestly as I could. There *were* hard passages to endure. However, my over-arching feeling is gratitude—what good fortune to have lived in the family that both Daddy and Mother secured with such competence, hard work, and love.

There is a simple occasion that serves as a mark of renewal for me; it represents a kind of covenant that Daddy and I have with the Earth and with each other. It happened one early summer day, sometime in the 1980s, when I'd brought some lilies-of-the-valley seedlings home to Corson Castle for him. We all associated the delicate white flower bells and sweet fragrance of these plants with Daddy in springtime.

"Daddy," I said, "Remember how we used to pick lilies-of-the-valley for you on your birthday? The stalks were so hardy that they grew up and bloomed even after someone piled a stack of boards on top of them, at the back of The Building."

"Oh, yes, I remember—we cleaned up that area after that. Let's put these in the planter out by the back porch."

So we did, and when we finished, he said "They'll grow fine since you and I planted them together!"

I will never forget those words. In pilgrimage, sometimes the greatest treasure, after long traversing of the wide woolly world, is found back at home.

As I conclude this work, I realize that there are many questions about the war Daddy experienced for which I will never find answers. The question about why that man appeared in Sudan when he did with that unexplained message of Daddy's life narrowly spared is a mystery. But that story has led me to some reflections that I accept as answers in their own way. We can imagine that his revelation afforded an opportunity for Daddy to claim, more than ever, the gift of his survival, the shining forth of a YES despite so many possibilities of NO. The man's announcement appeared like a mystical illumination at the center of the labyrinth, a reminder of safe passage past the death-dealing minotaur.

I don't believe Mother hung a blue star in the window during

WWII to announce that she had a family member in the US military. Happily, she never had reason to display a gold star—it meant someone had died in service; I am deeply grateful not to have been one of the 183,000 US "gold-star children" who lost their dads in World War II. I send blessings to them all.

As a result of following my questions, I feel that I've become a citizen of a wider world, with greater scope for encompassing pain together with wonder and healing. I know that I forgive Daddy for the hard times in our relationship, and, through all I have learned, I hope that I am granted forgiveness for not understanding better the enormous dimensions of his gifts to me and to our country. I wish that I had been able to express that to him more fully during his lifetime.

I hope that there's a boon in this writing that goes beyond us and into the world. For me, the rose is a fitting symbol of this desire.

Afterword

I completed most of my writing about the "never-quite-ending war" by late 2016. But I've chosen this list of 2017 events and publications to carry my hopes and concerns about this theme into the future:

- National Rosie the Riveter Day passed in the Senate and became official on March 21.

- People continue to receive belated news about loved ones lost in the war. On May 29 our local newspaper reported a serendipitous meeting between the son of a German man, who as a boy had seen a plane crash near his home in Germany, and the lost pilot's brother who lives in Raleigh, NC. Both gained a sense of closure at last.

- Time Life Books' photos and stories include well-known and previously unknown *Heroes of World War II: Men and Women Who Put Their Lives on the Line*. Films appear like *The Zookeeper's Wife*, based on the true story of Antonina and Jan Żabiński, director of the Warsaw Zoo. They saved the lives of three hundred Jews imprisoned in the Warsaw Ghetto following the German invasion of Poland on September 1, 1939.

- In the March *Iowa Alumni Magazine*, there's Kathryn Howe's moving piece, "From Auschwitz to Iowa City." We learn that

"For 70 years, Michael Bornstein remained silent about his faded tattoo and the seven months he spent [at age 4] inside the concentration camp. The University of Iowa graduate [a Ph.D. pharmacist] finally shares his story."

⟿ Difficult stories surface, like Jessica Shattuck's March 25 opinion piece in *The New York Times*: "I Loved My Grandmother. But She Was a Nazi."

⟿ June 1—the president withdrew the US from the Paris Climate Accords, a missed chance for international cooperation to help build sustainability, peace, and security.

⟿ World War II vets and all who died defending the world against the Nazis were insulted in Charlottesville, Virginia, on August 12. Neo-Nazis, white supremacists, and KKK members marched with Nazi flags and salutes. The president neglected to quickly and firmly condemn this outrage.

⟿ Peter Sawtell's August 18 *Eco-Justice Notes* on "Prayer for Times of Turmoil." In brief: "Remember to keep the focus on what is good and right. Find the time and space for meditation and mindfulness. Practice forgiveness. Be strengthened by community. Be grateful."

⟿ In late September, I read Ilarion Merculieff's book, *Wisdom Keeper: One Man's Journey to Honor the Untold History of the Unangan [Aleut] People*. He represents indigenous peoples worldwide who know that in a sense we are all suffering from PTSD caused by violence toward others, ourselves, and all Creation. He cites Hopi Elders: "Seek not to fight evil, let goodness take its place." That is our challenge for restoration and healing.

Thanks

Thanks to my husband, Howard Carter, for his invaluable editing and steadfast encouragement of this project. And my gratitude for the hospitality and insights of the Morning Group in "Forms of Autobiography," at the annual meetings of the Society for Values in Higher Education. Many thanks to my sisters, Marilyn Keeser, Bette Jane Weeks, and Janet Corson Mac-Neil and to my daughter, Rebecca Alice-Carter Rincon, for our shared stories of life with Daddy and Mother. Janet's booklet "The Life and Times of Dorothy Virginia Corson: In Honor of Her 80th Birthday, April 21, 1999" is an invaluable source of family data. Thanks to Ian MacNeil for his help.

I am grateful for Carol Henderson's writing consultations; they helped launch the whole project. I also thank Joyce Allen and my colleagues in her classes for their helpful companionship. My great praise for Nora Gaskin Esthimer's and Kelly Prelipp Lojk's editing and designing to finally bring this work into the world.

Truly, "it takes a community to raise a child." I have boundless gratitude to my parents for all the ways in which they fostered my education, in reading, in learning, and in life. I have been blessed by many wonderful teachers—from grade school on; among my most cherished are students and colleagues at Eckerd College, especially my husband Howard. They have brought me both delight and healing.

I am grateful to my contemporaries who have shared their stories, from Muncy High School and elsewhere. I honor those who have taught me to be more patient, loving, and attentive—in short, those who encourage me to listen deeply to others and to the Earth. I honor all whose lives have been touched by war and, despite its ravages, have become peacemakers.

Endnotes

[1] Jay Price, "France Bestows the Legion of Honor on Aging N.C. WWII Vets," *The News & Observer*, 4 February 2015, sec. A.

[2] "Ignorance Inspired WWII Documentary," *The News & Observer*, 26 November 2006, sec. A.

[3] Virginia Cunningham, *Heroes and Holidays* (Park Ridge, Ill.: Whitman Pubs., 1948), n.p.

[4] Charles Baxter, "Shame and Forgetting in the Information Age," *The Business of Memory*, ed. Charles Baxter (Saint Paul: Graywolf Press, 1999), 153.

[5] Neal Paris, "Our Post-War World," *The News & Observer*, 9 November 2015, sec. A.

[6] Roger Cohen, "Where the Road From Auschwitz Ends," http://nytimes.com/2015/03/11/opinion/roger-cohen-where-the-ro… (10 March 2015).

[7] Aron Heller, "Israel Honors GI Who Told the Nazis, 'We are all Jews'," *The Times of Israel*, 2 December 2015, www.timesofisrael.com/israel-honors-us-gi-who-told-the-nazis-we-are-all-jews/?fb… (1 June 2017).

[8] Susan Donaldson James, "Suicide Rate Spikes in Vietnam Vets Who Won't Seek Help," 3 May 2012, abcnews.go.com

[9] William Stafford, "The Mob Scene at McNeil," *Every War Has Two Losers: William Stafford on Peace and War*, ed. Kim Stafford (Minneapolis: Milkweed Editions, 2003), 13–23.

[10] Janet MacNeil, "The Life and Times of Dorothy Virginia Corson" (unpublished, 1999).

[11] Steven Verburg, "Kids of Soldiers Battle Reality of War at Home," *Wisconsin State Journal*, 1 February 2011, http://host.madison.com/wsj/news/local/article_406b3f34-2ca5-11e0-9ca5-001cc4c03286.html (5 March 2012).

12 "War Children," http://en.wikipedia.org/wiki/War_children (5 March 2012).

13 Bill Mauldin, *Up Front* (1945; repr., New York: W.W. Norton & Co. Inc., 1968), 7–8.

14 Mauldin, 148.

15 Mauldin, 130.

16 "Mission Background Information," http://www.graveyardofthe atlantic.com/USS_Background.htm (15 April 2014).

17 "World War II Troop Ships: Queen Mary," www.ww2troopships. com/ships/q/queenmary/crossings1944.html (6 March 2012).

18 "D-Day Remembered," *The St. Petersburg Times,* 25 May 1994, special sec. 2.

19 Jane Curry, *Miss Sniff* (Park Ridge, Ill.: Whitman Pubs, 1945).

20 Mauldin, 160–62.

21 President Dwight D. Eisenhower, "Farewell Address," 17 January 1961,

22 Rainer Maria Rilke, *Rilke on Love and Other Difficulties,* ed. John J. L. Mood (New York: W.W. Norton & Company, Inc., 1975), 9.

23 The Library of Congress, *I'll Be Home for Christmas: The Spirit of Christmas During World War II* (1999; repr., New York: Gramercy Press, 2006), 153.

24 "German Vengeance Weapons 1942–45." http://www.theotherside. co.uk/tm-heritage/background/v1v2.htm (6 March 2012).

25 Gaston Bachelard, *The Poetics of Space* (1958; rpt., Boston: Beacon Press, 1969), 15.

26 *Farming in the 1940s: Allis-Chalmers Tractors,* www.livinghistory-farm.org/farminginthe40s/machines_0202.html (10 April 2014).

27 Bachelard, 25.

28 "Brigid, Celtic Goddess of Fire," http://www.goddessgift.com/goddess-myths/celtic-goddess-brigid.htm (6 March 2012).

29 Kurt Vonnegut, "The Blood of Dresden," http://forum.woodenboat. com/showthread.php?87447-Vonnegut-s-Take-on-Dresden-Bombing&p=199065 (5 March 2012).

30 "US Army Rations World War II," http://www.qmfound.com/army_rations_...background.htm under general site: http://www.ww2incolor.com/forum/showthread.php?3551-US-Army-Rations-World-War-II (6 March 2012).

31 Timothy Snyder, review of *The Taste of War: World War II and the Battle for Food* by Lizzie Collingham, *The New York Times Book Review* (6 May 2012): 18.

32 S.M. Enzler, "The Impact of War on the Environment and Human Health," www.lenntech.com/environmental-effects-war.htm (6 March 2012).

33 Mauldin, 66–68.

34 "US Army Rations World War II."

35 "What Is Anger?", This Emotional Life, 2011, http://thisemotional-life.org/topic/anger/what-anger (20 December 2017).

36 Mary Carmen Cupito, "Gift of Transplants," *The St. Petersburg Times*, 25 December 1984, sec. B.

37 Terese Svoboda, *Black Glasses Like Clark Kent: A GI's Secret From Postwar Japan* (Saint Paul: Graywolf Press, 2008), 70.

38 "World War II Troop Ships: Queen Mary: Information About Specific Crossings" ww2troopships.com/ships/q/queenmary/cruiserecord1944.htm (23 August 2017).

39 *History of the 182D Ordnance Depot Company,* 5 typescript pages from The Memories Project, George C. Marshall Foundation Library, Lexington, Virginia.

40 "The Flaming Bomb," Stars & Stripes' G.I Stories, 1944–45, http://www.lonesentry.com/gi_stories_booklets/ordnance/index.html (6 March 2012).

41 ———.

42 Lida Mayo, *The Ordnance Department: On Beachhead and Battlefront,* (1968; rpt., Washington, D.C.: U.S. Army Center of Military History, 1991), 250, http://www.archive.org/stream/ordnancedepartme-00mayo/ordnancedepartme00mayo_djvu.txt (6 March 2012).

43 ———, chap. 16.

44 "World War II Database, Normandy Campaign, Phase 2, 25 July–22 August 1944," http://ww2db.com/battle_spec.php?battle_id=112 (6 March 2012).

45 W. C. Heinz, *When We Were One: Stories of World War II* (Cambridge, Mass.: Da Capo Press, 2002), 209.

46 Heinz, 225.

47 Kenneth Slawenski, "Holden Caulfield's Goddam War," *Vanity Fair,* 20 January 2011, http:/www.vanityfair.com/culture/2011/02/salinger-201102 (20 May 2015).

48 Jay McInerney, review of *J. D. Salinger: A Life,* by Kenneth Slawenski, *The New York Times Sunday Book Review* (13 February 2011): 1.

49 Casey McGrath, "Rosie the Riveter, a Reluctant Symbol of Patriarchy," https://www.msu.edu/~mcgrat71/Writing/Rosie%20the%20Riveter,%20a%20Reluctant%20Symbol%20of%20Patriarchy.pdf (8 April 2015).

50 Leon J. Pollom, "Post Office Murals Bring History to Life," *Williamsport Sun-Gazette*, 2 February 1992, sec. A.

51 C. Tyler, *You'll Never Know: A Graphic Memoir. Book One: A Good and Decent Man* (Seattle: Fantagraphics Books, 2009); *You'll Never Know: A Graphic Memoir, Book Two: Collateral Damage* (Seattle: Fantagraphics Books, 2010); *You'll Never Know: A Graphic Memoir, Book Three: Soldier's Heart* (Seattle: Fantagraphics Books, 2012).

52 *Souvenirs: Healing After War*, dir. and narr. Mara Pelecis, 1 hr. 28 min., Documentary Media, LLC, 2011, DVD.

53 *Souvenirs: Healing After War*, dir. and narr. Mara Pelecis, 1 hr. 28 min., Documentary Media, LLC, 2011, DVD.

54 George Packer, "Home Fires: How Soldiers Write Their Wars," *The New Yorker*, 7 April 2014, 69–73.

55 William Grimes, "Doris Bohrer, World War II Spy for Allies, Dies at 93," *The New York Times*, 22 August 2016, www.newsdiffs.org/diff/.../doris-bohrer-world-war-ii-spy-for-allies-dies-at-93.html (2 June 2017).

56 Sheryl Sandberg and Adam Grant, "Speaking While Female," *The New York Times*, 12 January 2015, https://www.nytimes.com/2015/01/11/opinion/sunday/speaking-while-female.html (2 June 2017).

57 Petula Dvorak, "WWII Pilot Elaine Harmon Breaks One Last Barrier at Arlington National Cemetery," *The Washington Post*, 7 September 2016.

58 Robert Hass, *The Essential Haiku: Versions of Bashō, Buson, & Issa* (Hopewell, N.J.: The Ecco Press, 1994), 61.

59 Eric Talmadge, "US Joins Hiroshima Commemoration for the First Time," Associated Press, 5 August 2010, cnsnews.com/news/.../us-joins-hiroshima-commemoration-first-time (6 March 2012).

60 Nancy Corson Carter, *Near the End of the Rainy Season: Poems from Japan* (Columbus, Ohio: Pudding House Publications, 2008), 31.

61 Laura Hillenbrand, *Unbroken: A World War II Story of Survival* (New York: Random House, 2010), 347.

62 Michi Weglyn, *Years of Infamy: The Untold Story of America's Concentration Camps* (New York: William Morrow and Company, Inc., 1976), 77.

63 Jeanne Wakatsuki Houston and James D. Houston, *Farewell to Manzanar* (1973; rpt., New York: Random House, 1995), 123.

64 Michael Doyle, "They Fought on Two Fronts," *The News & Observer*, 3 November 2011, sec. A.

65 Mark Sherman and George Katagiri, eds., *Touching the Stones*

(Portland, Ore.: Oregon Nikkei Endowment, 1994), 103.

[66] David Rosen and Joel Weishaus, *The Healing Spirit of Haiku* (Berkeley: North Atlantic Books, 2004), 2.

[67] Marilyn Hazelton, "Telling the Truth about War," http://www.indiegogo.com/projects/233309 (25 March 2013; site now discontinued).

[68] Carter, 32.

[69] Matsuo *Bashō, The Narrow Road to the Deep North and Other Travel Sketches* (London: Penguin Books, 1966), 107.

[70] Clark Strand, *Seeds from a Birch Tree* (New York: Hyperion, 1997), 2–3.

[71] David Vandermast, review of *American Chestnut: The Life, Death, and Rebirth of a Perfect Tree* by Susan Freinkel, *American Scientist* 96:4 (July–August 2008): 345.

[72] Barbara Demick, "The Remains of Pearl Harbor Sailors Are Finally Coming Home," *Los Angeles Times,* www.latimes.com/nation/la-na-pearl-harbor-burials-20161129-story.html (2 June 2017).

[73] "D-Day Remembered," *The St. Petersburg Times,* 25 May 1994, special sec., 5.

[74] Andrew Lycett, "Breaking Germany's Enigma Code," 17 February 2011, www.bbc.com/history/worldwars/wwtwo/enigma_01.shtml (3 June 2017).

[75] Navajo Code Talkers: World War II Fact Sheet, http://www.history.navy.mil/faqs/faq61-2.htm (6 March 2012).

[76] "She Gave Her Long Hair for the War Cause," *St. Petersburg Times,* 19 November 1990, sec. A.

[77] Jason Cumming, "The Disaster That May Have Saved D-Day—D-day 65 Years Later," 5 June 2009, www.nbcnews.com/id/30977039/ns/world...d.../disaster-may-have-saved-d-day (3 June 2017).

[78] Tom Brokaw, *The Greatest Generation* (1998; rpt., New York and Toronto: Random House, Inc., 2004), 92.

[79] ———, 298.

[80] Ruth Sheehan, "After 65 Years, His Due: Seymour Johnson Honors a WWII Airman Shot Down Three Times," *The News & Observer,* 29 August 2009, sec. B.

[81] John Matthis, "65 Years Later, WWII Veteran Opens Up" *The News & Observer,* 25 November 2010, secs. D, C.

[82] Lucas Selvidge, "The Sacrifices They Made: My View," *Chapel Hill News,* 23 September 2012, sec. A.

[83] Bachelard, 67.

[84] ———, 68

85 Henry David Thoreau, *Walden* in *Walden and Civil Disobedience*, ed. Owen Thomas (1854; rpt., New York: W.W. Norton and Co., Inc., 1966), 76.

86 Wendell Berry, *Home Economics* (San Francisco: North Point Press, 1987), 144–45.

87 Rainer Maria Rilke, *Rilke's Book of Hours: Love Poems to God*, trans. Anita Barrows and Joanna Macy (New York: Riverhead Books, 1996), 96.

88 Dee Follin, "Searching for Home" (lecture for the C.G. Jung Society of the Triangle, Chapel Hill, NC, 28 January 2011).

89 Helena Meyer-Knapp, *Dangerous Peacemaking* (Olympia, WA: Peace-Maker Press, 2003), 199–200.

90 J. E. Cirlot, "Key," *A Dictionary of Symbols* (New York: Philosophical Library, 1962), 159.

91 "Memory Unearthed: The Lodz Ghetto Photographs of Henryk Ross" at MFA Boston, www.mfa.org/exhibitions/memory-unearthed (27 October 2017).

92 Wendell Berry, *The New Collected Poems* (Berkeley: Counterpoint Press, 2012), 354.

93 *Instructions for American Servicemen in Britain 1942* (1942; rpt., Cambridge: The University Press, 2004).

94 "Britain Honors Last WWI Army Veteran," 6 August 2009, http://www.cnn.com/2009/WORLD/europe/08/06/ww1.funeral/index (6 March 2012).

95 Martin Fackler, "Retired Japanese Fighter Pilot Sees an Old Danger on the Horizon," *The New York Times*, 3 April 2015, http://www.nytimes.com/2015/04/04/world/asia/retired-japanese-fighter-pilot-sees-an-old...(3 June 2017).

96 ———.

97 Gardiner Harris, "Obama Visits Place 'World Was Changed,'" *The New York Times*, 28 May 2016, https://www.nytimes.com/2016/05/28/world/asia/obama-hiroshima-japan.html (3 June 2017).

98 Michael S. Schmidt, "Japanese Leader Offers Condolences in Visit to Pearl Harbor," *The New York Times*, 27 December 2016, https://www.nytimes.com/2016/12/27/us/politics/pearl-harbor-abe-obama-visit.html (3 June 2017).

99 Black Elk, *Black Elk Speaks; Being the Life Story of a Holy Man of the Oglala Sioux* (1932; rpt., Lincoln: Univ. of Nebraska Press, 1989), 194–95.

100 Robin Marantz Henig, "Scientists are Closing in on an Inescapable Conclusion: Pesticides May Be a Cause of Parkinson's Disease,"

Onearth Magazine, Summer 2009, 49–53.

[101] Painton Cowen, *Rose Windows* (London: Thames and Hudson Ltd., 1979), 99.

[102] Clay Risen, "The Environmental Consequences of War: Why Militaries Almost Never Clean Up the Messes They Leave Behind," *The Washington Monthly,* January/February 2010, www.unz.org/Pub/WashingtonMonthly-2010jan-2g00008 (27 April 2015).

[103] Joanna Macy, "A Wild Love for the World," transcript of interview with Krista Tippett, 17 March, 2011, http://being.publicradio.org/programs/2011/wild-love-for-world/transcript.shtml (6 March 2012).

[104] Nancy Corson Carter, "War and Environment: Breaking Covenant With God, Earth, Ourselves, and Our Children," *Church and Society,* November/December 2005, 34–44.

[105] Sarah Ruth van Gelder, "Love and Resistance in Wartime: Sarah Ruth van Gelder Interviews Chris Hedges," *YES! A Journal of Positive Futures,* 32 (2005), 18–19.

Sunday Dinner at the Farm

(2016, Finishing Line Press, Georgetown, Kentucky)

When I was a child, my father drove Mother, my sisters, and me to visit his parents' farm in central Pennsylvania each Sunday. This tradition lasted until Grandpap died in 1957 and Grammy moved to town. Late one night many years later, I traveled in my imagination back to my grandparents' farm. As I walked about the house and land, I began to map what I call a geography of the heart. The results are the poems and photos in this volume. I think of them as a celebration of my experience and an invitation to my readers to remember their own special "heart maps." Available for purchase at **www.finishinglinepress.com**

"Carter's poems make your mouth water and your heart expand as her grandparents and parents come to life as we read. The book ends with the lines 'I remember! I remember!' and she makes us remember, too."

— **Peter Meinke**, Poet Laureate of Florida

"Touched by nostalgia, but formed from precise observations, these poems consistently evoke engaging reminders of a nearly vanished way of life."

— **Gary Fincke**, Charles B. Degenstein Professor of English and Creative Writing, Susquehanna University

CPSIA information can be obtained
at www.ICGtesting.com
Printed in the USA
FSHW04n1707070318
45215FS